John Morley at the India Office, 1905–1910

JOHN, VISCOUNT MORLEY, O.M.
Photograph by Downey. Courtesy Radio Times Hulton Picture
Library, London.

John Morley at the India Office

1905-1910

by Stephen E. Koss

New Haven and London, Yale University Press   1969

Library of Congress catalog card number: 72-81423

Designed by John O. C. McCrillis,
set in Baskerville type,
and printed in the United States of America by
the Vail-Ballou Press, Inc., Binghamton, N.Y.
Distributed in Great Britain, Europe, Asia, and
Africa by Yale University Press Ltd., London; in
Canada by McGill University Press, Montreal; and
in Mexico by Centro Interamericano de Libros
Académicos, Mexico City.

Published with assistance from the Louis Stern Memorial Fund.

For e.

Acknowledgments

The present study had its first incarnation as a Columbia University doctoral dissertation under the joint sponsorship of Robert K. Webb and Ainslie T. Embree. Professor Webb subjected the manuscript to the painstaking scrutiny that is his hallmark, and Professor Embree read and criticized several drafts, always with encouragement and good humor. To both of them I am immeasurably grateful.

A year's research in British archives was made possible by a grant from the United States Educational Commission in the United Kingdom. During this period I received many valuable suggestions from Professor Hugh Tinker and Dr. S. R. Mehrotra of the School of Oriental and African Studies. I share with many students a profound debt to Dr. Mehrotra, who gave his counsel and friendship so unsparingly. I hope this book, in which his influence is so deeply felt, will not disappoint him.

Grateful acknowledgment is also due the librarians and staffs of the many depositories I visited: of these, I should mention especially Stanley Sutton of the India Office Library, London, and Dr. Richard Bingle of his staff; Dr. Thomas I. Rae of the National Library of Scotland, Edinburgh; and D. S. Porter of the Bodleian Library, Oxford. The Earl Spencer permitted me access to the muniment room at Althorp and, on several occasions, Viscount Harcourt kindly allowed me to consult his family papers at Stanton Harcourt. I received advice about bibliography from Professor Kenneth Ballhatchet, now of the School of Oriental and African Studies, and enjoyed helpful interviews with A. F. Thompson of Wadham College, Oxford, and Robert Rhodes James, now of All Soul's College, Oxford. I profited too from innumerable conversations with Professor Chilton Williamson, who stirred my interest in imperial thought and policy, and who has been my teacher, colleague, and friend.

Chapter 8 appeared, in amended form, in the *Journal of Asian*

Studies of May 1967. I have also borrowed in my earlier chapters from a note I contributed to the *English Historical Review* of July 1967.

I have mentioned in my introduction (page 12) two works that appeared after my book was completed and delivered to the publisher. I must add a third, D. A. Hamer's admirable study of *John Morley, Liberal Intellectual in Politics* (London, 1968). Though it is not concerned to any extent with Morley's India Office years, I would have liked to refer to it in my early chapters.

My wife's contribution, impossible to calculate, made my work go more quickly and all the more pleasantly. She has excelled as research assistant, typist, and critic, and graciously shared our early years of marriage with Lord Morley. This project holds many fond memories for both of us, and to these I dedicate this book.

S. E. K.

Barnard College,
Columbia University

Contents

Introduction

Morley in Spite of Himself

John Morley's contemporaries, who attributed so many differing qualities and opinions to him that they became powerless to discern the man behind the myth, considered his acceptance of office in December 1905 as a watershed which separated all that came before from all that was to follow. Historians of early twentieth-century India and of Morley's five-year tenure at the India Office have readily accepted this interpretation and have refused to trouble themselves with earlier controversies; they have tended to regard the Secretary of State for India as a distinctly new Morley, who came into the twentieth century without a past worthy of consideration by the student of Indian or imperial history. In the same way, historians of nineteenth-century British politics have virtually ignored the final decade of Morley's public life.

Morley himself would never have agreed that his acceptance of the Indian secretaryship at the age of sixty-seven marked a departure, or that his belated preoccupation with Indian affairs required the diversion of his career into new and hitherto unexplored channels. The decisions that he was called upon to make as Secretary of State for India admittedly introduced him to a wide range of new issues, conditions, and criteria, but the veteran parliamentarian took up his post armed with the battle-scarred ideological weapons he had accumulated over the decades. To John Morley, his move to the India Office in 1905 was merely a change of address and not in any way a change of profession.

Yet it is hardly surprising that a career which spanned so many decades, controversies, and colleagues should have been compartmentalized, often to the point of abstraction, for reasons of historical expediency. The trend had set in long before his death in 1923, and it was abetted by Morley himself. Though he was haunted by

1

recollections of past defeats and disappointments, Morley did not particularly mind if others dismissed his inglorious past from their minds. He intended to employ his secretaryship to redeem his reputation and to attain the victory that had eluded him in parliamentary battles over Irish Home Rule, assorted imperial ventures, and the Boer War. Morley, who in spirit and deed remained W. E. Gladstone's lieutenant, preferred to identify himself—only half-facetiously—as a student of the classics, a literary critic, or as the curator of his impressive private library. "What humble man of letters," he boasted to Sir Sidney Lee, "has been made a Secretary of State since Addison?" [1]

Parliamentary pressures had long since put an end to Morley's literary pursuits. Though he never ceased to picture himself as a miniature Colossus of Rhodes who straddled both professions with a foot firmly planted in each, it was apparent soon after he entered the Commons in 1883 that he had shifted his full weight to the foot at Westminster. Nor had he found it possible to further that healthy intercourse between politics and journalism which, in his opinion, had been achieved across the Channel under the Third Republic.[2] He had intended to use his experiences in each field to supplement the other, explaining to Joseph Chamberlain that "it is exactly because I hope to become a thoroughly useful political writer that I lean to Parliament." [3] But even before he delivered his maiden speech, Morley was forced to concede that T. H. Huxley had been "right about the mire of politics. I used to think that I could perhaps improve politics; so far it looks as if politics has rather *dis*improved me." [4]

Morley had experienced far too many setbacks and unmitigated failures along the way ever to be absolutely certain that he had acted wisely in forsaking his library for a seat on the Liberal back benches. His deliberations on the matter are a direct measure of the successes or disappointments he encountered at various stages of his public career. At a particularly bleak moment in 1898 he told Frederic Harrison, "Whenever I see you, I always say 'Thou

1. Morley to Lee, December 11, 1905, Lee Papers (Bodleian Library, Oxford).

2. "Valedictory," *Fortnightly Review*, n.s., 32 (1882), 516. This was the last issue of the *Fortnightly* Morley edited.

3. Morley to Chamberlain, January 3, 1878, Chamberlain Papers (University Library, Birmingham).

4. Morley to Huxley, January 22, 1883, Huxley Papers (Imperial College, London).

hast chosen the better part.' " [5] His outlook had improved decidedly when he assured Sir Austen Chamberlain that "not for untold publishers' royalties would he exchange the satisfaction of saying 'Yea' or 'Nay' in great affairs of State for the solitude, the nervous exhaustion, the introspection of the life of letters." [6] Morley fought a continual duel with his alter-ego as to the comparative values of his two vocations. J. H. Morgan has described the intensity of this debate in Morley's later years, when the would-be philosopher-king could never resolve whether he would prefer to be "Gibbon or Pitt, Macaulay or Palmerston." [7] The passing years took with them his opportunity and, ultimately, his ability to devote himself to literary efforts, and his awareness of this was undoubtedly responsible for much of his irascibility at the India Office. Aside from a posthumously published account of his controversial resignation of August 1914, he wrote only two works after his release from Indian duties. In 1913, he "amplified" the text of the inaugural sessional address he had delivered the previous year at Victoria University, Manchester, "into the most ungodly jumble that was ever seen." [8] Both he and his public were considerably more satisfied with his two volumes of *Recollections* which followed four years later; but except for portraits of friends and colleagues, the best-written and most illuminating portions of this work were gleaned from diaries, memoranda, and correspondence, and the author's major creative effort consisted of wielding his editorial blue pencil. By 1918, he could not do even this, and he was forced to refuse, with profound regret, piquant wit, and a trembling hand, the Gladstone family's invitation to prepare a new, abridged edition of his *Life of Gladstone:* "Alas, it is impossible for Beethoven to take a hand in cutting down his own 3 volume symphony." [9]

Few had a more difficult time distinguishing Morley the statesman from Morley the author-philosopher than India's nationalist

5. Morley to Harrison, April 24, 1898, Harrison Papers (British Library of Political and Economic Science, London).

6. Cited in J. H. Morgan, "More Light on Lord Morley," *North American Review,* 221 (1925), 488; see also Sir Austen Chamberlain, *Down the Years* (London, 1935), p. 198.

7. "The Personality of Lord Morley," *Quarterly Review,* 241 (1924), 179.

8. Morley to Harrison, September 7, 1913, Harrison Papers.

9. Morley to Mary Gladstone Drew, March 3, 1918, Mary Gladstone Papers, British Museum Add. MSS. 46, 240, fol. 127.

leaders. But the fact that their appreciation of Morley's previous literary and political efforts led them far afield can by no means be attributed to an ignorance of his writings. Surendranath Banerjea professed to "have read his works again and again," and to "teach them to my scholars" at Calcutta University in order to "saturate their minds with lofty principles of political wisdom." [10] Gopal Krishna Gokhale, a more moderate leader of the Indian National Congress whose word the Indian secretary was less inclined to doubt, maintained that "large numbers of educated men" in India "feel towards Mr. Morley as towards a Master," and he expressed confidence that "the reverent student of Burke, the disciple of Mill, the friend and biographer of Gladstone" would not, in the course of his secretaryship, "cast a cruel blight on hopes which his own writings have done so much to foster." [11] The great pity is that Morley's critics, including those Indian politicians who thought that they knew him best, interpreted his pronouncements too literally and failed to discern his subtle distinctions between European situations and their semblances elsewhere. Those who insisted that they held the nineteenth-century Morley in highest esteem were often those who most bitterly condemned the twentieth-century Morley as a traitor to his predecessor's noble principles. A less hasty and more thoughtful investigation of his record would have saved India's nationalist leaders considerable inconvenience and disillusionment and would have absolved John Morley, for better or worse, from the charge of treachery.

Secretaries of State for India were traditionally selected according to the dictates of intraparty politics, with little if any consideration of personal qualifications. Though Morley's appointment was no exception, its significance was and continues to be heatedly debated. Never had an announcement of an appointment to the India Office aroused as much enthusiasm, interest, and speculation as Morley's; and nothing in his ensuing secretaryship—certainly not the reform scheme that overhauled the Indian council structure and conceded the elective principle to India—had so profound an effect on the course of Indian nationalism as the wild hopes it engendered.

10. Speech at Caxton Hall, Westminster, July 13, 1909, Banerjea, *Speeches and Writings* (Madras, 1920?), p. 370.
11. Presidential address, 1905 Indian National Congress, Gokhale, *Speeches* (Madras, 1916?), p. 841.

The Liberal Government's Indian secretary was hardly an unknown political commodity when he crossed the threshold of the India Office, though he was much misunderstood. In India as in Great Britain, he was either revered or despised for reasons which few men could honestly recall and which fewer still would consent to reexamine. His loyal admirers had idealized in Honest John a martyr to absolute truths which the flesh-and-blood Morley had long recognized as politically expendable. His critics were divided into two camps, each equally steeped in versions of the philosopher-statesman reflecting a bare minimum of reality. The first group, its membership steadily increasing, dismissed Morley as an impractical theorist, a scholar who long ago had taken a wrong turn and had obtained a seat in the House of Commons chamber rather than in the House of Commons library for which he was obviously better suited. The second group tended to discern more method than madness in Morley's doctrinaire pronouncements, but it was itself divided between those (mainly British) who argued that Morley was attempting to subvert imperial power in the name of ideology, and those (mainly Indian) who maintained that he employed the same pretense to achieve the reverse effect.

It is in the diverse misunderstandings of Morley's character and ideals, mostly innocent but some quite deliberate, that one may perceive the reasons why his appointment in 1905 was so celebrated, and why, despite his vigorous disclaimers, it lifted the expectations of Indian nationalists to heights of delirium from which they could only fall. It was by no means necessary for him to issue an encouraging statement to galvanize the Indian national movement; his mere presence at the India Office was more than sufficient.

No one could have been more acutely aware than Morley of the implicit dangers of exciting expectations, even unintentionally, which neither his assessment of the Indian situation nor the structure of the British Raj would permit him to fulfill. In a remarkably prophetic letter to Lord Lamington, Governor of Bombay, he declared his intention to move cautiously, and he enumerated the reactions that might result from an injudicious step on his own part:

An atmosphere of general excitement may be created, with all sorts of vague expectations, aspirations, and violent non-

sensical babble. The European population [of India] may fly
into an ugly panic, and won't forget that we are only fifty
years from the Mutiny.

The Mahometans may show their teeth against changes
that they may regard as too favourable to the Hindoos.

The Hindoos, or at any rate the Bengalis, may lose their
heads—not very solid heads at the best, some say.

The Princes may turn glum, for they are not really in love
with the Raj, whatever they may profess.

In short, the cauldron which is simmering may begin to
boil.[12]

It proved impossible, however, even for a John Morley who
minced words, to avoid the pitfalls of popularity. By the time that
he and his fellow Liberals assumed office, Indian nationalists were
poised to cheer heartily, as much for their liberation from Curzonian controls as for the replacement of that intractable Viceroy and
his Conservative colleagues at Westminster with more sympathetic
administrators. The fact that John Morley's name was announced
converted that well-rehearsed chorus of approval into spontaneous
cries of exultation.

Not until the general election in January 1906, a month after
the formation of the Campbell-Bannerman ministry, could the
British voters make clear their vehement rejection of Conservative
leadership. But long before the first indications of Tory defeat
were evident, India had already proclaimed that she would gladly
welcome the party of Gladstone, Bright, and Ripon back to power.
Lord Curzon did not wait until his colleagues had been turned out
of office to resign the viceroyalty; his well-publicized antagonism
to Lord Kitchener, Commander-in-Chief of the Indian forces,
occasioned his premature return to England in November. Lord
Minto, though appointed to succeed Curzon during the last weeks
of the Balfour Government, was nonetheless more palatable to
Indian tastes than his predecessor had been. Yet the replacement
of a deeply resented Viceroy by a comparatively congenial one was
insufficient to appease India's nationalist spokesmen; they welcomed Minto with one eye firmly fixed on political developments
in London, anticipating that "during Minto's regime the British

12. Morley to Lamington, August 24, 1906, Lamington Papers (India Office
Library, London).

Government will pass into the hands of the Liberals." [13] The Governor of Madras diagnosed a "recrudescence of agitation" in the week preceding Balfour's resignation which he attributed "entirely . . . to the hopes which are engendered in the minds of the [Indian] politicians by the change of Viceroys and the impending change of Government at home." [14]

India's moderate politicians, who patterned their aspirations and their strategies upon nineteenth-century Liberal models,[15] convinced themselves that this revival of liberalism in the West implicitly augured the success of the Indian National Congress and its moderate ideology. Gopal Krishna Gokhale, who presided over the twenty-first Congress session, celebrated the fact that "in England, for the first time since the Congress movement began, the Liberal and Radical party will come into real power." [16] Gokhale had recently returned from a mission to Britain, where his modest contribution to the impending Liberal victory had been rewarded with assurances "that many of the aspirations which animated his mind would be carried into practice." [17] Among the representative Liberal politicians whom he had consulted during his fifty-day lecture tour was John Morley, destined to assume the burdens of Indian administration within a month's time. Although Morley found their November 22 interview "immensely interesting," [18] it remains highly improbable that Gokhale, by appealing to his conscience or imagination, persuaded Morley to come to India's rescue.[19] There can be no doubt, how-

13. *Daily Hitavadi* (Calcutta), November 18, 1905, cited in *Bengal Native Newspaper Reports, 1905.*

14. Ampthill to Brodrick, December 7, 1905, Ampthill Papers (India Office Library, London).

15. In a speech delivered at the National Liberal Club, London, on November 15, Gokhale professed that "we, in India, are struggling to assert those very principles which are now the accepted creed of the Liberal Party in England." Gokhale, *Speeches,* p. 1073. On the same day, in an address to the New Reform Club at the Trocadero Restaurant, he bolstered his arguments with allusions to Morley's *The Life of William Ewart Gladstone* (3 vols. London, 1903). Ibid., p. 1092.

16. Presidential address, 1905 Indian National Congress, Gokhale, *Speeches,* p. 841.

17. Speech by Lord Coleridge, November 15, 1905, cited in Gokhale, *A Debate on the Awakening of India* (London, 1905?), p. 6.

18. Morley, *Recollections* (2 vols. New York, 1917), 2, 139.

19. Sir William Wedderburn, a retired Anglo-Indian active in Congress affairs, presumed that Gokhale had been "in considerable measure" responsible for Morley's decision to accept the India Office. Stanley Wolpert implicitly accepts this

ever, that the Congress emissary and his compatriots were sincerely delighted when Morley's appointment to the Indian secretaryship was subsequently announced. They were confident that "the repressive policy of Lord Curzon," from which they had grievously suffered, was no more than "the backwash of that 'Imperialism' which is associated in England with the name of Mr. Chamberlain." [20] With considerably less justification, they looked to the most ardent and eloquent opponent of Chamberlain's South African designs to rectify the jingo abuses of Chamberlain's Indian accomplice, particularly the 1905 partition of Bengal which had so incensed nationalist opinion.

Who was it whom Indian leaders believed they were welcoming, and precisely what did they expect of him? In the mind of at least one prominent congressman, John Morley was credited as "the statesman who pacified Ireland" and who, it was consequently presumed, might "be safely trusted . . . to pacify Bengal." [21] Nine months before the advent of the Campbell-Bannerman ministry, amid speculation about Morley's eventual assignment, one Indian journalist professed:

> Perhaps there is no author living or dead about whom we are more unanimous in our admiration than we are about Mr. John Morley. . . . To the political wisdom and philosophic spirit of his masters, Mr. Morley has added that rare genius of understanding different phases of character and alien modes of belief—of grasping the ideals cherished by men far removed from his own line of thought.[22]

It would be unfair to ascribe the optimism of educated Indians exclusively to naïveté or self-deception, though each undoubtedly played its part. Certainly the classic texts of nineteenth-century liberalism—including those written by Morley—had encouraged the belief that education could overcome any social handicap. India's university graduates, who took for granted that intellect

---

interpretation. See Wedderburn to Gokhale, December 14, 1905, cited in Wolpert, *Tilak and Gokhale* (Berkeley, 1962), p. 173.

20. *Report of the Twenty-first Indian National Congress*, p. 23.

21. Rash Behari Ghose, Opening address, Twenty-second Indian National Congress, Calcutta, December 26, 1906, *Report*, p. 7.

22. Hira Lal Chatterji, "Mr. John Morley," *Indian Review, 6* (1905), 252.

and not color was their outstanding attribute, considered themselves full-fledged English liberals; one of their number had even obtained membership in the parliamentary Liberal Party.

It came as a shock to educated Indians that Morley, from whose words they had derived both inspiration and encouragement, did not share their high opinion of themselves. The new Secretary of State could not be persuaded that either a diploma or a frock coat conferred English citizenship upon its owner. He admitted "a gross philistine weakness" on his own part against "Orientals," and professed that "when I have to [deal] with them I'd rather dispense with Parisian, Cosmopolitan, or even London varnish." He particularly disdained the facility with which the Aga Khan affected a Western manner, and found the unassuming Gokhale more congenial company.[23] Nothing could have been more painful to members of India's educated elite than the failure of British Liberals to return their respect and loyalty. Gandhi, a young barrister traveling in South Africa, believed that his "faultless English dress" would insure him a first-class railway accommodation, but in such eyes as those of Winston Churchill he would always remain a "half-naked fakir."

The applause for Morley in December 1905, considerable as it was, was not nearly so universal as the belief that Honest John had never considered Indian problems.[24] The imperialist press at home and in India consoled itself that Morley's inexperience in Indian affairs would blunt the edge of his much-dreaded Little Englandism. Sir William Wedderburn, the aged ally of the Indian national cause, greeted Morley's appointment with full confidence that the Indian secretary's open mind would more than compensate for his previous lack of interest in Indian affairs. "On the whole," Wedderburn reasoned, "I do not think that we could have a better man." Paying no attention to the views that Morley had expressed in Parliament, in the editorial columns of nineteenth-century journals, and in nearly a dozen published volumes, Wedderburn anticipated the greatest benefits for Indian nationalism from Morley's supposed shortage of preconceptions: "Now that he

23. Morley to Minto, October 26, 1906, and February 18, 1909, Minto Papers (National Library of Scotland, Edinburgh).

24. The anonymous author of an article in the *Spectator*—possibly Sir Alfred Lyall—proved a notable exception (December 16, 1905), p. 1025.

is responsible for India, he will feel it his duty to go thoroughly into the facts, and his historical experience will lead him to the right conclusions." [25]

Other partisans were even more explicit in divorcing Morley from his namesake who had come up through the Liberal Party ranks. "We have, for a Secretary of State," wrote a distinguished Muslim scholar, "not, thank heavens, a 'practical politician,' which usually means one who can see just a few paces further than his nose, but what Mr. Morley would himself call 'that abject being, a philosopher.' " [26] Bipin Chandra Pal, among the most vociferous of Indian extremists, shared the same impression:

> A child of the French Illumination, brought up on the philosophy of Mill and Bentham and the nineteenth-century individualistic rationalism of England, Lord Morley is, in spite of his superior culture and mentality, an anachronism in twentieth-century thought and life.[27]

For personal as well as ideological reasons there were Englishmen, too, who denounced Morley as an "ideologue," ill-equipped to contend with the political forces which he had, in fact, helped to create. John Buchan's biographical endeavor to rehabilitate the memory of Lord Minto offers a portrait of Morley that has considerably more in common with the subjects of his literary efforts —Rousseau, Voltaire, and Diderot—than with such political intimates as Gladstone, Harcourt, and Chamberlain. At the India Office, Buchan alleged, Morley behaved not like a responsible statesman, but like a "scholar," who, when "transferred to the seat of power, is always apt to order things with a high hand, because he has little knowledge of the daily compromises by means of which the business of the world is conducted." [28]

25. Wedderburn to Gokhale, December 14, 1905, cited in Wolpert, *Tilak and Gokhale*, p. 173. An editorial in the *Indian Review* (6 [1905], 820), congratulated Sir Henry Campbell-Bannerman for Morley's appointment; acknowledging that "the lions in the path" of the new Indian secretary were "many and of a most determined character," it nonetheless presumed that "Mr. Morley may bring to the consideration of the great problems that are pending, a historic mind which is at once open and just." An advertisement for Morley's *Life of Richard Cobden* (London, 1905), followed at the foot of the page.

26. Mohamed Ali, *Thoughts on the Present Discontent* (Bombay, 1907), pp. xi-xii.

27. Bipin Chandra Pal, *Nationality and Empire* (Calcutta, 1916), pp. 273-74.

28. John Buchan, *Lord Minto: A Memoir* (London, 1924), p. 222.

With a decade of public service still before him, John Morley found himself the prisoner of a reputation that spoke louder and often more eloquently than his own feeble voice and that allowed him little room for creative maneuver in either Indian affairs or domestic politics. Nothing he could do in his capacity as Secretary of State for India was sufficient to deprive him of the amateur status to which he was consigned by overenthusiastic supporters in unwitting league with carping critics. His actions, even when they were obvious reapplications of measures that he had framed for Ireland or that he had vainly advocated for Egypt or the Transvaal, have been invariably identified as ad hoc, for his contemporaries had forgotten—and subsequent historians have chosen not to recall—the youthful predecessor of the elder statesman whom they presumed to know.

Because Morley's performance from 1905 to 1910 reflected more a fidelity to past commitments than any vision for Indian constitutional growth, it is necessary to appreciate the precise nature of those commitments and to recognize how intensely and self-consciously Morley was a product of his Gladstonian heritage. Only as exercises in nineteenth-century Liberal statesmanship do his twentieth-century decisions emerge as components of a coherent program. It was with reference to the first Earl of Lytton, whom Disraeli appointed to the viceroyalty in 1874, that Morley had framed his views on the distribution of constitutional powers between Simla and Whitehall. During his two terms as Chief Secretary for Ireland he had defined his attitudes toward coercion and nationalist agitation. His struggles as an anti-imperialist and a pro-Boer had intensified his opposition to military leaders and their expansionist designs. It is with reference to the events and controversies of earlier decades that one may best understand his view that responsible institutions would prove not only a failure but also a liability in a non-Christian, non-westernized society; and it was this belief, rather than any intention to divide and rule, that convinced him to endorse reluctantly Lord Minto's proposals for communal electorates. In each instance, his position was dictated by his adherence to Gladstonian principles and by his determination to speak as his master's voice. It was his misfortune—and India's—that by the time he returned to office in December 1905, that voice carried little authority and less conviction.

The wealth of quotable material in Morley's correspondence

with Lord Minto, recently made available, has elicited a number
of scholarly inquiries of which this is neither the first nor, in all
likelihood, the last. The sources are too rich, the personalities too
fascinating, and the issues too complex for any single account to
exhaust them. Most recently Stanley A. Wolpert, a fellow American, has written of *Morley and India, 1906-1910*.[29] Though our
books cover some of the same ground, they differ in concept and
interpretation. Wolpert portrays Morley as "a leading architect of
India's political future," determined to advance India's progress
toward "the goal of parliamentary self-government." The present
study, viewing Morley from another vantage point, offers conclusions quite different.

Unlike Wolpert's book and those of our predecessors in the
field, this is not in a strict sense a work in Indian history: India is
little more than a backdrop against which emotional and intellectual issues are projected. But Morley, it must be remembered, was
not in a strict sense an "Indian" administrator: he came no closer
to India than his weekly dispatches from Lord Minto, and all the
while his preoccupation remained British society and institutions.
Rather than duplicate the efforts of previous scholars by providing
a narrative of events in India during these five years, I will place
Morley and his policies within the intellectual and political context of British liberalism. It is in this context, and not simply in
that of Indian history, that these must be examined. Before one
can judge whether his actions were either the fulfillment or be-
trayal of past principles, one must establish precisely what those
principles were. As R. J. Moore has noted, there persist "large
gaps in the ideological framework for the study of British India."[30] Following his own admirable example, I am making a
modest attempt to fill one such gap, a crucial one, in the pages that
follow.

29. Berkeley, 1967. I should point out that the present study was written before
the publication of either the Wolpert book or *Servant of India: A Study of Imperial Rule from 1905 to 1910 as Told through the Correspondence and Diaries of
Sir James Dunlop Smith*, ed. Martin Gilbert (London, 1966). The latter, a most
valuable primary source for the period, gives strong reinforcement to several of
my arguments.

30. *Liberalism and Indian Politics, 1872–1922* (London, 1966), p. 1; see also a
seminal article by Moore, "John Morley's Acid Test: India, 1906–10," *Pacific Affairs,*
40 (1968), 333-40.

1   The Sorcerer's Apprentice

In his autobiographical *Recollections,* published nearly two decades after Gladstone's death, John Morley recounts an after-dinner conversation with Mrs. Gladstone, his hostess, on the evening of January 9, 1894. The Grand Old Man and another guest, Lord Armitstead, were rattling the dice on the backgammon board while Morley, as the authorized emissary of his Cabinet colleagues, informed Mrs. Gladstone that "the pride and glory of her life was at last to face eclipse, that the curtain was falling on a grand drama of fame, power, acclamation." [1] Within a month Gladstone had presided over his last Cabinet, had delivered his final speech in the House of Commons, and the Queen, without summoning him for consultation, had designated Lord Rosebery as his successor.

Quite appropriately it was John Morley who, after a decade in which he perfected his Gladstonianism, laid to rest one of the last vestiges of Gladstonian liberalism: the Indian policies which his mentor had evolved during a half-century of public life. With the exception of Morley's imperial policies for India, and the other attitudes he embodied, there was a minimum of Gladstonian content to the Liberal Governments of the twentieth century. Herbert Gladstone had neither the perseverance nor sufficient support among his colleagues to conduct Home Office affairs along Gladstonian lines, and James Bryce was transferred to the Washington Embassy after an undistinguished year at the Irish Office. As Indian secretary from 1905 to 1910, and again from March to May 1911, Morley learned from his recurrent failures the extent to which the Gladstonian world had been transformed in both hemispheres.

Historians have thoroughly destroyed the familiar portrait of

1. 2, 5. This incident does not appear in Morley's three-volume *Life of Gladstone* (London, 1903) .

W. E. Gladstone as a "Little Englander," [2] that elusive breed
whose characterstics Morley has often been said to have shared.[3]
There are, in addition, equally strong grounds on which to oppose
Sir Philip Magnus's contention that Gladstone "seldom thought
about India." [4] His references to Indian affairs are not many, but
they are explicit, and his speeches in Midlothian in 1879–80 are
testimony to an abiding concern. Even in Gladstone's earliest parliamentary years, he revealed an awareness of Indian issues and
often a fascination with them; this is reflected in a letter that, a
novice in the Commons, he wrote to his father: "You will see by
your *Post* that I held forth last night on the Universities Bill. The
House I am glad to say heard me with the utmost kindness, for
they had been listening previously to an Indian discussion in
which few people took any interest, though indeed it was both
curious and interesting." [5] In the years that followed, he retained
a lively interest in Indian problems, which was nourished by contacts with Richard Cobden and John Bright.

Neither the personalities with whom he had to contend nor the
incipient forces of Indian nationalism had ever compelled Gladstone to promulgate far-reaching Indian proposals. But he compensated for this deficiency by demonstrating a respect for constitutional liberties and a determination to fulfill the "great duty
towards India" that justified British rule. "We have no interest in
India," he declared, "except the wellbeing of India itself, and
what that wellbeing will bring with it in the way of consequence." [6] Morley, for one, could not have been in more complete
agreement. A decade earlier, he too cited the moral responsibilities of the Government of India: "At whatever cost, we are bound
to pay the most solemn and scrupulous respect to treaties [with
native rulers] and to the ideas and interests of the native popula-

2. See John S. Galbraith, "Myths of the 'Little England' Era," *American Historical Review,* 67 (1961), 34-48.

3. E.g. W. Menzies Whitelaw, "Lord Morley," in H. Ausubel et al., eds., *Some Modern Historians of Britain* (New York, 1951), p. 156.

4. Sir Philip Magnus, *Gladstone* (London, 1954), p. 443; more recently, R. T. Shannon, while correctly stressing that the "ideal of the beneficent sway of an imperial master race had no attraction for him," mistakenly concludes that "India seems hardly to have entered his thoughts." *Gladstone and the Bulgarian Agitation* (London, 1963), p. 8.

5. July 28, 1834, cited in Morley, *Life of Gladstone, 1,* 113.

6. Gladstone, "Aggression on Egypt and Freedom in the East," *Nineteenth Century Review,* 2 (1877), 151-53.

tion . . . for whom solely, our government is held in trust." [7]

The Morley-Gladstone partnership, which was erected on a foundation of mutual respect and intellectual compatibility and which was welded by a joint approach to the Irish problem, was, in fact, initiated by a common interest in Lord Lytton's Indian administration. Before the late '70s Morley, like most Radicals, had tended to be skeptical of Gladstone's intentions and critical of Gladstone's policies. The Grand Old Man had not even obliged the editor of the *Fortnightly Review* with a contribution to his journal.[8] Gladstone, at this time, was no longer the official head of his party, but it was to him that Liberals looked for direction; they were not disappointed. In his condemnation of Conservative aggressions along a route which circumvented Africa, touched the Balkans and Central Asia, and terminated at the conference table in Berlin, Gladstone cited India as a particular evil of Disraeli's imperialism.

The issues on which Gladstone waged his successful Midlothian campaigns grew mainly from the foreign and imperial policies of the Beaconsfield administration. Morley was gratified by Gladstone's choice of ammunition, delighted with Gladstone's pronouncements, and impressed by the clarity and vigor with which they were expressed: "It is needless to say," he wrote to the Prime Minister, "how heartily I exult in the magnitude and completeness of the victory which you have won." [9] Otherwise Morley found little in which to "exult," for his personal bid for a share in the Liberal victory had been rejected by the electors of Westminster, a fact he ascribed to deficient party organization and a shortage of campaign funds, and to which his reputation as a freethinker also contributed.[10] Still, the "magnitude and completeness" of Gladstone's triumph softened the blow of his own defeat. The recent campaign had revealed important points of agreement

7. Morley, "England and the European Crisis," *Fortnightly Review*, n.s., *1* (1867), 624.

8. "The *F.R.* is the only magazine in which he does *not* write—the voluminous animal," Morley fumed to Joseph Chamberlain. "Still, he's a famous mortal." Morley to Chamberlain, September 30, 1878, Chamberlain Papers. Among the compensations for Morley in the triumph which the Liberal Party enjoyed was Gladstone's first contribution to the *Fortnightly*, an astute analysis of "The Conservative Collapse" which appeared in the May 1880 issue over the by-line "Index."

9. Morley to Gladstone, April 7, 1880, Gladstone Papers, British Museum Add. MSS. 44,255, fol. 14.

10. Morley to Chamberlain, March 29, 1880, Chamberlain Papers.

between Morley and Gladstone, and each agreement was a bridge that brought the former closer to membership in the Gladstonian camp. Of these, it was Gladstone's appraisal of events in India that was most significant at the moment and that proved most notable in its long-range effects.

Morley's attention had undoubtedly been attracted to Indian affairs because Lord Lytton, the Conservative Viceroy, had been his close friend and a frequent contributor of poetry to the *Fortnightly*. Morley's so-called Little Englandism had not prevented him from celebrating Lytton's appointment in 1876: "My mind is rather full of the dazzling prize Lytton has got," he wrote to Joseph Chamberlain. "He is a kind, affectionate soul, and I can't but rejoice at his good fortune." [11] Lytton was not nearly so enthusiastic about his political plum when he contemplated his prospects in a letter to Morley a few days later: "I have not courted, or willingly accepted, the crushing gift of such a white elephant." The newly appointed Governor-General added: "I have been re-making my will; I may as well mention that I have left you a small legacy. Perhaps one of these days it may help to cover your election expenses. If so, remember the Tory source of it—and be merciful." [12] But even without Lytton's contribution, Morley amassed sufficient backing to stand, unsuccessfully, for a second time in 1880, and a rousing condemnation of his friend's Afghan and Indian policies was prominently featured among his denunciations of the Beaconsfield Government.

At the cost of a precious friendship, Morley learned valuable lessons about imperialism and Indian affairs that decisively influenced his thinking in the decades that followed. He witnessed the metamorphosis of Lord Lytton, under the Indian sun, from a poet to a potentate, thereby demonstrating the alarming ease with which jingoism destroyed British equanimity. The new Viceroy had no sooner been subjected to tropical temperatures than he ceased to contemplate esthetics and turned to projects which could not fail to antagonize his Radical friend. As he cruised through the Red Sea, Lytton related proposals to annex Egypt and to support the South African expansionist policies of Morley's bête noire, Sir Bartle Frere.[13]

11. Morley to Chamberlain, January 7, 1876, Chamberlain Papers.

12. Lytton to Morley, January 9, 1876, Lytton Papers (India Office Library, London).

13. Lytton to Morley, March 27, 1876, Lytton Papers.

There had been symptoms of Lytton's susceptibility to the imperial fever in letters to Morley before he began his viceroyalty, but these isolated passages do not appear to have disturbed their close relationship. He had touched upon two of Morley's particular sore spots, royal expenditure and the pageantry of empire, when he condemned the "lamentable exhibition of the English working class mind in the Debate on the Prince of Wales' Indian Expenses! It is not the grudging [of] the money that matters. It is the incapacity to take an imperial view of affairs. How can we hope to remain a great Empire if this tone of mind becomes prevalent?" [14] Once Lytton had been ensconced at Calcutta, it was no longer easy to discount his remarks as idle digressions. "What alienates me from the English radicalism of the day," he proclaimed to Frederic Harrison, who could be depended upon to communicate the revelation to Morley, "is its utter want of patriotism and practical common sense. So far as I can judge, it would willingly burn down every rafter of the great fabric of the British Empire in order to roast in the ashes some of its own little half-addled theoretical eggs." [15]

Self-conscious of the theoretical eggs in his own basket, Morley became steadily less impressed with the viceregal powers which his friend had inherited, and more fearful of them. Lytton had previously expressed the view that "efficient government of alien races by means of a parliamentary civilisation is an impossibility." [16] The implications of this argument first dawned upon Morley when Lytton's successive Indian policies took effect. It was with reference to Disraeli's Viceroy and to Lord Salisbury, then Secretary of State for India, that Morley evolved theories of Indian administration: the Indian Empire, he insisted to Chamberlain in 1876, could be properly administered under "our parliamentary system" only by shifting the preponderance of power to the Indian secretary at Whitehall.[17] Morley was later given the opportunity to redefine the imperial authority which, a quarter century earlier, Lord Lytton had abused.

Lytton's administration has been heavily criticized in two distinct areas: his projects for imperial expansion and his tacit denial

14. Lytton to Morley, July 26, 1875, Lytton Papers.
15. Lytton to Harrison, April 2, 1878, *Personal and Literary Letters of Robert, First Earl of Lytton,* ed. Lady Betty Balfour (2 vols. London, 1906) , 2, 98.
16. Lytton to Morley, July 26, 1875, Lytton Papers.
17. Morley to Chamberlain, March 18, 1876, Chamberlain Papers.

of the Indians' occupational and political aspirations. The Lytton years reaffirmed Morley's resolute opposition to frontier warfare—whether in Afghanistan, Burma, the Sudan, or South Africa—and they prompted him to contemplate the uneasy constitutional relationship between the Governor-General and his superiors at Whitehall; that they wholly failed, however, to enlist Morley as an advocate of representative institutions for India was demonstrated by his silence when Indian reform became a topic for parliamentary debate in 1892.

Morley's evaluation of imperial ventures hinged to a great extent on their effects upon the British Exchequer: "Anything more abominable than Lytton's Afghan scrape cannot be imagined," he told his sister. "The British people will have to pay for their Tory whistle. . . . Get your money ready, my dear." [18] Gladstone, too, deplored the Government of India's frequent recourse to deficit finance and Lytton's "spirit of expenditure." [19] It was not the source of the money but the waste of it that he decried, and he found no consolation in the fact that imperial efforts consumed funds from Indian rather than British pockets. Gladstone argued that by sending Indian troops to the eastern Mediterranean in 1877, "with the charge defrayed at the moment out of the Indian Treasury," Disraeli had repudiated the terms of the Government of India Act.[20] But his views on Indian and imperial issues were not dictated exclusively by his well-publicized tight-fistedness. British rule in India could be tolerated and even championed so long as it did not incur heavy public expenditures, distract the British people from more immediate and vital concerns, or prove detrimental to Her Majesty's Indian subjects. The policies implemented by Lord Lytton, presumably with the approval of Lord Beaconsfield, failed to satisfy Gladstone on any count.

Although Morley's opposition to Lytton also grew out of domestic considerations, it was, like Gladstone's, by no means devoid of concern for subject peoples. "The Afghan affair is really too bad," he wrote to Chamberlain, "and the idea of saddling India with a war, foolish in itself, just after a famine, or indeed after two fam-

18. September 20, 1879, cited in F. W. Hirst, *Early Life and Letters of John Morley* (2 vols. London, 1927), 2, 83.

19. Speech at Edinburgh, November 29, 1879, Gladstone, *Political Speeches in Scotland* (2 vols. Edinburgh, 1880), 1, 143-45.

20. [Gladstone], "The Conservative Collapse," *Fortnightly Review*, n.s., 27 (1880), 619.

ines, is one of the worst that ever entered a ruler's head." [21] At
this point in his checkered career, Chamberlain was inclined to
agree; he deplored Lytton's "Affghan War (Are there 2 F's, by the
way?)" and stated, "If we are to pose as a *great* nation, we must be
content to pay for our grandeur." [22] Employing a rhetoric the
paternity of which the future Colonial Secretary might have hesitated to acknowledge, Chamberlain urged Morley to extend the
attack into the pages of the *Fortnightly Review:*

> What's especially desirable to make clear is that this infernal
> Afghan business is the natural consequence of Jingoism, Im-
> perialism, British interests, and all the other phrasing of this
> mountebank government. It is in perfect harmony with the
> acquisition of Cyprus and the Protectorate of Asia Minor;
> and it is perhaps fortunate that before going farther in the
> latter bargain we should have a practical specimen of the sort
> of work we have so lightly undertaken.[23]

There is some justification for F. W. Hirst's remark that in criticizing Lytton's border policy, the *Fortnightly* "was rather tender
towards the culprit." [24] At least until the final months of Lytton's
viceroyalty, Morley treated the Governor-General more kindly in
print than in private. He admitted that on one occasion he had
expurgated a harsh condemnation of Lytton which "it would be
most painful for me to be responsible for." [25] In the issue for
January 1879, M. E. Grant Duff attempted an exoneration of
Lytton's character which contradicted Morley's well-known personal views.[26]

If Morley felt any compunction in criticizing the Viceroy and
his deeds in the pages of the *Fortnightly Review*, which had more

21. Morley to Chamberlain, September 28, 1878, Chamberlain Papers.
22. Chamberlain to Morley, September 29, 1878, Chamberlain Papers.
23. Chamberlain to Morley, October 15, 1878, Chamberlain Papers.
24. Hirst, *Early Life*, 2, 65.
25. Morley to Chamberlain, September 28, 1878, Chamberlain Papers.
26. "Sir Stafford Northcote—a Rejoinder," *Fortnightly Review*, n.s., 25 (1879),
132. Morley had received assurances from Lytton that "I am resolved that my
foreign policy should be my own" (Lytton to Morley, March 14, 1876, Lytton
Papers), and he could therefore feel secure in his conviction that the Afghan wars
had not been foisted upon Lytton by his superiors at home. Individual members
of the Beaconsfield Cabinet, Morley told Chamberlain, "are very wroth in their
hearts against Lytton, but of course he will be supported until the war is over."
Morley to Chamberlain, September 28, 1878, Chamberlain Papers.

than once boasted Lytton's name in its table of contents, he did not hesitate to inveigh against both in the *Pall Mall Gazette,* which had come under his editorial wing in May 1880. Lytton's Afghan adventures merited front-page diatribes in the *P. M. G.,* even after the hapless Viceroy had returned to England.[27] In Morley's opinion, the significance of these campaigns could not be overestimated. Decades later he remained convinced that rampant jingoism had not only "ruined Lytton," but had "contributed more than either Bulgaria or South Africa to the overthrow of Poor Dizzy." [28] When Morley became Secretary of State for India, the deep imprint of Lytton's experiences was still evident. He evoked plaintive images of the Tory Viceroy whenever the men on the spot threatened to embark upon military projects. "Depend upon it," he admonished Lord Minto, "an Afghan war will overthrow the statesmen responsible for it, whether in India, or on the quarter-deck here. Don't let us forget the fate of poor Lytton and his chiefs at home." [29]

Lord Lytton's military campaigns had provided the keynote of Gladstone's eloquent denunciation of Beaconsfield's global designs, but Gladstone was equally incensed by other Lyttonite policies. His selection of Lord Ripon to succeed Lytton, like his previous unsuccessful attempt to appoint John Bright to the India Office, testifies to the fact that he had not seized upon Indian issues for mere political advantage. He had deprecated Lytton's "increased taxation upon that impoverished population," [30] and he duly advised Ripon that he could not sanction an Indian income tax.[31] He had condemned the "ruinous, unjust, destructive war in Afghanistan," [32] and he instructed his Viceroy to conclude a hasty and conciliatory peace. Gladstone had raised strong objections to Lytton's 1878 Vernacular Press Act, better known in India as the "Muzzling Act," which imposed severe restrictions upon Indian journalism; it was in no way comparable, he insisted, to legislation

27. See issues of May 18, June 3 and 8, 1880, January 11 and March 4, 1881.

28. Morley to Minto, April 30, 1908, Minto Papers.

29. Morley to Minto, September 10, 1908, Minto Papers.

30. Speech at Glasgow, December 5, 1879, Gladstone, *Political Speeches in Scotland, 1,* 200.

31. Gladstone to Ripon, November 24, 1881, Ripon Papers, British Museum Add. MSS. 43,515, fols. 5-6.

32. Speech at Glasgow, December 5, 1879, Gladstone, *Political Speeches in Scotland, 1,* 200.

passed for Ireland: "We did not restrain the Irish Press for mere disaffection, but for the security of human life." [33] It was apparent to Gladstone that this discriminatory measure would not only generate further interracial enmity but would guarantee "that those who rule cannot get at the true mind and meaning and desires of those who are ruled." [34] Lord Ripon could not have doubted the Prime Minister's feelings on the matter when he was told: "That monstrous Vernacular Press Act, of Lytton or Salisbury or both, I am content to have in your hands." [35]

While Gladstone settled down to his second tenancy at Downing Street, Ripon set to work to contradict the impression bequeathed to India by the Lytton regime "that in all ways, in foreign policy, in finance, in such measures as the Vernacular Press Act and the Arms Act, the interests of the Natives of India were sacrificed to those of England." [36] Ripon found the Prime Minister's guidance and encouragement invaluable to him in his task, and he received both in abundant measure. It would be difficult to overemphasize Gladstone's personal contribution to the removal of the grievances, if not the aftertaste, of the Lytton viceroyalty. His constant support and gentle prodding were essential.[37] It is to his credit that his influence was exerted with tact and humility, and that the majority of the promises he made to the Indian people at Midlothian were ultimately fulfilled.[38]

33. *Parliamentary Debates*, 3d ser., *242*, cols. 44 ff. (July 23, 1878).

34. Speech at Glasgow, December 5, 1879, Gladstone, *Political Speeches in Scotland, 1*, 200.

35. Gladstone to Ripon, November 24, 1881, Ripon Papers, Add. MSS. 43,515, fols. 5-6. Gladstone's concern for "those principles of public law and respect for other peoples which Disraeli, Salisbury, and Lytton were deemed to have overthrown," is made evident in the introduction by S. Gopal to his excellent study, *The Viceroyalty of Lord Ripon* (Oxford, 1953).

36. Ripon to Gladstone, October 22, 1881, Gladstone Papers, Add. MSS. 44,286, fol. 257.

37. See Ripon to Gladstone, October 22, 1881, in which the Viceroy contemplates the delays involved in "getting rid of" Lytton's Vernacular Press Act (Gladstone Papers, Add. MSS. 44,286, fol. 252). Ripon subsequently advocated postponement of his Criminal Procedure Bill, but the Prime Minister—joined by Kimberley, Northbrook, and Hartington—protested that this would advertise his Government's timidity. "I cannot help feeling," Kimberley told Gladstone, "that Ripon is frightened by the agitation and that he misunderstands public opinion here on the subject." Kimberley to Gladstone, October 13, 1883, Gladstone Papers, Add. MSS. 44,228, fol. 124.

38. Of all Lytton's repressive legislation, only the Arms Act was allowed to remain on the statute books, though Gladstone had criticized it as a demonstration

Neither the Indian policies of Gladstone's second Government nor those subsequently promulgated by the Grand Old Man were themselves sufficient to guide John Morley in his administration of Indian affairs in the early twentieth century; Indian nationalism and British liberalism had each undergone a profound transformation in the intervening years. But Gladstone's Midlothian oratory brought into focus the considerations that were to shape Morley's Indian legislation as well as to embitter his relations with Lord Minto: a distaste for bureaucratic intolerance, a dread of military despotism, and an opposition to imperial expenditures. Two decades of collaboration with Gladstone reinforced Morley's views on these subjects until, when he arrived at the India Office, he was in a position to translate his mentor's doctrines into imperial policies.

---

of "a mistrust of people." Speech at Glasgow, December 5, 1879, Gladstone, *Political Speeches in Scotland, 1, 199-200*. The obstacle to repeal was Lord Ripon's confidence in the need for such a measure. Ripon to Gladstone, October 22, 1881, Gladstone Papers, Add. MSS. 44,286, fol. 252.

2   Gladstone's Lieutenant

John Morley was introduced to Gladstone early in 1876 at a meeting of the Metaphysical Society, to which they both belonged. "I have had only one good talk with him," he promptly informed Frederic Harrison, "and I quite feel his attraction—his simplicity, and freedom from small egotism and self-consciousness." [1] Yet it would be premature to date Morley's conversion to Gladstonianism from this first encounter. Morley, who had made one unsuccessful attempt to enter Parliament, would make another before he ultimately succeeded, and Gladstone had recently vacated the Liberal leadership presumably never to return. Only after the general election of 1880 did it become possible to regard the Grand Old Man as a permanent fixture in British political life, and this was a prerequisite to Morley's conversion. Indeed, Morley learned his lesson so well that he continued to rely upon Gladstonianism long after it had ceased to be practicable.

Gladstone's return to the premiership was a source of relief and satisfaction to Morley, who, to a greater extent than those Radicals with ministerial aspirations, had come to depend upon the veteran parliamentarian as a double-edged weapon against the Whigs within the party and the Tories without. "Mr. Gladstone will commit errors and society will shriek," he prophesied in the editorial columns of the *Pall Mall Gazette,* "but his errors will be the small intellectual waywardnesses of a judgment which is erratic in small things, but sure when it is in the presence of the greater interests of mankind." [2] It would be wrong, however, to assume that his celebration of Gladstone's reemergence signified that Morley had either issued his last criticism of the Prime Minister or suffered his last disappointment at Gladstone's hand. But henceforth there is a marked change in the emphasis and tone of Mor-

1. Morley to Harrison, February 16, 1876, Harrison Papers.
2. May 20, 1880, p. 1.

ley's criticisms. Though from time to time he attacked the Liberal Party's policies for being insufficiently Gladstonian either in content or application, he invariably found a way to absolve the party leader. As a reporter of parliamentary affairs and, from the spring of 1883, as a participant in them, Morley dedicated himself to the defense of the Gladstonian position even when W. E. Gladstone, for reasons of expediency, departed from it.

It is vital to an understanding of Morley's political career, through the Home Rule struggle and down to his resignation from the Cabinet on August 4, 1914, to observe that his allegiances were primarily to personalities and only through them to his party. It continued to be Gladstone's personality, rather than specific policies, which attracted him. At a time when the Liberal program offered little to cheer a Radical heart, he consoled himself that "public affairs are in the hands of a man who grapples with political difficulties instead of evading them or covering them up with phrases." [3] In a letter to Robert Spence Watson, who presided over the Liberal Party machine at Newcastle, Morley surmised that "if Gladstone were to leave the Government, the rest of the Cabinet would be straight Jingo. So let us pray for him." [4]

Was it wishful thinking or shrewd observation which led Morley to see the Grand Old Man as a bulwark against the jingoes who eventually dominated both sets of benches in the House of Commons? Morley's suspension of Radical disbelief, a vital ingredient in his conversion to Gladstonianism, was as much the product of personal predilection as the result of any encouragement he received from Gladstone. As a journalist, he regarded Gladstone as a maker of news; as a historian, he regarded him as a maker of history. In a note to Gladstone which accompanied a complimentary copy of his biography of Richard Cobden, he apologized that "the narrative will seem very thin and shadowy to a prominent actor." [5] Justifiably impressed with Gladstone's previous accomplishments, Morley, not unreasonably, expected to see herculean feats performed by a well-proved Hercules.

If the benefits he had anticipated took an unusually long time to accrue, Morley could reflect that age and his years in retirement

3. *Pall Mall Gazette* (November 9, 1880), p. 1.

4. Morley to Spence Watson, February 24, 1884, Hirst, *Early Life*, 2, 193.

5. Morley to Gladstone, October 24, 1881, Gladstone Papers, Add. MSS. 44,255, fol. 29.

had conspired to render the Grand Old Man a bit rusty, and that Gladstone had foolishly burdened himself with Whig colleagues who forced him to drag his heels.[6] Morley's close attention to parliamentary affairs and the accounts he received from friends inside the Government confirmed his suspicion that if any individual could stem the imperialist tide, it was Gladstone. There were numerous occasions in the early '80s when the latter interfered to veto or at least to dampen imperialist activity, and while others complained that he lacked energy and foresight, Morely enthusiastically applauded.[7]

It was a good deal more difficult for Morley to applaud the Government's 1882 intervention in Egypt, which was followed by catastrophe in the Sudan. These crises put his incipient Gladstonianism to the test, and revealed that it was stronger than he himself had perhaps suspected. Like Gladstone, he had expressed vehement opposition to previous proposals for British interference in Egyptian affairs. Yet he would have chafed at Sir Philip Magnus's unqualified assertion that it was "simple, honest self-deception" which permitted the Prime Minister to boast: "We have carried out this war from a love of peace, and, I may say, on the principle of peace." [8] Morley could appreciate the subtle distinction between past Tory imperial aggressions and the invasion of Egypt to which the Liberals had reluctantly assented. Personally, he could condone neither the British entry into Egypt nor his countrymen's continued presence there, but he saw no reason to impugn Gladstone's lofty motives.

Like the vast majority of his contemporaries, including members of the Cabinet,[9] Morley was confident that the British had in-

6. Morley found it difficult to forgive Gladstone—who, he insisted, was "not by his antecedents and traditions a Whig himself"—for surrounding himself with Whigs; he cited this as an example of Gladstone's ignorance of political currents and ingratitude to his Radical supporters (see "Home and Foreign Affairs," *Fortnightly Review*, n.s., 27 [1880], 865-66; also *Recollections, 1,* 167) , and he ascribed to this fact all the misfortunes of Gladstone's second ministry, including the dispatch of General Gordon to the Sudan in 1884. *Parliamentary Debates*, 3d ser., *294*, cols. 1071 ff. (February 23, 1885) .

7. Sir Charles Dilke transcribed accounts of these incidents from his diaries to assist Morley in his work on the *Life of Gladstone;* see especially entries for January 6, 1882; June 12, 1883; July 5 and December 14, 1884, Dilke Papers, British Museum Add. MSS. 43,942, fols. 29, 57, 88, 102.

8. Speech at Penmaenmawr, October 3, 1882, cited in Magnus, *Gladstone,* p. 315.

9. Sir William Harcourt, who took a particular interest in defining British aims in and for Egypt, circulated a memorandum among his Cabinet colleagues on

tervened only to return a safer and sounder Egypt to Egyptian hands. But this prospect grew more remote as successive diplomatic and East African exigencies impeded the withdrawal of British troops; of these, the most dramatic was the defeat by Sudanese insurgents of General Charles Gordon at Khartoum. Morley could not disguise the fact, which he later admitted to James Bryce, that this was "indeed a dismal tale: the one business in which I think Mr. G. cuts a weak and hopeless figure." [10] He deplored the selection of Gordon, the mission that had been entrusted to him, and the Government's failure to provide him with sufficient and sufficiently prompt support to prevent him from becoming a martyr to the jingo faith.[11] Yet again he was convinced that Gladstone's motives, if not his tactics, were defensible. On February 15, 1884, Morley rose in the Commons to deliver a speech which backhandedly supported the Government, declaring opposition to British penetration into the Sudan, which was no more than Gladstone had done, and advocating a withdrawal from Egypt at the earliest possible moment, which Gladstone had repeatedly promised.[12] At a time when Radicals angrily disparaged the Prime Minister's liberalism and Conversatives cast aspersions upon his patriotism, Morley's temperate language sounded like a shower of praise to Gladstone. The next morning, Morley was rewarded with a telegraphed invitation to dinner at Downing Street. "He congratulated me," he reported to Spence Watson, "and said he was in agreement with most of it. I said to him 'It looks as if you and I were the last of the Cobdenites.' " [13]

What remained to separate Morley from a fellow Cobdenite in

March 27, 1884, soliciting their opinions on this issue; the replies he received, which are among the Harcourt Papers at Stanton Harcourt, were unanimous in rejecting a permanent occupation.

10. Morley to Bryce, December 23, 1902, Bryce Papers (Bodleian Library, Oxford). Bryce assisted Morley in the preparation of this chapter in the *Life of Gladstone*. Morley expressed similar sentiments to Lord Cromer, who also contributed his recollections to the Gladstone biography. Morley to Cromer, April 3, 1901, Cromer Papers, PRO/FO 633/7.

11. Morley, *Life of Gladstone, 3*, 160.

12. *Parliamentary Debates*, 3d ser., *284*, cols. 1031 ff. (February 15, 1884) ; Morley used essentially the same technique a year later, when he moved an amendment opposing further military action in the Sudan "while refraining from expressing an opinion on the policies pursued by Her Majesty's Government." Ibid., 3d ser., *294*, cols. 1071 ff. (February 23, 1885) .

13. Morley to Spence Watson, February 24, 1884, Hirst, *Early Life, 2*, 193.

whom he recognized only the most virtuous motives and the most noble aspirations? One of the first votes Morley cast in the Commons reveals the nature of the last obstacle on his road to Gladstonianism: on March 14, 1883, he supported Charles Stewart Parnell and the Irish members, against the Government, on a Bill which had been introduced to amend the provisions of the 1881 Land Act.[14]

The origins of Morley's interest in the Irish problem are not obscure. His friends in political life may have approached the subject with disdain or trepidation, but he had friends in literary circles who were very much taken with it. Among them were the Positivists—including Harrison, Richard Congreve, E. S. Beesly, and Henry Crompton—who had petitioned Parliament in May 1867 on behalf of Irish political prisoners. Twenty years before Gladstone promulgated his first Home Rule Bill, the English disciples of Comte had founded the Ireland Society, which issued an appeal "for Irish Nationalism, [rather] than for a Parliament in Dublin"; [15] this fell far short of Home Rule, but it went further in that direction than anything else in its day.

As early as 1877, Joseph Chamberlain had chided Morley for his excessive concern with the Irish problem: "I think you have a half-kindness for these rascally Irishmen who are bound to give us a great deal of trouble." [16] Others, too, suspected Morley's latent sentiments and shared Chamberlain's misgivings. "A leading Whig came to me," Morley reported to Chamberlain in 1879, "very uneasy at my supposed leanings to Home Rule." [17] Yet it was not until the fall of Gladstone's second Government in June 1885, when he was convinced that nothing less than Home Rule would restore Irish stability and parliamentary decorum, that Morley committed himself to that course.

Morley had hitherto condemned the Liberal Government for responding to Irish disorders with repressive legislation. "It is worse than the loss of many a parliamentary seat to English Liberalism," he reckoned, "that the greatest of popular orators should never again be able to tell his countrymen that force is no rem-

14. *Divisions, House of Commons, Session 1883*, p. 77. It was prophetic that Morley and Joseph Chamberlain went into different lobbies on this division.

15. Frederic Harrison, *Autobiographic Memoirs* (2 vols. London, 1911), *1*, 322-23.

16. Chamberlain to Morley, October 3, 1877, J. L. Garvin, *Life of Joseph Chamberlain*, (3 vols. London, 1932), *1*, 273.

17. Morley to Chamberlain, November 8, 1879, Chamberlain Papers.

edy." [18] Yet Morley, not wholly without justification, was loath to consider the Coercion Act of 1881 a Gladstonian product. As he saw it, the Prime Minister's hand had been forced by overzealous colleagues, particularly W. E. Forster, the Irish Secretary. Morley was soon encouraged by news of Forster's resignation,[19] and by the release of Parnell and the Land Leaguers from Kilmainham Gaol. He consoled himself that if Gladstone had acted without foresight, he had at least acted without enthusiasm and had been honest enough to admit his errors. Morley undoubtedly realized too that opportunities for a creative, purposeful Irish policy would be lost as soon as the Liberal leadership passed to Hartington, Harcourt, or even Chamberlain. "I have never been an adulator of the Prime Minister," he assured one assailant, "but I must say that I believe that there has never been a time in his career when the country was better pleased to see him in control of our affairs than it is at this moment." [20]

It was not until Gladstone assumed the premiership for a third time, in February 1886, that he confirmed what many had begun to suspect, that he had adopted the cause of Home Rule.[21] Six weeks earlier, Herbert Gladstone, convinced that his father's hold upon the party was in danger, had launched his "Hawarden Kite," implying his father's conversion. Herbert's remarks, published at the close of a three-week-long general election, had—despite Gladstone's prompt denial—given rise to suspicions that the Grand Old Man had either connived to suppress news of his true sympathies until every ballot had been counted, or that he had conveniently acquired such sympathies only when it had become

18. "England and Ireland," *Fortnightly Review*, n.s., *29* (1881), 407.

19. With self-satisfaction, Morley recorded Harcourt's remark to Chamberlain that "your mischievous friend, J.M.," had prompted Forster's resignation by persistent attacks in the *Pall Mall Gazette* (*Recollections*, *1*, 175 ff.) ; it is more probable, as Morley realized, that Forster resigned because he disapproved of Gladstone's attempt to conciliate Parnell.

20. *Parliamentary Debates*, 3d ser., *298*, cols. 215-16 (May 11, 1885).

21. There is a lucid account of Gladstone's conversion in R. C. K. Ensor, *England, 1870–1914* (Oxford, 1963), pp. 92-97 and Appendix A. The versions in Viscount Gladstone's *After Thirty Years* (London, 1928) and Morley's *Life of Gladstone* are equally disappointing. Herbert Gladstone is intent upon self-defense, not on a reasoned explanation of his father's views. This incident is among the few in Morley's work in which the biographer allows his sentiments to intrude; the effect is not so much distortion as confusion.

apparent that his restoration to office would require Irish support. Though Morley later expressed distaste for Gladstone's "machinations of December, 1885," [22] he accorded his leader unstinting public support and dismissed Herbert's divulgence as the figment of a youthful imagination.[23] By this time, Morley's fellow Liberals had already come to look upon him as an apologist for Gladstonian policy; hours before Morley's Newcastle speech of December 21, Reginald Brett, later Lord Esher, advised Lord Rosebery that "no public figure" had yet supported Gladstone, "but I fancy J. Morley will supply the deficiency tonight." [24]

It is futile to quibble about who converted whom to whose Irish formula. Morley arrived at his decision to endorse Home Rule at an earlier date than Gladstone, but chivalry and political strategy led him to deny as "pure moonshine" allegations that his arguments had converted the Grand Old Man.[25] Whatever the origins of the Gladstonian Home Rule program, Morley was proud and eager to defend it to skeptical Liberals and hostile Tories. Yet it came as a surprise to him, as it did to senior politicians, that he was permitted to issue his defense of it not only from a place in Gladstone's third ministry, but from the office of the Chief Secretary for Ireland.

Two days before his appointment, he speculated to Brett that he would "be offered some miserably small place outside the Cabinet," which he would probably refuse.[26] When Lord Spencer, among the few who shared Gladstone's recognition of Morley's capabilities, dined with Sir William Harcourt and his son Lewis (Loulou) on January 27, he "ridiculed" their proposal to reappoint Sir Henry Campbell-Bannerman to the Irish Office and argued "that John Morley should go to carry out the reforms in the Government there." [27] The defection of prominent Liberals in 1886, the irreparable schism in the party ranks, and his exten-

22. Morley to Hamilton, July 31, 1902, Hamilton Papers, British Museum Add. MSS. 48,619.

23. Speech at Newcastle, December 21, 1885, *The Times* (December 22, 1885), p. 6.

24. Brett to Rosebery, December 21, 1885, *Journals and Letters of . . . Viscount Esher*, ed. M. V. Brett, *1* (London, 1934), 120.

25. Morley, *Life of Gladstone*, *3*, 296 n.

26. Lewis Harcourt's Journals, January 29, 1886, Harcourt Papers.

27. Ibid., January 27, 1886.

sive knowledge of the Irish issue combined to confer upon Morley an importance which Lord Acton considered "excessive," [28] but which Spencer and Gladstone recognized as invaluable.

Morley's appointment as Chief Secretary was an affirmation of the Prime Minister's intention to proceed with Home Rule and, as such, it was heavily criticized. *The Times* insisted that it was "impossible to overestimate the political importance of this selection," [29] and even those Liberals who proved willing to subscribe to Gladstone's Irish policy regretted his decision to rub salt in Whig wounds by naming as his Irish Secretary "the most conspicuous and unqualified advocate of Home Rule." [30] Sir William Harcourt conceded that Morley's "position and abilities entitle him to a place in the Cabinet," yet he felt impelled to protest to Gladstone that Morley's appointment to this particular post would hamstring the Government in its relations with rebellious Irishmen on the one hand and recalcitrant Liberals on the other.[31] Not all of the criticism leveled at the appointment was as well reasoned: Lord Salisbury's counsel was required to convince the Queen to accept a minister who was "in fact a Jacobin." [32] But the disapproval that was most painful to Morley came not from the lady at Osborne, but from the member for West Birmingham. Joseph Chamberlain resented Morley's appointment for two reasons: he regarded it as "a direct and immediate pronouncement in favour of a separate Parliament" for Ireland,[33] and he realized that it rendered virtually certain an early conflict between himself and Morley. As Austen Chamberlain later explained to his father's friend: "It put you in the forefront of the struggle on the very question on which you and he disagreed." [34]

Though Morley, to a more obvious extent than Chamberlain,

28. Cited in Morley, *Recollections, 1,* 218. Morley resented this comment by a "particularly well-informed critic," and explained that the secret of his success was "quite simple. In moments like this, it is the men who know their own mind[s] that are important even to excess."

29. February 3, 1886, p. 9.

30. A. G. Gardiner, *Life of Sir William Harcourt* (2 vols. London, 1923), *1,* 562.

31. Harcourt to Gladstone, January 31, 1886 [copy], Harcourt Papers.

32. The Queen consoled herself that the selection of a free-thinker to administer Roman Catholic Ireland would hasten the fall of Gladstone's Government. Elizabeth Longford, *Victoria, R.I.* (London, 1964), p. 487.

33. Lewis Harcourt's Journals, January 31, 1886, Harcourt Papers.

34. Austen Chamberlain to Morley, January 1, 1917, Austen Chamberlain Papers (University Library, Birmingham).

cherished the illusion that their thirteen-year-old friendship remained inviolate, there had been numerous indications that the two would be unable to maintain their political partnership. Morley was not only estranged by his friend's pronouncements on the situations in Egypt, the Sudan, and Ireland, but by Chamberlain's ambitions within the Liberal Party. Morley had come to rely increasingly upon Gladstone at the same time that Chamberlain, for personal reasons, desired to see the Grand Old Man step or be pushed aside.[35] The fact that Morley's confidence in Chamberlain had been shaken did not help matters at the Round Table conferences held in the spring of 1887 at Harcourt's London house in an attempt to restore Liberal unity. Of the five participants, Morley was most completely identified with the former Government's Irish policy, but Harcourt and Lord Herschell were equally staunch defenders of their chief; it was their task to reach an understanding with Chamberlain and Sir George Trevelyan, the two renegades from Gladstone's third Government. Their weeks of discussion left Morley and Chamberlain even more contemptuous of each other's policies, methods, and motives, and a Valentine's Day dinner at Trevelyan's home was hardly conducive to personal or political reconciliation.[36] Chamberlain concluded that Morley fancied himself Gladstone's successor;[37] and Morley took the view that only in Chamberlain's absence could the Liberal Party pursue a morally justifiable course.[38]

There exists an unfortunate tendency in accounts of John Morley's attitudes and behavior—whether in the Home Rule crisis, the interparty struggles of the '90s, his India Office years, or his Cabinet resignation in 1914—to attribute too much if not everything to his admittedly thin skin. The fact that Morley was too easily offended by a casual remark should not be taken to imply that he spent three decades in a perpetual pique, let alone that his

35. Lewis Harcourt learned from Brett on May 19, 1885, that "Chamberlain hopes and expects to be Prime Minister in the next Parliament, but this John Morley and all C's friends see to be impossible *yet*." Lewis Harcourt's Journals, Harcourt Papers.

36. Ibid., February 17, 1887; on this subject see the valuable study by Michael J. Hurst, *Joseph Chamberlain and Liberal Reunion* (London, 1967).

37. Sir William Harcourt assured Chamberlain that rumors of such aspirations on Morley's part were unfounded. Harcourt to Chamberlain, March 1, 1887, cited in Gardiner, 2, 36-37.

38. Morley to Gladstone, January 28, 1888, Gladstone Papers, Add. MSS. 44,255, fols. 237-38.

susceptibility to both insult and praise governed his political allegiances and decisions. This is not the place either to refute the notion that Morley's single consistency was his political opportunism, or to evaluate the extent to which vanity and spite influenced the decisions of his long and diverse career. Yet it would be an oversimplification to dismiss Morley's falling out with Chamberlain as a clash of personalities.

Approximately a year before he took his seat at the Round Table, Morley had finally declared his allegiance to Gladstonianism. Because of the precise circumstances of his conversion, it was his view that his new faith was epitomized by an adherence to Home Rule. If equally loyal Liberals, and perhaps even Gladstone himself, failed to conceive of Gladstonianism in precisely the same sense, that does not diminish the fact that early in 1886, Morley had pledged himself to tenets to which he remained faithful beyond the duration of his political career. He realized, quite rightly, that he was the single participant in the 1887 negotiations convinced of the moral as well as the political necessity of Gladstone's Irish policy.[39] If personal animosity played any part in his attitude toward Chamberlain, it was incidental to his determination to defend the Gladstonian faith from threats posed by Unionist heretics.

The Morley-Gladstone alliance strengthened in the face of adversity. Reginald Brett recorded in his journal a poignant description of Gladstone during the 1886 Home Rule debates, "with a rump of his old following . . . [and] Morley alone giv[ing] him help."[40] Yet neither Gladstone's influence nor his young lieutenant's ardor were sufficient to win enough votes to pass the controversial measure. Gladstone dissolved Parliament and appealed to the electorate, which revealed an antipathy to Home Rule that exceeded even that of its elected representatives. The Liberals trailed the Conservatives in the new Parliament by over two hundred seats, and the support they received from the eighty-five Par-

---

39. Lord Ripon counseled Morley to remain "firm. . . . We must not 'clink down' as the Yankees say. . . . I have complete confidence in you, but I cannot say so much for your colleagues." Ripon to Morley, January 17, 1887, Ripon Papers, Add. MSS. 43,541, fols. 10-11. Morley was equally displeased with "the constitution of the Conferences" and complained to Lord Spencer that "Herschell is weak on the question . . . and Harcourt is apt to fly off at a tangent." Morley to Spencer, January 3, 1887, Spencer Papers (Althorp).

40. May 20, 1886, *Journals and Letters*, ed. Brett, *1*, 126.

nellites was a small and an often humiliating compensation. Gladstone immediately ended his third and shortest-lived ministry, and Morley was succeeded at the Irish Office by A. J. Balfour.

Morley's years on the opposition front bench brought him frequent reminders that it was Gladstone and not their consciences that prevented his party from abandoning Home Rule, and it is during this period that one may perceive the origins of his political allegiances of the '90s. Harcourt and Lord Rosebery both disappointed him by appearing to renege in their devotion to the official Liberal policy toward Ireland. The latter suggested that the party redefine its intentions in a bill framed by a commission of jurists and civil servants. Morley, who wanted to retain a voice for himself, told Gladstone that this proposal found "no favour with anybody that I have seen: nor does it deserve favour." [41] Nor did Rosebery attempt to conceal his imperialist tendencies which, Morley feared, would shift national attention away from Home Rule. Rosebery's susceptibility to jingoism had more obvious consequences and elicited more bitter opposition from Morley when, within a few years, Rosebery assumed successively the Foreign Office and the premiership.[42]

Although Morley felt reasonably comfortable with Sir William Harcourt's pronouncements on matters of foreign and domestic policy, he had good reason to doubt Harcourt's fidelity to Home Rule. Harcourt still bore the taint of his past Whiggery and had been an unenthusiastic convert to Gladstone's Irish policy in 1886. Exposed to prolonged parliamentary opposition, the thin veneer of his Home Rule sentiments began to crack and peel away at the edges. Their respective responses to the Parnell scandal, which broke late in 1890, illustrated rather than created the gulf that separated Morley and Harcourt, and that influenced Morley's ill-considered decision to support Rosebery for the premiership in 1894. Like many Liberals who had never taken warmly to their party's alliance with Parnell, Harcourt was glad "to have done with such a rascal," [43] and he seized the opportunity presented by

41. Morley to Gladstone, April 14, 1889, Gladstone Papers, Add. MSS. 44,256, fol. 8.

42. In the meantime, Morley and Rosebery divided over the Anglo-German agreement of June 1890; see Robert Rhodes James, *Rosebery* (London, 1963), pp. 200-03. An excellent portrait of Rosebery as an imperialist is to be found in Robinson and Gallagher, *Africa and the Victorians* (London, 1963).

43. Harcourt to Lady Harcourt, November 29, 1890, cited in Gardiner, 2, 87.

the O'Shea divorce case to free his party from its Home Rule shackles. Calculating that a general election was imminent, Harcourt proposed that as the fall of Parnell had "fatally checked our positive advance in the direction of Home Rule," the Liberals should resign themselves to "operate on . . . negative and defensive lines, as against coercion." [44] Morley was outraged by such a suggestion, and replied that a change in Irish policy "would be taken to justify Parnell's charge that Mr. G. seized the divorce as a pretext for getting rid of H.R. by getting rid of the leader." [45] Heated words were exchanged, and it was not until almost a year had passed that their correspondence shows evidence that Harcourt's apostasy had been forgiven if not forgotten.

In July 1892, a new House was elected in which the Liberals and their Irish nationalist allies outweighed the Tory-Unionist combination by forty votes. Within a month's time, Gladstone returned to Downing Street for a fourth and final time, and Morley, who had held his seat at Newcastle by an uncomfortably slim margin,[46] resumed work at the Irish Office. The Irish secretaryship was neither socially nor geographically attractive to most English politicians, but Morley was aware that at this particular juncture, it afforded an unusual opportunity for creative maneuver and conferred an extraordinary prestige. Until early February, he added to the duties of his office the task of drafting a second Home Rule Bill.[47] Then, for a further eight months, he defended that ill-fated measure against its formidable critics in the Commons.

The old team, its ranks reduced but tightened, was reassembled; to it was added the Earl of Rosebery, a distinct asset in dealings with the royal household, foreign capitals, and the electors of Scotland. It was Morley who had lured Rosebery out of premature retirement and back to the Foreign Office.[48] In so doing, he had unwittingly weakened the cause that he believed Rosebery's presence would reinforce. Rosebery immediately introduced proceed-

44. Harcourt to Morley, December 23, 1890, Harcourt Papers.

45. Morley to Harcourt, December 26, 1890, Harcourt Papers.

46. When Morley, as was required of all Cabinet appointees, submitted himself for reelection seven weeks later, he was returned—much to his surprise—with a healthier majority than the last; see *Recollections, 1,* 326-27.

47. The other members of this committee were Gladstone, James Bryce, Sir Henry Campbell-Bannerman, and Lords Herschell and Spencer. It is significant that neither Rosebery nor Harcourt was included.

48. See Morley, *Recollections, 1,* 311 ff.; also Gardiner, *2,* 179; James, pp. 244-45.

ings to annex Uganda which Morley condemned as a "folly [which] would be stupendous and criminal." [49] A feverish debate persisted through the autumn months, and despite equally vehement opposition to the project by the Prime Minister, Harcourt, Asquith, Trevelyan, and Shaw Lefevre,[50] Rosebery won first a compromise from his colleagues and ultimately permission to proclaim a protectorate in East Africa. These results were less a tribute to Rosebery's manipulative skills than a testimonial to the strategic position he reluctantly occupied. Individual considerations prompted each of his Cabinet colleagues to swallow their pride and their principles in order to placate the melancholy Rosebery, rather than risk his probable resignation and the further weakening of their Government.

Morley, who remained "very strong against the whole Uganda policy," [51] nonetheless urged his associates to conciliate Rosebery. His reasons, however mistaken, are obvious. Robert Rhodes James has suggested that Morley's "surprisingly mild" behavior was a gesture of gratitude for Rosebery's unaccepted offer to defray the expenses of his Newcastle by-election; [52] there is no reason to question the sincerity of Morley's gratitude, but it should be pointed out that neither a similar offer from Lord Lytton in 1876 nor a financial dependence upon Chamberlain during his early parliamentary career prevented Morley from publicly denouncing his friends' policies. It is probable that Morley was less concerned with the feelings of his would-be benefactor than with the fate of the Irish reform scheme that would soon be introduced. He had waited six years for this occasion, and he did not intend to "wreck the Irish policy [or] the future of the Party by driving Rosebery out, or [by] going himself and perhaps taking others with him." [53]

It is not surprising that Morley's concerns were parochial during these months. He was confident that there would be ample op-

49. Morley to Gladstone, September 25, 1892, Gladstone Papers, Add. MSS. 44,256, fol. 253.

50. Lewis Harcourt's Journals, September 23, 1892, Harcourt Papers; he might have added to this list Campbell-Bannerman, Herschell, and Spencer.

51. Ibid., November 5, 1892.

52. James, pp. 268-69.

53. Lewis Harcourt's Journals, November 5, 1892, Harcourt Papers; "I have sold my soul . . . for the Irish Question and have accepted Uganda and many other things I detest for the sake of it," Morley subsequently professed to Gladstone. Ibid., February 11, 1894.

portunity, once Gladstone's Bill had passed, to discipline the Foreign Secretary and, if need be, to topple the Government. Meanwhile, both as Chief Secretary and as the minister most devoted to Gladstone's project, he would do nothing to imperil its chances of success. The lack of enthusiasm among his fellow Liberals disturbed him: "none of them cared for Home Rule," he complained to Lord Acton, "but he, Asquith and Mr. Gladstone." [54] Harcourt particularly embittered Morley by dismissing the measure as "merely a Bill *pour rire*—it is ludicrous and impossible," [55] and Morley lamented to Sir Algernon West that "Harcourt is doing what he can to break up and destroy the Bill." [56]

The provisions of the 1893 Home Rule Bill were announced by Gladstone on February 13, and Morley moved the first reading four days later. On September 1, after a total of eighty-five sittings, the Commons passed the third reading of the Bill by a margin six less than the combined Liberal-Irish-Independent Labour majority of forty votes. Thereafter, the measure passed to the House of Lords, where it was considered for fewer days than the Commons had taken months. After a week, their Lordships discarded the Bill, deflated and lifeless, by a resounding vote of 419 to 41.

Although Morley remained unshaken in his belief in the moral righteousness of Gladstonianism, he was forced to acknowledge the fact that Gladstone's leadership had lost its dynamism and authority, first within the Cabinet and in each successive Parliament. He observed signs that Gladstone's abdication was imminent, and that, according to the inviolable rules of nature, this retirement was fated to be final. By this time, Morley had reached the painful conclusion that the eighty-five-year-old statesman, whose cause had long been his own, was no longer insurance for but rather an impediment to the survival of Gladstonian ideals in any future blend of liberalism. Morley was sufficiently realistic to be aware that Gladstone's physical disabilities and political inflexibility had contributed to the failure of Home Rule, and were threatening to shatter the party organization which the Gladstone name had held

54. Cited in Sir Algernon West, *Private Diaries* (London, 1922), pp. 92-93. Morley's previous reliance upon Asquith made it especially difficult to forgive him for his backsliding on Home Rule after the turn of the century; see Asquith's speech at Earlsferry, October 11, 1905 (*The Times*, October 12, 1905, p. 4) and Morley's reply at Forfar, October 20, 1905 (*The Times,* October 21, 1905, p. 13).
55. Cited in James, p. 277.
56. West, p. 121.

intact for decades. As soon as it became apparent that the Prime Minister lacked sufficient time and strength to accomplish his mission, Morley could only hope that Gladstone would bequeath to his successor a Liberal Party with the electoral and ideological fortitude to carry out those tasks which he would leave undone.

The initial prospect of Gladstone's absence filled Morley with alarm and with regrets that there would never be "much chance of the revival of Home Rule." [57] But he soon grew convinced that a well-executed withdrawal would allow Gladstone to preserve his reputation and would avert "disaster to our new policy in Ireland." [58] His decision to persevere as a Gladstonian without his chief was reached only after the Prime Minister had refused repeated requests to reconsider his stand on the naval appropriations issue.[59] Forsaking all hope that Gladstone might agree to a compromise, Morley threw in his lot with the majority of his colleagues, who argued that the single chance for party solidarity lay in a new leader. Once he reached his decision, Morley remained steadfast. Though he "was miserable at the shattering of his idol," he had served too long and too intimately with the Grand Old Man to see him reduced to nominal control of the Government and the party. "If, after all this anguish, these tragedies, Mr. Gladstone was to stay," Morley vowed that "he would have no part or parcel in it, as Mr. Gladstone would have lost all authority." [60] However unfilial Morley might appear, he had Gladstone's interests at heart as well as his own and those of their party: Gladstone recognized "the gap which really severs me from (especially) my Commons colleagues," [61] and he pitiably compared his plight to that of Lady Burdett-Coutts, who had scandalized late-Victorian society by marrying a man a full generation her junior.[62]

In order to insure his political survival and thereby the survival of Gladstonian doctrines in a post-Gladstone world, Morley was obliged to assume an active, perhaps a decisive, role in the machinations that filled the early months of 1894. While Gladstone cal-

57. Lewis Harcourt's Journals, January 6, 1894, Harcourt Papers.

58. Morley to Gladstone, February 2, 1894, Gladstone Papers, Add. MSS. 44,257, fol. 151.

59. See Peter Stansky, *Ambitions and Strategies* (Oxford, 1964), p. 33.

60. West, p. 241.

61. Gladstone to Morley, January 5, 1894, Gladstone Papers, Add. MSS. 44,257, fol. 144.

62. West, p. 351.

culated the strategic moment to announce officially his historic decision, his colleagues engaged in strategies of their own, which
grew more frantic and devious as Gladstone's announcement became overdue. To deny Morley's complicity in these often unsavory proceedings would be foolhardy; but to divorce his actions
and those of other combatants from all ideological considerations,
attributing them exclusively to vanity or personal ambition,
would be equally absurd. It is neither a defence of Morley's unedi-
fying campaign, nor a commendation of his maladroit tactics, to
acknowledge the principles which prompted him to engage in the
intense struggle for the Liberal Party leadership.

Others must share the blame if Morley, the son of a Blackburn
physician, exhibited an inflated ego during the 1894 leadership
crisis. His Radical philosophy had persuaded him that modest birth
and income were not serious liabilities in the political game, and
this impression had been reinforced, to his immense satisfaction,
by a flood of invitations to Malwood, Mentmore, Barnbougle,
Althorp, and Hawarden. But Morley quickly perceived that he
offered more than a literary reputation and a talent for witty conversation as qualifications for a prominent position in the reconstituted Liberal Party. After all, he was the single member of the
outgoing Government who had energetically and consistently
identified himself as an exponent of Gladstone's views, and he was
confident that he deserved full consideration not only for his own
merits, but as the acknowledged repository of the Gladstonian tradition. To Reginald Brett, among others, Morley represented "the
moral element in our Party," and the only Liberal who could be
depended upon to "bear onward the torch when it falls from Mr.
G.'s hand." [63] Neither Brett nor Morley anticipated the haste
with which the Gladstonian torch would be jettisoned as soon as
the Grand Old Man had departed.

The fact that Morley felt entitled to greater compensation than
he ultimately received does not imply that his ambitions were disproportionate to his capabilities, nor does it imply that he had
carefully defined his goals. Basically he remained, as Sir William
Harcourt had described him in 1887, a politician afflicted with "a
somewhat excessive distrust of his own powers and claims." [64]

63. Brett to W. T. Stead, October 25, 1891, *Journals and Letters*, ed. Brett, *1*,
154.
64. Harcourt to Chamberlain, March 1, 1887, cited in Gardiner, *2*, 36-37.

Lord Rosebery was convinced that Morley's frustrated designs upon the Foreign Office had been deliberately instigated by Loulou Harcourt in an attempt to purchase Morley's support for his father's candidacy or at least to implant a disaffection from Rosebery.[65] The precise station to which Morley aspired is impossible to ascertain. The opening weeks of 1894 were chaotic, and Morley's movements were among the most erratic of all. He was profoundly disappointed by his eventual reassignment to the Irish secretaryship, but how much more he expected can only be guessed.

A personality with many sides and few rounded edges, Morley was always a difficult piece to fit into the puzzle of cabinet-making. Undoubtedly it would have been to his advantage in 1894 if his efforts had slackened, if his role had been more passive and dignified. But he had been sheltered too long beneath Gladstone's protective wing to acquire the skills and discretion that normally come to those who occupy high office. Devotion to his Gladstonian ideals led him into battle. Vanity, too, was instrumental, but it reflected an overconfidence in his ideological position more than in his personal strength. Opportunism, which is the usual explanation, fails to account for his heightened fervor once it became apparent that his personal ambitions would not be fulfilled. Rather, he was fighting as ruthlessly as he knew how to prevent the doctrines he represented from sharing the oblivion that seemed in store for him. He sincerely believed, and he was proved right by later events, that only by obtaining a key ministry could he impose upon his colleagues a continued adherence to Home Rule.

Morley was aware that neither Harcourt nor Rosebery, the two contenders for the party leadership, were dedicated to Gladstone's Irish formula, but he reasoned that if the Liberals were to be led by a lukewarm Home Ruler, it was preferable to have him in the Lords, where he could do minimal damage to the cause. And Morley anticipated that a Prime Minister in "another place" would allot him a more prominent position on the Government front bench. If he delayed his choice, it was not to extract greater concessions for himself, but for his Irish policy. He withheld his sup-

65. Lord Rosebery provided a personal account of the events of January through March 1894 in an untitled memorandum which has been published in *History Today, 1* (1951) and *2* (1952) and again as an appendix to James' *Rosebery;* in the latter, see p. 504.

port from Harcourt, thereby playing into Rosebery's hands, not because the latter had outbid his rival, but because Morley perceived that, under Harcourt, Home Rule as a policy was not likely to have the recognition that he would have achieved for it at the Foreign Office or Exchequer.

Although his blunders contributed to his failure to find a place for himself and his doctrines in the new Liberal order, it is doubtful whether he would have succeeded even had he performed with the dexterity of an Asquith or the affability of a Campbell-Bannerman. He realized that he had been too closely identified with the ancien régime to escape the disapprobation in which it was held by its heirs.[66] He returned grudgingly to that "back kitchen," [67] the Irish Office, which—now that Home Rule had been shelved—no longer afforded its occupant a major role in policy-making. For the sixteen months that the Rosebery ministry performed the excruciating feat of clinging to power "by its eyelids," [68] Morley enjoyed only the dubious consolation that Harcourt's success in the leadership struggle would have proved equally disastrous to his Irish designs.

Morley had entered the Rosebery Government with full knowledge that he would be isolated, physically and ideologically, but he had had no idea how humiliating that could be. On the afternoon of March 12, Lord Rosebery received his colleagues at the Foreign Office. With the obvious intention of placating Morley, whose outstanding service to the Irish cause he cited, Rosebery affirmed that Home Rule "would be pressed to the forefront, and, as far as in me lies, pressed to a definite and speedy conclusion." [69] Morley's satisfaction, if any, was short-lived; within hours, the Houses of Parliament assembled to hear an address from the Throne from which the expected Liberal pronouncement on Home Rule had been self-consciously omitted.

The Rosebery Government's Irish policy, when it could be discerned, was an insult and an embarrassment to its authorized

66. See *Recollections*, 2, 8, where Morley quotes from a diary for 1894 which, in all probability, has since been destroyed according to instructions in his will.

67. Morley described the Irish Office in this way to Rosebery on March 1, 1894; see Rosebery's memorandum, James, Appendix 3, p. 509.

68. This was Robert Rhodes James' pungent description of his subject's accomplishment, p. 369.

69. Cited in James, p. 337.

executor. But Morley found it no more humiliating than the Government's foreign and imperial policies, which flatly contradicted his Gladstonian principles. Here, at least, he had Harcourt on his side, and though the latter continually berated him for having perpetrated their common misfortune, they closed ranks to oppose Rosebery's expansionist, inherently anti-French policies. Despite frequent threats to resign, Morley remained a member of a ministry that offered the single chance, though a steadily less promising one, for the eventual revival of Home Rule.

On June 24, 1895, Harcourt announced to the Commons the Government's decision to resign. It was thereupon Lord Salisbury's task to form a Government and to schedule a general election. Morley made immediate preparations to defend the seat at Newcastle he had held since 1883. He reminded his fellow Liberals of their unfulfilled promise to the Irish nation,[70] and he vowed a personal determination to "fight on Home Rule—and on that alone." [71] If his intentions were unmistakable, his defeat by the electors of Newcastle was not any less so.

The "unexpected repulse" [72] which Morley suffered in the 1895 general election cannot, with justification, be attributed to any single factor; it was the symptom of profound personal shortcomings as well as the product of a complex political situation. He was among a handful of eminent Liberals who were spurned by their constituents, and his particular plight offers insights into the contemporary political scene, local and national, and into the political concerns of late-Victorian Englishmen. It was not vanity, but astute political sense, which prompted him, in a flood of letters to friends and associates, to consider his fate at Newcastle more a blow to his party than to himself. His defeat attested to deficiencies in the Liberal program which could have been discerned even before the vestiges of power had been wrested from Gladstone's hands: in particular, an inability to harness the still untold energies of a mass electorate and an incompetence to deal with the emergent forces of social democracy. The Liberal Party, despite the freak recovery that awaited it, had ceased to be a viable ideological force and an effective tactical unit.

70. Speech of July 4, 1895, cited in Gardiner, 2, 368.
71. Lewis Harcourt's Journals, June 27, 1895, Harcourt Papers.
72. See Morley, *Recollections*, 2, 47.

As Morley reportedly realized in a particularly candid moment,[73] his political efficacy had perished, along with the cohesion of his party, in the paroxysms of the mid-'90s. Yet he also realized that neither his temperament nor his commitments to Home Rule would permit him to stand idly on the sidelines while others reconstructed the Liberal Party. He required a minimum of prodding from his former colleagues to "cross the Rubicon and the Tweed"[74] and contest a Scottish constituency in a February by-election. But he approached the prospect of returning to Westminister with considerable doubts whether he wanted "to go back to the parliamentary vomit at all. My aversion deepens as time goes on."[75] His spirits revived with the news that he had obtained a plurality of nearly two thousand votes at Montrose. "The battle is over," he rejoiced in a letter to an emigrant Scotsman, Andrew Carnegie, "and I am once more where I do believe that I ought to be."[76] And he jested to Gladstone that his "only complaint is that the constituency is not compact, and one has to sleep in too many beds."[77]

Morley's temporary absence from the Commons chamber had kept him aloof from party intrigues. During these months as well as those which followed his reelection, he was content to sulk in his corner, nursing the bruises he had received from both rivals for the Liberal leadership. He wished neither Harcourt nor Rosebery to triumph and to be in a position to impose his will upon the party; for this reason, he urged Lord Spencer to organize a second front which might reestablish the party's equilibrium without recourse to either of its feuding leaders.[78] When this failed to materialize, Morley hoped that Harcourt and Rosebery might somehow resolve their differences and thereby negate each other's in-

73. R. B. Haldane to his mother, April 13, 1896, Haldane Papers (National Library of Scotland, Edinburgh).

74. Morley to Campbell-Bannerman, November 23, 1895, Campbell-Bannerman Papers, British Museum Add. MSS. 41,223, fol. 42.

75. Morley to Campbell-Bannerman, November 18, 1895, Campbell-Bannerman Papers, Add. MSS. 41,223, fol. 40; also Morley to Harcourt, November 15, 1895, Harcourt Papers.

76. Morley to Carnegie, February 28, 1896, Morley-Carnegie Correspondence (Microfilm, Bodleian Library, Oxford).

77. Morley to Gladstone, March 1, 1896, Gladstone Papers, Add. MSS. 44,257, fols. 200-01.

78. Morley to Spencer, August 18, 1895, Spencer Papers.

fluence.[79] This possibility was ruled out early in October 1896, when Rosebery unexpectedly stepped down from the party leadership, citing as his reason a lack of support from prominent Liberals of whom Morley no doubt was one. Harcourt, who had been leading the Liberal forces in the Commons, assumed the de facto leadership of the party. He and Morley initiated an intimate collaboration that had eluded them in previous years, when it might have worked to their mutual advantage and satisfaction.

In the years that followed, the British nation betrayed Morley's confidence, and the Liberal Party betrayed its remaining Gladstonian principles. Early in 1898, Morley surveyed the national and international scenes and told Lord Spencer that "the outlook strikes me as very black." [80] Yet not all the tragedies which Morley experienced that year were confined to political and diplomatic affairs. At Hawarden on May 19, Gladstone died in his eighty-ninth year. Since 1874, he had frequently reminded his colleagues of his mortality, but he had as frequently convinced them that he would survive forever.[81] Morley visited him for the last time six days before the end, and described the occasion to Lord Acton:

> I saw him for five minutes, and I don't think he knew me. The nurse seized the moment as being favourable, but it hardly proved so—and I have a suspicion that such moments are rare, and only for a flash or the twinkling of an eye.[82]

With Gladstone's death, Morley suffered profound grief. He had lost a valued friend as well as a partner in an alliance that transcended not only their personal relationship, but also the lifetime of its senior member.

At the invitation of the Gladstone family, Morley began work that autumn on the most ambitious of his literary projects: a three-volume biography of his mentor, which was published in 1903. He

79. Sir Edward Hamilton's Diary, January 24, 1896, Hamilton Papers, British Museum Add. MSS. 48,668, fols. 94-95.

80. Morley to Spencer, January 11, 1898, Spencer Papers.

81. "Mr. G. [is] 87 today!" Morley had exuberantly reminded Harcourt a year and a half earlier; "20 years older than you, 30 than me, and so on. I look to him to write a short obituary of me for Knowles (19th century)." Morley to Harcourt, December 29, 1896, Harcourt Papers.

82. Morley to Acton, May 14, 1898, Acton Papers (Cambridge University Library).

approached the monumental task with misgivings, amply fore-
warned by Harcourt, among others. "I have a strong instinct that
you are absolutely right," he admitted to Harcourt before commit-
ting himself to the venture. "The thing would be to go into a
long, black tunnel, of which I would never see the end." [83] But
by late August, when he received Herbert Gladstone's formal
offer, Morley had come to the conclusion that a "long, black tunnel" would provide a welcome refuge from the furious winds of
jingoism; besides, the assignment would afford him an irreproach-
able excuse for standing on the parliamentary sidelines until imperial and party storms had abated.

Yet even sequestered in the archives at Hawarden, Morley
found it impossible to prevent the pains of the moment from in-
truding upon the treasured memories of the past. He had intended
the Gladstone biography to be not only a posthumous tribute to
its subject, but a proselytizing tract on behalf of the waning Gladstonian faith. Soon, however, he craved a more dramatic means to
propagate his doctrines. His absence had failed to produce the stir
he had intended on the Liberal front bench. There sat Sir William Harcourt, whose leadership of the Liberal Party had dissi-
pated into an absurd fiction. Together with Harcourt, he devised a
strategy to compel the party to mend its ways.

Harcourt's behavior at the close of 1898 was hardly as enigmatic
as that of his accomplice. He had already reached an advanced age
and had surrendered any expectation of leading his shattered party
back to power. His son, Loulou, rightly regarded as the family's
political propelling force, had announced plans to terminate his
bachelorhood, which aroused immediate speculation that the elder
Harcourt would soon seek more leisurely pastures.[84] It is doubtful
whether anyone but Loulou shared Morley's intimate knowledge
of Harcourt's intentions, let alone his concern about them. By October 1898, Harcourt was fiercely determined to step down, and
Morley appears to have assured his friend of similar plans. Yet it is
probable that at this date, Morley contemplated nothing more
than devoting his full time to the Gladstone biography.[85] At the

83. Morley to Harcourt, July 15, 1898, Harcourt Papers.

84. See Sir Edward Hamilton's Diary, December 1, 1898, Hamilton Papers, Add.
MSS. 48,674, fol. 6.

85. See Harcourt to Morley, October 10, 1898, and Morley to Harcourt, October
13, 1898, Harcourt Papers.

same time, he reluctantly realized that it would suit the majority of his fellow Liberals if he elected to accompany Harcourt.[86] Early in December, the scheme was formulated that led to Harcourt's retirement and to Morley's continued distress. As he had promised, Morley delivered his friend's letter of resignation, along with his meticulously worded reply, to the editorial offices of *The Times;* both were published on the fourteenth, and neither achieved the effects for which their authors had hoped. Harcourt's intentions were immediately apparent, but Morley's remained obscure. Sir Edward Hamilton, who had all along expected Morley to follow Harcourt's lead, inferred from the published correspondence that Morley was reluctant "to throw in his lot with Harcourt." [87] But H. H. Asquith, who disapproved of Harcourt's maneuver and deplored Morley's complicity, recalled that Morley's letter had been "generally interpreted as meaning that he had resolved to share Harcourt's retirement." [88]

In a note to R. B. (later Lord) Haldane, hours before the disclosure, Morley alluded to Harcourt's withdrawal, but neither stated nor implied that his own political fate was at stake.[89] Yet, to Morley's dismay, this was precisely the conclusion that his fellow Liberals drew from the two letters that appeared in print. Morley's opinions were not solicited—or worse, they were ignored —during the feverish weeks in which a new party chief, Sir Henry Campbell-Bannerman, was chosen. Infuriated by his party's readiness to take him at his word, Morley allowed himself to be goaded into pronouncing his own political death sentence.

Morley followed up his cryptic announcement of mid-December with a more explicit statement to his constituents at Brechin six weeks later which stands out as his most illuminating appraisal of himself and his ideological difficulties. In it, he reiterated his decision to refrain from taking "an active and responsible part in the formal councils of the heads of the party." No more than a recognition of the status quo, in effect it spelled an end to his pretensions to a place in the party hierarchy. He clarified his recent behavior as well as Harcourt's by discussing their estrangement

86. Morley to Spencer, December 2, 1898, Spencer Papers.
87. Sir Edward Hamilton's Diary, December 14, 1898, Hamilton Papers, Add. MSS. 48,674, fol. 17.
88. Asquith, *Fifty Years of Parliament* (2 vols. London, 1926), *1*, 263-64.
89. Morley to Haldane, December 13, 1898, Haldane Papers.

from Liberals who had succumbed to the lures of jingoism. He was aware that the majority of Liberals, like the majority of Englishmen, were enthusiastically applauding Kitchener's audacity at Fashoda and pledging their support to the Uitlander cause in South Africa. Yet he declared that he would persevere on the Gladstonian path, the path of retrenchment, antimilitarism, and Home Rule. "One thing I will not do," he vowed: "I will not go about the country saying fine things or listening to fine things about Mr. Gladstone, and at the same moment sponging off the slate all the lessons that Mr. Gladstone taught us and all the lessons that he set." [90] On the following day, Morley resumed his tour through the towns of his constituency. Breaking his journey at Arbroath, he delivered a eulogy of the Grand Old Man at a public meeting to raise funds for a Gladstone memorial, to which he pledged a personal contribution of fifty guineas.[91]

What remained of Morley's political career after his speech at Brechin in January 1899? His seat in the Commons, for one thing. Morley had failed to instruct his constituents to shop for another candidate, and their sympathetic response to his plight, coupled with the encouragement he received from old friends, persuaded him to stand for reelection the following year. But failing health, the paralysis of Britain's two-party system, and the "detestable war" in South Africa made him despondent, and led him to "[draw] more and more within my humble little shell." [92] It was from this shell that Morley emerged, for a purpose that he would have been the last to anticipate, when his party recovered power, if not its Gladstonian principles, at the close of 1905.

90. Speech at Brechin, January 17, 1899, *The Times* (January 18, 1899) , p. 6.
91. *The Times* (January 19, 1899) , p. 11.
92. Morley to Spencer, January 26, 1900, Spencer Papers.

3   Reemergence

In the months before his fellow Liberals emerged from their decade in the political wilderness, John Morley had vacillated between offering either a bid for a position in the reconstituted party hierarchy or a unilateral declaration of withdrawal from public life. A dissolution expected momentarily and a Liberal majority at the polls widely forecast, he explained to Sir Henry Campbell-Bannerman from the writing desk in his library: " 'Tis not that I want to be idle, but I believe that industry here will be more fruitful for the universe (there's vanity for you!) than attendance on the bench." [1] Assuming that Morley sincerely intended to withdraw from public life—or at least to retain the distance from the Liberal front bench that followed his controversial "resignation" speech at Brechin in 1899—what could have induced him to accept a post in the new Government?

In his *Recollections* Morley describes a meeting with Campbell-Bannerman on January 19, 1905, at which irrevocable decisions were taken:

> "What are your predilections?" he asked. . . . He would not listen to my *nolo episcopari*. "Within limits you would have what you like." I wrote down a list of a possible Cabinet. The upshot in his mind India for me, Bryce Ireland. [2]

It is, however, highly improbable that these discussions assumed the significance that Morley, who had a passion for pinpointing

1. Morley to Campbell-Bannerman, May 21, 1904, Campbell-Bannerman Papers, Add. MSS. 41,223, fols. 130-31; see also Campbell-Bannerman to Herbert Gladstone, April 24 [1904] [copy], Viscount Gladstone Papers, British Museum Add. MSS. 45,988, fol. 93.

2. 2, 131; at this time, Morley did not want his appointment to the India Office to appear accidental and wished to scotch rumors that he would have preferred the Exchequer. On December 30, 1906, Lord Esher advised the King that Morley resented the fact that Campbell-Bannerman had not asked him to approve Bryce's appointment as Irish secretary; this would further disprove Morley's account of the January 19, 1905 deliberations. See *Journals and Letters*, ed. Brett, 2, 211-12.

historic occasions, retrospectively asserted. Even after he had allegedly accepted the India Office as his eventual assignment, he
continued to contemplate his retirement before another Parliament assembled at Westminster. On scattered occasions, he
alluded to his possible participation in the impending Liberal
ministry, but he did not regard his post as a certainty. At least for
the purpose of argument he postulated to Herbert Gladstone that
he would be stationed at his familiar desk at the Irish Office,
though he sardonically begged his correspondent to "excuse my
intolerable presumption and absurd ambition." [3] But on the
whole, Morley devoted considerably less thought to his eventual
place in the Liberal Cabinet than to the fulfillment of the
promises he had made to himself over the last decade. Weeks before he accompanied the Liberals on their triumphant march to
power, he confided to Lord Spencer:

> One single short sentence is hovering in my brain, and I ex-
> pect that I shall find courage to launch it. You may guess what
> it is—the hint, or even the plain statement, of my *exit*. Only
> to you do I owe any warning of this purpose; so kindly keep it
> to yourself, and on no account give yourself the friendly
> trouble to reply or otherwise notice what would be a very
> trivial event after all—or rather, as Talleyrand said at the
> death of Napoleon—" 'Tis not an event; 'tis only a piece of
> news." [4]

Yet when the fateful moment at last arrived, Morley declined to
utter that "single short sentence." Perhaps he belatedly realized
that political controversy was the stuff of his daily existence. In
any event, he was tremendously encouraged by recent evidence—
including the Order of Merit and the reception accorded his three-
volume *Life of Gladstone*—that he had been absolved of his pro-
Boer stigma: in recent years, he recalled, he had been "a voice
crying in the wilderness," but now "the wilderness was quite populous and sociable." [5] Though he was relieved by the failure of
the Liberal Imperialists, who had lacked the assistance of their

3. Morley to Gladstone, April 11, 1905, Campbell-Bannerman Papers, Add. MSS.
41,217, fol. 219.

4. Morley to Spencer, October 11, 1905, Spencer Papers; it may be presumed that
by this time Morley realized that the India Office was the best he could hope for.

5. Speech at Walthamstow, November 20, 1905, *The Times* (November 21, 1905),
p. 12.

elusive standard-bearer, Lord Rosebery, he felt obliged to bol-
ster Sir Henry Campbell-Bannerman against renewed assaults.
Campbell-Bannerman would have to retain actual as well as nominal control of the Liberal forces if there was to be any hope of returning the errant party to the Home Rule path from which it had
long deviated.[6] Above all, Morley reluctantly assumed his place in
the Campbell-Bannerman Cabinet—and that place was largely in-
consequential—in order to imbue that body with a measure of his
own Home Rule spirit.

Morley was also lured into the political arena by the Indian secretaryship itself, but for reasons quite unlike those which Indian
nationalists took for granted. He initially accepted the India Office
not because it offered a laboratory for Gladstonian experiments,
but because it conferred a maximum of political authority at the
same time that it promised to entail a bare minimum of administrative responsibility. It was particularly easy to draw such conclusions from the administration of his predecessor, St. John Brodrick.[7] Sir Arthur Godley (later Lord Kilbracken), the veteran
undersecretary at the India Office, correctly perceived Morley's in-
clinations, though he failed to anticipate the interests which the
Secretary of State would subsequently evolve. In early November,
Godley reported to an anxious Lord Minto rumors of Morley's
impending appointment, and related:

> I know John Morley well . . . and I venture to prophesy
> that, if we get [him] here as Secretary of State (an arrange-
> ment which would be quite agreeable to me personally) , we
> shall not get his undivided attention for Indian affairs. A
> good deal of his time and thought will be devoted to the

6. Although it is extremely doubtful whether his assistance was in any way instrumental, Morley's immediate designs were realized. One by one, the Liberal Imperialists—with the exception of Rosebery—returned docilely to the fold, and
Campbell-Bannerman resisted their attempts to catapult him into the upper chamber. Morley could not repress his delight when writing to Sir Charles Dilke, a less
fortunate Liberal: "The crisis was acute. . . . At the eleventh hour E[dward] G[rey]
changed his mind, C.B. was victorious, and the situation was saved. . . . If C.B.
had been bullied into going to [the] H. of L., the effect would have been in every
way disastrous." Morley to Dilke, December 10, 1905, Dilke Papers, Add. MSS.
43,895, fol. 259.

7. "So far as I can see," Morley, reviewing the Curzon-Kitchener controversy,
remarked to his undersecretary, "the S. of S. might as well have been non-existent
since his Dispatch of Nov. 18, 1904." Morley to Godley, March 19, 1906, Kilbracken
Papers (India Office Library, London) .

amenities which will be pressing between him and one or more of his colleagues in the Cabinet.[8]

And, finally, Morley took the India Office in 1905 because it fell to him by default. There was no more likely candidate for the position and no more likely position for him. "I am in Niagara Falls," he reported to his American friend Nicholas Murray Butler, president of Columbia University. "Like the Ancient Romans, we distribute great posts by lot." [9]

There are ample indications that Morley had, in fact, expected to be rewarded with a more impressive assignment. As early as 1899, F. W. Hirst had brushed aside his hero's rejoinders and had predicted that as soon as the Liberals were restored to health and to office, "Mr. Morley will certainly not return to Ireland. I think he would lean towards the Exchequer. I hope so. . . . As Chancellor he would be able to put in some sledgehammer blows at the bloated armament estimates." [10] More seasoned political analysts shared Hirst's view of Morley's aspirations. W. T. Stead, Morley's assistant and successor at the *Pall Mall Gazette,* reported that Morley, "the custodian of the Gladstonian tradition," entertained "a desire to walk in the steps of the G. O. M. so literally as to have wished to seat himself in the Treasury as Chancellor of the Exchequer." [11] While the nation awaited the list of Campbell-Bannerman's appointments, *The Times* backhandedly boosted Morley's stock by conceding that "no one in the Party can prefer stronger claims" to the chancellorship, "though the City may be surprised at his appointment." [12] On the following day, St. John Brodrick, the outgoing Indian secretary, informed Lord Minto that Morley, who had been "favored by C. B.," had lost the Exchequer to Asquith "after a terrible struggle," making it "pretty certain that we shall get Morley here." [13] As soon as Mor-

8. Godley to Minto, November 10, 1905, Minto Papers. Before arriving at the India Office, Godley had served as Gladstone's private secretary. The Grand Old Man later commended him as "my East Indian conscience." Gladstone to Godley, November 27, 1891, Kilbracken Papers, British Museum Add. MSS. 44,901, fol. 67.

9. Morley to Butler, December 16, 1905, Butler Papers (Columbia University Library, New York).

10. Diary, August 28, 1899, cited in Hirst, *In the Golden Days* (London, 1947), p. 176.

11. W. T. Stead, *The Liberal Ministry of 1906* (London, 1906?), p. 47.

12. *The Times* (December 7, 1905), p. 9.

13. Brodrick to Minto, December 8, 1905, Minto Papers.

ley's assignment was made known, E. S. Beesly, a Positivist friend since *Fortnightly* days, offered him a message of sympathy and expressed the hope that "the India Office will not cut you off too much from other affairs." [14]

Morley's personal references to his political ambitions were few and self-belittling. By this time he had thoroughly mastered the knack of promoting his claims unobtrusively. Moreover, there were few political associates in whom he chose to confide. On November 25, he discussed the allocation of ministries with Sir Edward Grey, a close friend notwithstanding their fundamental disagreements over policy. Morley promptly related the details of this two-hour conversation to Campbell-Bannerman, taking particular care to mention Grey's revelation that the Liberal Imperialists "supposed that *I* should wish to be C[hancellor] of E[xchequer]." Morley professed to be thoroughly surprised though flattered by the proposal and assured Campbell-Bannerman: "When he asked me about myself, I said, as I said to you without affectation, that I doubted if at the last moment I should not stand out." [15] In his intentionally unassuming way, he had conveyed his message to his party leader. But the chancellorship was evidently a higher price than his colleagues were prepared to pay for his participation.

Morley's fellow Liberals were intent upon presenting an image of thoroughly restored unity to the electorate, and it suited their purpose as little as it did Morley's temperament for the most prominent Gladstonian and pro-Boer to abstain from office in the new Government. "He long occupied a midway position between the elder parliamentary hands and the younger school of Liberal politicians," Augustine Birrell, who took the portfolio for education and then the Irish Office, explained. "No Liberal Cabinet in recent times could have been complete without him." [16] For his part, Morley was notably less enthusiastic. "I would rather have stood aside," he told Dilke, "but they would not have it, so I am at the India Office." [17] To accommodate both his colleagues and his

14. Beesly to Morley, December 15, 1905, Morley Papers (India Office Library, London).

15. Morley to Campbell-Bannerman, November 25, 1905, Campbell-Bannerman Papers, Add. MSS. 41,223, fols. 164-65.

16. Augustine Birrell, "Lord Morley of Blackburn, O.M.," *Empire Review, 38* (1923), 1361.

17. Morley to Dilke, December 10, 1905, Dilke Papers, Add. MSS. 43,895, fol. 260.

interests, he accepted what he and others believed to be a noncontroversial assignment on an interim basis. "I did not much wish to return, but they told me that honour and credit and duty demanded," he insisted to Sir Edward Hamilton, assuring him that he had absolutely no intention of recasting his retirement plans: "Depend upon it, the 65 rule is sound." [18]

Morley was himself struck by the incongruity of the appointment, and marveled how "odd" it was "that from that beginning I should end at this office." [19] But the assignment was no more unconventional than those of David Lloyd George to the Board of Trade, John Burns to the Local Government Board, or Winston Churchill, a recent apostate from Tory ranks, to the undersecretaryship at the Colonial Office. Quite unmistakably, the India Office was refurbished in 1905 to accommodate its occupant's vanity, not his ideology. *The Times,* with obvious relief, expressed full confidence that the Indian realm would afford "ample scope for his abilities." [20] There was more than a grain of truth to one Anglo-Indian journal's candid assertion that Morley "has been given the India Office with the idea that he will do least mischief there." [21] Morley might have recalled that he had jumped to exactly the same conclusion two decades earlier, when Lord Randolph Churchill had been allotted the Indian secretaryship in Lord Salisbury's first ministry; as editor of the *Pall Mall Gazette,* Morley observed at the time that Salisbury had shrewdly

> selected the India Office for his irrepressible colleague merely in order to intern him where he can do little or no mischief. The ponderous machinery of the Indian Government is too massive to be affected materially by the buzzings of the mosquito which for the moment is allowed to poise itself on the axle of the driving wheel.[22]

He probably remembered, too, that John Bright had bypassed the India Office in Gladstone's first Cabinet, citing failing health, but with the view that King Charles Street was a highly unsuitable address for any conscientious Radical. Morley contemplated with

18. Morley to Hamilton, December 21, 1905, Hamilton Papers, Add. MSS. 48,619.
19. Morley to Harrison, December 12, 1905, Harrison Papers.
20. *The Times* (December 9, 1905), p. 11.
21. *The Englishman* (December 12, 1905), p. 4.
22. *Pall Mall Gazette* (June 18, 1885), p. 1.

amusement "what [John Stuart] Mill (who had refused a seat on India Council) would say if he knew that his friend were S. of S. for I." [23]

When Campbell-Bannerman solicited contributions for the forthcoming Royal Address, Morley, who remained primarily concerned with obtaining an explicit declaration of adherence to Home Rule, refused to divert attention to Indian matters: "I hope you understand that *I* do not wish you to say *anything* about *India*." [24] As in 1894, he notified the Prime Minister that his energies were reserved for the affairs of his own department, though he vainly expressed a willingness to be drawn into intimate collaboration on Irish policies. Yet his self-denying ordinance proved no more effective under Campbell-Bannerman than it had under Lord Rosebery. "When I took office," Morley told Lord Minto, "I had a very firm intention to become a purely departmental Minister, and to stand aside from other questions. Easier said than done." [25] On a subsequent occasion he complained: "It is not easy, however much I seek it, to be a purely departmental Minister." [26] When the pages of his agenda became too crammed, or when he took exception to the policies his colleagues pursued, he retreated into his shell and reaffirmed his India-only rule: "There is no chance of my being ready to speak," he advised Campbell-Bannerman on June 20, 1907. "You sent me to the Ganges and Brahmaputra, and I stick to the business of my department. I am sorry, as I told you the other night, to be so little use to you, but so it is." [27] But Morley's reticence was not the result of mere petulance. As time wore on, he found it increasingly difficult to apportion his efforts among too many causes: "I labour under the disadvantage of having been accustomed for most of my life to concentrate upon one subject at a time, and mainly in my serene library, notwithstanding my over-abundant platform exercises about Home Rule, or the Boer War." [28]

"Electioneering crowds out all else," Morley exuberantly in-

23. F. A. Hirtzel's Diary, May 15, 1906, *1*, 44 (India Office Library, London).

24. Morley to Campbell-Bannerman, December 20, 1905, Campbell-Bannerman Papers, Add. MSS. 41,223, fol. 178.

25. Morley to Minto, June 22, 1906, Minto Papers.

26. Morley to Minto, November 29, 1907, Minto Papers.

27. Morley to Campbell-Bannerman, June 20, 1907, Campbell-Bannerman Papers, Add. MSS. 41,223, fol. 252.

28. Morley to Minto, February 14, 1908 [copy], Morley Papers.

formed Lord Minto soon after he assumed office; "happily India is not drawn in." [29] It was wholly Morley's doing that Indian controversies were ignored during the 1906 general election. He preferred to focus the nation's attention on more traditional concerns. Though his own reelection was virtually assured, he campaigned vigorously during the first weeks of the new year, concentrating upon Joseph Chamberlain's Tariff Reform proposals, the South African situation, disestablishment and, of course, his perennial favorite, Home Rule. Indian affairs were mentioned only in hasty replies to questions from the floor.

Chastened by successive decades of disappointment, Morley entertained few hopes of a decisive Liberal victory. The crippled state of the Unionist Party guaranteed his colleagues a working majority, but he envisioned a return to the parliamentary distribution which had hamstrung both Gladstone and Rosebery during the previous decade. "Some say all will end in a tie, as in 1885: *i.e.* Liberals = Unionists + Irish," he told Lord Ampthill, Governor of Madras. "Others give us a clear majority of 30 or 40 over the two." [30] Winston Churchill, with ebullient expectations for the party he had recently joined, visited Morley

> in the small but highly ornamental circular room in the India Office. I found him despondent. "Here I am," he said, "in a gilded pagoda." He was gloomy about the forthcoming election. He had had too long experience of defeat to nourish a sanguine hope.[31]

The ultimate Liberal majority of eighty-four seats more than twice exceeded Morley's wildest expectations, and was sufficient to convince even the most seasoned skeptic that a bright new day was dawning. "What times!!" Morley exclaimed to his undersecretary: "Who shall interpret them? For my own part I look on with grim, truculent, and bloodthirsty satisfaction—like an ancient Roman when he turned his thumb up (or was it down?) for the despatch of the fallen gladiator." [32]

During the campaign, Morley had accorded Lord Minto his solemn promise: "From the 20th January to the last day of my

29. Morley to Minto, January 2, 1906, Minto Papers.
30. Morley to Ampthill, January 4, 1906, Ampthill Papers.
31. Winston Churchill, *Great Contemporaries* (New York, 1937), p. 80.
32. Morley to Godley, January 17, 1906, Kilbracken Papers (I.O.L.).

being at the India Office, I shall be an Indian and nothing else." [33]
By and large, Morley kept his word, but it proved difficult for
him to disown the issues with which his name had been identified
for decades. "India is entitled to claim at present his immediate attention," one of his admirers conceded; "but Ireland has prior and
stronger claims which undoubtedly will be enforced when the crucial moment arrives." [34] As Lord Esher explained to the King, a
considerable number of Irish M.P.s continued to regard Morley
"as the repository of the Gladstone tradition," and they "naturally" conferred with him on matters of common interest.[35] Morley retained close contacts with John Dillon and other nationalist
spokesmen, and he rarely hesitated to convey their proposals and
his own suggestions to Campbell-Bannerman.

But Morley's continued interest in Irish affairs did not preclude
a growing attachment to his own office. At the close of 1905, King
Edward informed Lord Minto of a lengthy discussion with the
Secretary of State, "who is an old friend of mine. He is immensely
impressed with the importance of the duties which now devolve
upon him." [36] Morley's undersecretary at the India Office noted
that "the Secretary of State's interest in foreign affairs, frontier
questions, and military questions, increases as time goes on." [37]

It was a gradual process by which Morley was awakened to the
unusual opportunities for political self-expression which the India
Office afforded its tenant. His predecessors had traditionally been
appointed to satisfy the dictates of party strategy and had rarely revealed aptitude for Indian affairs; they, too, had tended to be preoccupied with issues beyond their compass and, on the whole, had
been content to rely extensively upon their retinue of civil
servants—particularly the permanent undersecretary at the India
Office—hesitating to explore those areas in which they might employ the creative powers they had inherited. While most Indian
secretaries flitted through Whitehall on their way to more coveted
assignments, Morley remained to preside over Indian affairs for
five years, during which he utilized his position to the utmost of its

33. Morley to Minto, January 11, 1906, Minto Papers.
34. W. J. Johnston, "Mr. Morley and Ireland," *Westminster Review, 165* (1906),
476.
35. Esher to King Edward, December 30, 1906, *Journals and Letters,* ed. Brett,
2, 211-12.
36. King Edward to Minto, December 22, 1905, Minto Papers.
37. Godley to Minto, March 8, 1907, Minto Papers.

and his own capacities; as he painfully realized, neither he nor his doctrines had any place else to go.

Morely's initial disclaimers of any interest in his post were interlaced with signs that on no account would he serve as a figurehead. "Please do not give me an under-secretary without consultation," he remonstrated to Campbell-Bannerman on December 8. "I have views." [38] It soon became apparent that, despite his comparative unfamiliarity with Indian problems, he would not permit the competing bureaucratic machines at Calcutta and Whitehall to function without his close scrutiny. At least in his own opinion, his direct encounters with Irish nationalism and his academic experience with continental nationalisms more than compensated for any lack of intimacy with the Indian variety. To a remarkable degree, his self-confidence was fully justified, and the lessons he had learned in more temperate climates proved as relevant as those which most Indian administrators learned by experience.

Morley's appointment coincided with and, in part, presaged an acceleration of Indian nationalist agitation which afforded the India Office new prominence and the Indian secretary new responsibilities. He was soon aware that he had undertaken more than he had intended, and, in all probability, than his fellow Liberals had intended to allow him: "India," he concluded with mixed emotions, "is now one of the front-rank problems for this country— along with, say, Navy, Army, Colonial Relations, and, (above all) National prosperity in Finance." [39] His colleagues reached similar conclusions and noted with relief that there was still service to be wrung from the veteran politician whom they had long dismissed as a spent force. Lord Esher recalled a fishing trip with Sir Edward Grey, who mused about

> the false perspective of politicians. No one foresaw when the administration was formed the real posts of difficulty and danger. He thinks it was providential, J. M.'s going to the India Office—in his opinion, *the* most dangerous post. No one can tell when the gathering storm there will burst, but none

38. Morley to Campbell-Bannerman, December 8, 1905, Campbell-Bannerman Papers, Add. MSS. 41,223, fol. 177; Morley subsequently selected as his parliamentary undersecretary J. E. Ellis, who had demonstrated his attachment to the Indian national cause as a member of the British Committee of the Indian National Congress.

39. Morley to Godley, June 16, 1908, Kilbracken Papers (I.O.L.).

of them but J. M., with his unimpeachable record, could have governed India just now, in the face of a sentimental Parliament.[40]

But Morley's effectiveness was tempered by the recurrent ailments of advancing years and by the lingering presentiment that each impending year would be his last. "I wish my 'inch of taper' were not so near being 'burnt and done,' " he brooded to Andrew Carnegie. "Then one might have had a chance of doing something for India." [41] He lacked the strength, if not the resolution, to juggle both the heavy burdens of Indian administration and his obligations to constituents. "I have to say with shame," he admitted to Lord Lamington, "that I am at the very bottom of the list of Ministerial votes!! In old days, I should have felt horribly guilty, and Mr. Gladstone when he was Prime Minister would never have stood such a neglect of duty." [42] His health, which had frequently broken down during the previous decade, was steadily failing. H. W. Nevinson, an acquaintance since their days of joint opposition to the Boer War, provided a pathetic portrait of Morley after an interview at the India Office on September 25, 1907: "Though he still had fifteen or sixteen years to live, he looked very old. . . . He looked like a mummied relic of the Gladstonian age who had somehow contrived to keep a glimmer of life in his mummy clothes." [43] Nor did Morley's exposure after 1908 to the rarefied air of the House of Lords return a healthy glow to his complexion. His predecessor at the India Office, who, as the Earl of Midleton, also preceded him into the upper house, echoed Nevinson's observations in letter to Lord Minto the following summer:

> What worries me a little is that I fear Morley is not himself physically at all strong. He has aged a good deal lately and saves himself everything, even doing his work some days at Wimbledon without coming to town at all. He practically never attends the House of Lords except when Indian subjects are under discussion and Asquith told me the other day he considered [Morley] was getting very old.[44]

40. Journals, September 29, 1908, *Journals and Letters*, ed. Brett, 2, 346.
41. Morley to Carnegie, December 28, 1906, Morley-Carnegie Correspondence.
42. Morley to Lamington, December 31, 1906, Lamington Papers.
43. Nevinson, *More Changes, More Chances* (London, 1925), p. 228.
44. Midleton to Minto, July 15, 1908, Minto Papers; also August 13, 1908, Minto Papers.

Alarmed by evidence of his debility—physical and political—Morley repeatedly proffered his resignation from the India Office, though he trembled at the irrevocable step.[45] As early as the spring of 1906, he hinted to F. A. Hirtzel, his private secretary, the intention to retire as soon as he had delivered his annual budget speech,[46] and he affirmed that intention the day he fulfilled that responsibility.[47] Within a few days, the ovation accorded his speech had changed his mind, and he proudly forwarded to the Prime Minister "a testimonial to [my] modest worth" from G. K. Gokhale, "the Native Champion," who professed that Morley had "taken a weight off his heart." [48]

At the close of his first year as Indian secretary, a few days before his sixty-eighth birthday, Morley made an attempt to surrender his seals of office. He pointed out to the Prime Minister that a vacancy at the India Office might facilitate Cabinet reconstruction, and he referred wistfully to plans for "a final piece of writing for which none too much time remains." [49] In a month's time, Morley repeated his request [50] and, confident that this had decided the matter, he wrote a note to Minto designed to cushion the impact of the impending announcement: "I sometimes feel as if the strain were beginning to tell on my vital energies," he confessed. "Ah, well, nobody is indispensable, and if I vanish back into my library, there are as good fish in the sea as ever came out of it." [51]

45. According to Campbell-Bannerman, Morley threatened during the early weeks of his secretaryship that there would soon be "a vacant stool at Whitehall." Cited in J. A. Spender, "John Morley," *Fortnightly Review*, n.s., *144* (1938), 671. In his apologia for the one resignation threat he carried through, Morley revealed:

> [I] felt acutely what Mr. Gladstone had often told me, that a public man can have no graver responsibility than quitting a Cabinet on public grounds. . . . Anybody can hold and advocate unpopular opinions; but withdrawal from a Cabinet is a definite act, involving relations for good or ill with other people, and possibly affecting besides all else the whole machinery of domestic government.

Memorandum on Resignation (London, 1928), p. 16.

46. F. A. Hirtzel's Diary, May 30, 1906, *1*, 48.

47. Ibid., July 20, 1906, *1*, 63.

48. Morley to Campbell-Bannerman, July 23, 1906, Campbell-Bannerman Papers, Add. MSS. 41,223, fol. 196.

49. Morley to Campbell-Bannerman, December 22, 1906, Campbell-Bannerman Papers, Add. MSS. 41,223, fol. 203.

50. Morley to Campbell-Bannerman, January 23, 1907, Campbell-Bannerman Papers, Add. MSS. 41,223, fols. 232-33.

51. Morley to Minto, January 24, 1907, Minto Papers.

But Morley's thinly veiled prophecy heralded nothing more than an anxious flutter in the Anglo-Indian pulse. Lady Minto presumed that Morley was "getting weary of his burden and means to go very soon," and she calculated that the Government of India might "fare very much worse if we had the engaging Winston in the big chair at the India Office." [52] Her fears proved unfounded, for by the time his letter reached the Viceroy, Morley had been persuaded to retain his ministry and to seek refuge in the House of Lords.

It is evident that, before the summer of 1907, when Morley alluded to retirement, he intended a complete withdrawal, not a seat in the upper house; the latter was a prospect which he had pondered and had flatly rejected. Moreover, the arguments with which he had persuaded Sir Henry Campbell-Bannerman to resist a peerage were still fresh in his mind. Shortly before his arrival at the India Office, Morley had hastened to assure Frederic Harrison:

> I shall not go to "another place," save in one contingency not at all likely to happen. I will never change my name. The H. of C., in spite of everything, is still the most *bracing, fortifying* and *testing* place in Europe.[53]

On February 25, 1907, Morley vowed to his private secretary that Easter would find him either in the Lords or on the Liberal back benches.[54] His conversion to the former was gradual and reluctant for, despite his colleagues' assurances to the contrary, he perceived that an Indian secretary in the upper house would forfeit a measure of his influence and a share of the glory. Yet a number of factors encouraged him to accept a peerage and continue at the India Office. The first and most obvious was his growing interest in Indian affairs, which proved more of a challenge than he had previously suspected. The moment seemed ripe for a historic move in a progressive direction, and Morley did not wish to deny either India the benefit of his Gladstonian experience or himself the opportunity to implement his mentor's doctrines.

Though Morley tentatively applied for a peerage early in

52. Lady Minto's Indian Journals, April 11, 1907, *1907-i*, 107 (Indian Institute, Oxford). Morley, more gleefully, also contemplated Churchill as his successor: "some say 'dangerous, but active'; perhaps I should say dangerous *because* active." F. A. Hirtzel's Diary, April 27, 1908, *3*, 42.
53. Morley to Harrison, October 4, 1905, Harrison Papers.
54. F. A. Hirtzel's Diary, February 25, 1907, *2*, 22.

1907,[55] he had yet to settle the matter in his own mind. For more than a year he continued to tantalize his colleagues, particularly Lord Minto, with reports that he intended to resign his seat in the Commons, his Cabinet office, or both. The parliamentary crisis made him reluctant to go to the House of Lords at the very moment that its fate hung in the balance, and by the time he sent his traditional New Year's greeting to James Bryce, he had become determined to remain a member of the Commons.[56] Yet on May 5, 1908, in a brief ceremony at which he "blushed like a girl," [57] John Morley was created Viscount Morley of Blackburn. Indian exigencies and failing health had prompted his move, but his decision was the result of less obvious political considerations.

Sir Henry Campbell-Bannerman waged a valiant struggle during the early months of 1908 against an illness which brought his resignation and death in April. A month earlier, Morley had warily prophesied that the Government would be reshuffled, with "Asquith inevitable." [58] He recognized the impregnability of his personal position, but he feared the ideological implications of Asquith's ascendancy. Morley found it extremely difficult to forgive Asquith for his machinations against Harcourt and Campbell-Bannerman, for his support of the Boer War, and for his implicit repudiation of Gladstone's Irish policy on the eve of the Liberal return to power. He confessed to Sir Frederic Hirtzel that when Asquith changed residences on Downing Street, it would be unpleasant for him " (who had been a Home Ruler all his life) to join" the reconstituted Cabinet.[59] By the spring of 1908, Morley had decided that "he would not accept office under Asquith and remain in the H. of C.," for he had no wish to be called upon to defend or sanction policies which he opposed. He jested to Lord Esher that "he would *like* to be Prime Minister himself. Failing that, he would like to go to the House of Lords." [60]

Morley conferred with the new Prime Minister on April 6, "and

55. Morley to Campbell-Bannerman, February 28, 1907, Campbell-Bannerman Papers, Add. MSS. 41,223, fol. 236.

56. Morley to Bryce, January 6, 1908, Bryce Papers.

57. Morley, an agnostic, was not required to swear the oath of allegiance, but instead affirmed it; see Esher to M. V. Brett, May 6, 1908, *Journals and Letters*, ed. Brett, 2, 310.

58. F. A. Hirtzel's Diary, March 10, 1908, *3*, 28.

59. Ibid., February 27, 1908, *3*, 25.

60. Journal, February 11, 1908, *Journals and Letters*, ed. Brett, 2, 284.

after placing the I[ndia] O[ffice] at his disposal (which Asquith would not hear of) arranged to go to H. of L. at once." [61] In the pages of his *Recollections,* he recounted that he had voiced "a claim from seniority of service for your place at the Exchequer, but I don't know that I have any special aptitude for it under present prospects"; instead, he told Asquith, he preferred to remain at the India Office, where "I am engaged on an extremely important and interesting piece of work." The Prime Minister, according to this account, was taken aback by Morley's decision to go to the Lords:

> "Why on earth should you go there?" "Because, though my eye is not dim, nor my natural force abated, I had a pretty industrious life, and I shall do my work all the better for the comparative leisure of the other place." [62]

The report of these deliberations which Morley furnished to Lord Minto was equally dramatic and equally improbable. According to this version, Morley was told "that if I wished for it, I might go to the Exchequer," but he replied that he was "too old to learn a new trade." Asquith, he told the Viceroy, "had pointed out to me in terms that my modesty won't allow me to write down, that my departure would be highly disadvantageous to the strength and credit of the administration." It was of course his intention—for strategic as well as personal reasons—not only to emphasize his own importance, but also to leave Minto on tenterhooks, and he reserved the right to give vent to "impulse" and renounce public life when the moment for final decision arrived.[63]

The most vehement opposition to Morley's ennoblement came from longtime friends, who articulated his own misgivings. "I don't like 'John Morley' decked out like an ordinary man with a title, when the Man is greater than the title," Andrew Carnegie protested. "The latter is ridiculous and though it cannot efface the

---

61. F. A. Hirtzel's Diary, April 6, 1908, *3, 36.*

62. *2, 251;* Morley provided Lord Esher with a less amiable account of his meeting with Asquith: "J.M. was remonstrated with by Asquith for leaving the H. of C. and merely said, 'I go altogether or I go to the Upper House.' 'When,' asked Asquith. 'Today, this very hour,' said J.M." Journal, April 10, 1908, *Journals and Letters,* ed. Brett, *2,* 303-04.

63. Morley to Minto, March 27, 1908, Minto Papers; Minto hastened to assure Morley: "I do understand so well the temptation of the library—but you can't be allowed to go there!" Minto to Morley, April 16, 1908, Morley Papers.

former, it does obscure it more or less, especially when the wearer cannot but be known to laugh at the silly gaud himself." [64] Morley promptly explained his move on grounds of expediency: "There is not a 'gaud' or 'bauble' about it. It is simply placing a steady workman where he can do his work best and with most justice to himself." [65] In his explanation to Robert Spence Watson, who had managed his Newcastle campaigns, Morley was considerably more defensive:

> I could not help it. I would have if I could. My disposition was all that way. Only, as you have found out many a time before now, in politics nobody can do what he likes—it would have been a sorry bit of vanity to quit a post of usefulness in India and in the Cabinet, rather than give up a name without a Nobiliary Tag.[66]

On the whole, the announcement of Morley's elevation was warmly applauded in the press and in most political circles. The *Spectator* reported widespread relief that Morley would remain at his post, and hailed his performance at the India Office as "one of the most conspicuous successes of the Liberal Government." [67] R. C. Dutt, on behalf of the Indian moderates, gratefully advised Morley that:

> All India thinks you have accepted the peerage in order to be able to serve India longer, in order not to leave your high office without leaving some mark on the administration which will be remembered for generations to come.[68]

Alert to the benefits to be derived from propagating this view, Morley professed to a biographer at the end of 1911 that, "having done for the cause of Indian reform all that he could accomplish as a Commoner, it was necessary for him to enter the House of Lords in order to finish the task." [69] But regardless of the altruistic motives he subsequently cited, Morley's decision to accept a peerage can be explained most convincingly in political terms. He was resolved to escape the moral as well as the physical burdens which

64. Carnegie to Morley, March 29, 1908 [copy], Morley Papers.
65. Morley to Carnegie, April 7, 1908, Morley-Carnegie Correspondence.
66. Morley to Spence Watson, April 20, 1908, cited in *Recollections*, 2, 252.
67. *Spectator* (April 18, 1908), p. 607.
68. Dutt to Morley, April 24, 1908, Morley Papers.
69. George M. Harper, *John Morley and Other Essays* (Princeton, 1920), p. 2.

accompanied a place on the Government front bench. His transfer to the Lords in no way explicitly furthered the cause of Indian reform; in fact, it probably had the opposite effect by subjecting him to more conservative influences.

So far as India was concerned, Morley's elevation was more the result of poor timing than strategy. In the spring of 1907, he confided to Lord Esher that he did "not like leaving the Commons while the 'unrest' lasts." [70] A year later, he naïvely hoped that the prospect of imminent reform would be sufficient to appease Indian agitators and to render unnecessary his continued presence in the lower house. He soon realized his mistake and, on the eve of the introduction of the Morley-Minto reform scheme, admitted to Asquith:

> If I had foreseen Indian difficulties last April, I should not have dreamed of going to the H. of L., for I should then equally have foreseen that the stage of action must be in the H. of C., and that the simpletons whom I had kept well at bay for 2½ years would get their chance. I should have left the I. O. and the Government, and nobody would have been a penny the worse.[71]

Morley backed into the parliamentary hornets' nest that he had helped to create with his earlier campaign to "end or mend" the House of Lords. Radical M.P.s demanded that the Morley-Minto reforms be promulgated in the Commons, an awkward arrangement with the Secretary of State in "another place." "What is the case?" Morley asked Asquith, for whom he reviewed the situation. "A statement of the very first moment is to be made—yes, of the *very first*. Be sure. Who can make it but the responsible Minister?" [72]

In his weekly letter to Minto, Morley snickered at the tempest in the Radical teacup:

> The Indian group in the House of Commons waxes more wroth every day that the arrogant, privileged, abominable House of Lords should have the early Indian asparagus and the first dish of green peas and all the other delicious *pri-*

70. F. A. Hirtzel's Diary, June 18, 1907, 2, 54.

71. Morley to Asquith, December 15, 1908, Asquith Papers (Bodleian Library, Oxford).

72. Morley to Asquith, December 14, 1908, Asquith Papers.

meurs from my oratorical garden hot-houses and forcing pits.[73]

Yet he belatedly realized that the dissension between the two houses and the controversial nature of the reform proposals made it advisable for the Secretary of State to sit on the Government front bench. As a consequence, he vainly appealed to Asquith "to relieve me of an office which I only took to oblige C. B., and which I only continue to oblige you." [74]

Convinced that he had outlived his usefulness, Morley was unable to celebrate his "grand glorification" with the enthusiasm that others displayed. "I have more to make me a little dismal than you have," he insisted to Frederic Harrison: " (1) I'm pinned to India (2) I'm pinned to H. of L." [75] Lady Minto, on a visit to London, visited Morley at the India Office on May 3, 1908, and was told: "I am in a bad temper today; I am unhappy at having to leave the House of Commons which has been the scene of all my Parliamentary tussles, and I have no wish to go to the Lords." [76] The Secretary of State lamented to the Viceroy:

> My intention almost to the last was to bolt from public life altogether, for I have a decent library of books still unread, and in my brain a page or two still unwritten. Before the present Government comes to an end, the hand of time will in any case have brought the zest for either reading or writing down near to zero, or beyond.[77]

But Morley was too fatigued to contemplate seriously either literary projects or political crusades; he was "within a few months of the Psalmist's allotted span," [78] and the House of Lords seemed as good a burial place as any.

Despite the few occasions when he chafed at his constitutional limitations, Morley learned to appreciate the tranquillity which the House of Lords, except for a few turbulent months in 1910, afforded. He regretted the unmistakable signs of old age more than

73. Morley to Minto, December 10, 1908, Minto Papers.
74. Morley to Asquith, December 14, 1908, Asquith Papers.
75. Morley to Harrison, April 27, 1908, Harrison Papers.
76. Mary, Countess of Minto, *India, Minto and Morley* (London, 1934) , p. 207;
also Morley to Lady Minto, May 4, 1908, cited in Ibid.
77. Morley to Minto, April 15, 1908, Minto Papers.
78. Morley to Minto, April 23, 1908, Minto Papers.

any of the effects of his peerage: "The H. of L. is full of interesting and important men," he reported to Minto, "and on good occasions produces an admirable debate. But it is for us Elders, not for the men in the fighting line of national politics and great issues." [79] The continuing need for strenuous exertions on India's behalf deferred the relief which Morley had anticipated in the spring of 1908. The hours he no longer devoted to attendance in the Commons were devoted instead to India's proliferating problems.

Morley's physical condition continued to deteriorate, and he waited in vain for the respite which the promuglation of the Morley-Minto reforms had deceptively promised. "Thankful am I," he told Minto, "that I had the courage to go to the H. of L. a year ago. In the H. of C. I should have been a dead man by this time." [80] But Morley's transfer to quieter pastures came too late to achieve a medicinal effect. "My bronchial tubes are slowly edging me towards finis," he wrote to Asquith during a Cabinet meeting on February 1, 1909.[81] His friends were alarmed by evidence of his further decline, and urged him to step aside once he had inscribed his name in the crowded pages of Indian history. "Victory is now perching upon your shoulders," Andrew Carnegie counseled.

> All parties agree you have managed well. Carrying out *your* policy is all that a Successor can do. . . . You cannot bear the strain long at best. Why struggle on until compelled to go— perhaps too late to place the needed cap upon the pyramid of your fame.[82]

Morley was inclined to agree with his friend, but he shared Gladstone's inability to extricate himself from political ties. Another major assignment remained before him and, despite his denials, it was one that he relished. "I am rather jaded, and I have a birthday of terribly high figure next month," he wrote to Minto in November 1909;

> I had promised myself a rest as soon as ever I got free of Reforms and Deportees. Unhappily I am not quite my own master for three or four weeks to come. They insist that I de-

79. Morley to Minto, August 6, 1909, Minto Papers.
80. Morley to Minto, June 17, 1909, Minto Papers.
81. Morley to Asquith, February 1, 1909, Asquith Papers.
82. Carnegie to Morley, December 6, 1908 [copy], Morley Papers.

nounce the House of Lords to their noble faces—a pastime
that would have given me lively satisfaction once, and I
should have produced an hour's oration with the utmost ease.
So I shall have to revive my memory of Pym, Hampden, Eliot
and King Charles.[83]

Caught between the pincers of Indian nationalism and the British
constitutional crisis, Morley could spare the time for only a short
excursion to the Continent at year's end. From Menton on December 21, a few days before his seventy-second birthday, he informed R. B. Haldane: "I have forgotten India and the House of
Lords, and the General Election, and am immersed in, what do
you think? *Goethe!!*" [84]

Neither the Indian riddle nor the dispute between the Houses
of Parliament were solved as quickly or as painlessly as Morley,
who supervised each of them in his capacities as Indian secretary
and leader of the Liberal peers, had anticipated. He gradually
wearied of trying to weather two storms at once, each of hurricane
proportions. "You had better let me go after Monday's crisis, if we
survive it," he advised Asquith in a heavily underscored memorandum dated April 14, 1910.[85] But he reluctantly agreed to hold
on a while longer, miscalculating that after its exhausting onslaught against the Lords, the Liberal Government would soon
fall.[86]

There was also the added inducement of surviving Minto,
whose viceroyalty was drawing to a close, as sole proprietor of
Indian affairs. "There may be some advantage," he told the Governor of Bombay, "in my having a chance of giving the new
Viceroy—whoever he may be—a good start on what I conceive to
be the right lines for his journey." [87] But neither his desire to initiate Minto's successor nor his heightened dedication to his duties
was sufficient to sustain the ailing Indian secretary. On September
12, he appealed to Asquith for a release from office, concluding
that "the next few years will require even more energy and clearer
vision than the last few, and I think you had better start these years

83. Morley to Minto, November 5, 1909, Minto Papers.
84. Morley to Haldane, December 21, 1909, Haldane Papers.
85. Morley to Asquith, April 14, 1910, Asquith Papers.
86. Morley to Clarke, May 13, 1910, Morley Papers.
87. Ibid.

with a new S.S., as well as a new Viceroy." [88] The Prime Minister persuaded him to "suspend the thing until we can discuss it, face answering to face," [89] but this time Morley's decision remained unaltered. When Asquith proved slow to take action, Morley reiterated his petition.[90] This was sufficient to relieve him of the burdens of Indian administration.

Doubts have been raised whether Morley expected his resignation—the next-to-last of many—to be accepted. "John Morley told me yesterday of his resignation," Lord Esher recorded in his journal on October 28, 1910.

> The truth is that he has been caught this time. Sore at not being asked to Balmoral, inclined to think that he was not being treated with consideration, he wrote to the Prime Minister saying that he was tired out and unable to go on.
>
> He did not receive from Asquith the sort of letter he expected, and after a delay, during which he expected *de faire prier,* he reiterated his wish to retire. He was taken at his word.[91]

But Morley had already prepared his Indian colleagues for the event of his abdication, which could not have been long deferred at best. And there can be no doubt that he was physically exhausted.

This would have been the logical moment for Morley to retire, but the veteran Liberal was too addicted to parliamentary and party affairs. "I grieve to quit the Cabinet as a whole," he confessed to Haldane,

> and still more to break off the daily intimacy with three men (or is it two?) of whom you are the first. But I don't feel up to the coming controversies, taken along with a heavy department. If I find myself drawn into the struggles ahead, I shall be better able to say my say from outside.[92]

88. Morley to Asquith, September 12, 1910, Asquith Papers.

89. Morley to Asquith, September 21, 1910, Asquith Papers.

90. Morley to Asquith, October 13, 1910, Asquith Papers.

91. *Journals and Letters,* ed. Brett, *3,* 28-29; J. A. Spender identified himself as "a competent witness to the fact that [Morley] was painfully astonished when one of his many resignations was finally accepted." *The Public Life* (2 vols. London, 1925) , *1,* 104.

92. Morley to Haldane, October 30, 1910, Haldane Papers.

It was not for another four years that Morley experienced the lonely solitude that he anticipated with such trepidation in the autumn of 1910. Winston Churchill convinced Asquith that he should "even now retain [Morley's] services in some great office without administrative duties," [93] and the Prime Minister re-shuffled his Cabinet to accommodate Morley as Lord President of the Council. Morley seized the opportunity,[94] confident that his new assignment would afford him comparative leisure and few headaches.[95] For another four years he remained an uneasy member of the Liberal Government, until the early days of August 1914, when fate and the German Imperial Army shattered the last remnants of his Liberal order.

By entering the Cabinet in 1905, John Morley inflicted innumerable punishments, both physical and ideological, upon his fragile constitution. He found himself isolated and sometimes alienated from the inner circle of ministers who propelled their party and shaped its policies. His colleagues delighted in his wit and respected his knowledge of parliamentary procedures; yet the homage he received as Liberal elder statesman—the minister who had served most years in the Commons—was largely empty. "To sit at a man's table is one thing, to sit at his feet another," philosophized Augustine Birrell, one of Morley's two close Cabinet friends. "Morley," he recalled, "always stuck to paths that, in the opinion of most of his younger political companions, were beginning to be *antiquas vias.*" [96] As a member of the prewar Liberal Governments, Morley watched his colleagues enact social programs which he could not readily endorse, promulgate an Irish settlement which implicitly repudiated his mentor's most sacred doctrines, and, finally, lead the British nation into a war which he

93. Churchill to Asquith, October 22, 1910, cited in Churchill, *Great Contemporaries,* pp. 83-84.

94. Morley to Asquith, November 2, 1910, Asquith Papers.

95. Morley had discussed the Lord Presidency a half year earlier with Sir Almeric Fitzroy, who "suggested that the attainment of [Earl Beauchamp's] eightieth year might very fittingly be used for another effort to induce him to retire." Fitzroy told Morley that the party chiefs had "opened communication with [Beauchamp's] family, and were assured by his daughter that it would kill him to insist upon the performance of his duties. 'Fancy,' said Lord Morley with fine scorn, 'anybody being killed by the duties of the Lord President of the Council.'" Sir Almeric Fitzroy, *Memoirs* (2 vols. London, 1925?) , 2, 405–06.

96. Birrell, "Lord Morley of Blackburn, O.M.," p. 1361.

could not condone and which nineteenth-century liberalism could not survive.

Each prominent Liberal inferred a different significance and a different promise from his party's electoral triumph in January 1906. To his distress, Morley soon perceived that this stunning victory was neither a belated vindication of his principles nor proof of the Liberal Party's recovery from two decades of internecine warfare. He expressed to Lord Minto his view that the 1906 Liberal majority had been "mainly due, in the huge extent of it, to furious detestation of Balfour and his tactics. No great issue was really settled." [97] Though the ensuing decade was punctuated by sharp controversies and fitful appeals to the electorate, the Liberal program remained amorphous, obstinately refusing to crystallize into its familiar nineteenth-century form. "We are still wondering and wondering about our [Budget] Crisis, action of the Lords, date of an Election, and so forth," a harried Secretary of State informed the Viceroy in 1909. "We all change our minds, as we change our clothes, at least once a day. I need not tell you what suit I am wearing this afternoon. By the time you get this, it might have gone clean out of fashion, and I may be ashamed of ever having worn it." [98]

For the most part Morley's advanced age and departmental duties excused him from taking a hand in projects which rubbed against his Gladstonian grain. His position among his fellow Liberals was a curious and uncomfortable one: those associates whose professionalism he respected—Churchill and Lloyd George—like those whose company he enjoyed—Haldane and Grey—were each advocates of policies that he resolutely opposed. He complained to his private secretary about

> the failure of this Government: utter weakness, want of courage, nerve and knowledge of what they were driving at. The only men who knew were Lloyd George and Winston. The others—Asquith, Grey, and Haldane—were able men, but they knew nothing about politics. They had utterly mistaken causes of majority of 1906; were wrong in wanting Rosebery instead of C[ampbell] B[annerman] as P. M.; wrong in wanting to kick C. B. up into the H. of L., in which they nearly

97. Morley to Minto, January 24, 1908, Minto Papers.
98. Morley to Minto, October 7, 1909, Minto Papers.

succeeded, and which would have been fatal; wrong in going in for Old Age Pensions when they might quite well have been kept out.[99]

To a limited extent, his isolation reflected his continued estrangement from the Liberal Imperialists, who came to control the three vital organs of prewar Government: the Foreign Office, the War Office, and the premiership. His past grievances were, in turn, inflamed by new issues, which arose to estrange him from fellow Liberals of non-Gladstonian persuasions.

The Liberal Government soon embarked upon extensive programs for social reform to which Morley could respond, at best, with resignation. In his opinion, such schemes were irresponsible maneuvers to purchase the working-class vote by discarding party principles. "Though I am as little of a capitalist personally as the most determined Socialist could desire," he told Minto, "I have all my life felt that there is no worse blow for the mass of working people than a blow that strikes capital."[100] In the autumn of 1906, he presided over a dinner party at the Athenaeum, where, his private secretary reported, he poured eloquent scorn upon the notion of old-age pensions and upon proposals to nationalize the railways. Lloyd George, among the guests, endorsed both projects, and defended their respective merits to his skeptical host.[101]

Although his opposition to the Eight Hours Bill, more than any other single factor, had cost him his seat at Newcastle in 1895, Morley expressed essentially the same views in 1908 when a deputation of his Scottish constituents urged him to support state assistance to the unemployed.[102] He decried the constitutional implications of proposed legislation to rectify abuses in the sweated industries, and "fortified" his arguments with quotations from the 1834 Poor Law Report and from the secular writings of Dr. Thomas Chalmers; as a last resort, he warned his colleagues "that if they supported it *as a Government,* he could not stay."[103] The members of the Liberal Cabinet were fully aware of Morley's aversion to any "socialist" remedies that exceeded the niggardly doses of the Newcastle Program which Gladstone had endorsed in 1891. Winston Churchill, who displayed fond reverence for Mor-

99. F. A. Hirtzel's Diary, September 28, 1909, *4,* 78.
100. Morley to Minto, April 7, 1909, Minto Papers.
101. F. A. Hirtzel's Diary, October 18, 1906, *1,* 89.
102. See *The Times* (January 8, 1908), p. 14.
103. F. A. Hirtzel's Diary, February 19, 1908, *3,* 22.

ley, expressed reluctance in 1908 to take charge of the Local Government Board, for fear that plans for a minimum standard would prove a personal affront to the veteran politician.[104] Fortunately, there seldom arose a need to enforce ministerial solidarity, as the party's parliamentary majority was sufficiently large to afford any dissenter frequent opportunities for tactful absences.

Long before he had entered Parliament, Morley exhorted his countrymen to "end or mend" the House of Lords, and the fate of the second Home Rule Bill had since made reform all the more imperative.[105] During the early years of the Campbell-Bannerman ministry, he expressed warm support for the Prime Minister's projected assault upon the upper house; here, after all, was a course which Gladstone had advocated on the eve of his retirement. "By the time you get this," he gleefully teased the Viceroy, "you will know for certain whether or not on your return home four or five years hence, you will find a H. of L. to shelter you, or will have to seek a seat in the H. of C. If the latter, allow me humbly to place the Montrose Burghs at your disposal." [106] Yet Morley's enthusiasm waned as the tenacity of his adversaries and the ferocity of his allies increased. Lloyd George, raised to the chancellorship in 1908, ignored Gladstone's 1894 proposals and defied the temperate spirit of Campbell-Bannerman's 1907 House of Commons resolution. Moreover, he threatened to convert the budget crisis from a constitutional into a social issue. "Lloyd George wants the guillotine," Morley's secretary recorded in his diary. "J. M. has said [all] along if they guillotine he will go." [107] Instead Morley exerted whatever influence he could muster to temper his colleagues' vengeance and to enlist the services of conciliatory peers.

Morley continually reproached himself for remaining in a Government which capitulated to the jingo clamor for Dreadnoughts. The Naval Estimates of 1909, he lamented, "ends an era—the era of Gladstonian retrenchment. The Liberal League has beat us." [108] Nor did he approve of the Cabinet's unpublicized commitments to continental powers which he knew about or suspected to a greater extent than he later cared to admit. Though his per-

104. Roy Jenkins, *Asquith* (London, 1964), p. 181.
105. See Morley's speech at Manchester, November 8, 1893, *The Times* (November 9, 1893), p. 4.
106. Morley to Minto, November 30, 1906, Minto Papers.
107. F. A. Hirtzel's Diary, July 14, 1909, *4*, 56.
108. Ibid., March 18, 1909, *4*, 23.

sonal predilections were consistently pro-French, he wished Great
Britain to dampen European rivalries by holding aloof. He had
explained his position to Gladstone in 1889: "All I care for is that
English Liberals should not be called anti-German, or anti-
French, or anti-anybody, and should give no excuse to German
Liberals for being anti-English." [109] Early in 1909, Morley expressed certainty that a European war was inevitable.[110] Knowing
that he could neither restrain nor influence his associates, he nonetheless remained in office. But by this time it was no longer Ireland, and certainly not India, but mere force of habit that kept
him there.

The Indian secretary was permanently estranged from his colleagues by his lonely vigil on behalf of Gladstone's Irish proposals.
He realized that the hope of implementing his Home Rule doctrines was more apparent than real.[111] By 1912, when the Government grudgingly promulgated a third Home Rule measure,
Liberal attitudes and Irish conditions had each been transformed
to an extent which rendered Morley's nineteenth-century views
inapplicable. Gladstone's lieutenant was disheartened, though
hardly surprised. He had witnessed the evolution of bitter antago-
nisms within the Irish nationalist movement as well as the sustained pusillanimity of his compatriots. His most painful blow had
come five years earlier, when Augustine Birrell, the Irish Secretary, outlined the miserly provisions of the Irish Councils Bill. As
John Redmond, parliamentary leader of the Irish Nationalists,
quickly pointed out, "Mr. Gladstone offered Ireland full self-
government and autonomy, but what his party was offer[ing] was
not Home Rule." [112] The Government, Morley informed Minto,
had betrayed its Irish allies by giving

109. Morley to Gladstone, January 15, 1889, Gladstone Papers, Add. MSS.
44,256, fol. 3.
110. F. A. Hirtzel's Diary, March 25, 1909, 4, 25.
111. At least in the sober opinion of *The Times*, Morley should have been
gratified by the Cabinet's position on Ireland (December 9, 1905, p. 11); but Goldwin Smith was a good deal more perceptive when he lamented that among the
members of the new ministry, "Mr. Morley alone seems to be firm in the faith,
and he is accordingly translated from Ireland to India. The rest either renounce
Home Rule or are manifestly seeking to get rid of it by infinite postponement."
Letter to the editor by Goldwin Smith, *Spectator* (December 30, 1905), p. 1119.
112. *The Times* (May 8, 1907), p. 11; *The Times* recalled that Gladstone had
dismissed such a devolution policy "as wanting in all the elements of permanence
and security." (May 2, 1907), p. 13.

a violent shake to that union of Irishmen with the British Liberals that Mr. Gladstone initiated twenty years ago. You, I know, thought him all wrong. I took his view and have stuck to it down to this hour, and shall go on sticking to it for the rest of my days, though I don't expect anything to come of it in my time.[113]

Not invited by his colleagues to contribute either ideas or oratory on Irish issues, Morley proclaimed himself "too full-blooded for this Government. I call them a Palmerstonian . . . not a Gladstonian Government." [114]

On the benches of the House of Commons, no less than in the Cabinet office, Morley felt increasingly isolated. Here, too, his discomfort resulted from the varied strains of advanced age, from his fidelity to an Irish formula that equally displeased Irish patriots and English politicians, and from a persistent inability to come to terms with the forces of incipient socialism. "I hope you will live long enough to feel as I do," he wrote ruefully to A. J. Balfour near the close of his ministerial career, *"vivre c'est survivre*—to live is to outlive." [115]

In mid-May 1904, from a Manchester podium that he shared with Churchill, Morley reiterated his optimistic view that whatever "a Labour candidate calls himself, when he comes to the House of Commons, the Labour man will be a Liberal." [116] The following March, he calmed the fears of younger Liberals with firm assurances that

whether they like to be called Liberals or not . . . ninety-nine times out of a hundred, [Labourites] will go into the Lobby with all of us. Or, if you like, we will go into the Lobby with them. I do not say they will make the lives of the new Ministers easier . . . but they will bring . . . a freshness, a vigour, a sincerity into the House of Commons of which it stands greatly in need.[117]

113. Morley to Minto, May 24, 1907, Minto Papers.
114. F. A. Hirtzel's Diary, February 25, 1907, 2, 22.
115. Morley to Balfour, February 18, 1914, Balfour Papers (British Museum).
116. Speech at Manchester, May 13, 1904, Morley, *The Issues at Stake* (London, 1904), p. 15.
117. Speech to the National League of Young Liberals, London, March 20, 1905, Morley, *An Address to Young Liberals* (London, 1906?), pp. 13-14.

Yet Morley was jarred after the 1906 general election by the
clamor of the Labour and Radical M.P.s who had been swept into
office. Though, for the most part, they shared his party label, these
left-wing arrivals shared little of his social outlook and few of his
opinions. "I have been spending an afternoon in the new H. of
C.," he wrote to Lord Lamington, who had sat for a London constituency two decades earlier. "You would hardly know the place;
most of the faces are new; the faces best known all gone. . . .
Some of the prevailing notions are unsound enough to my mind,
but there is nothing wild-cat, and we are all very decorous, cheerful, polite and well-behaved so far." [118] A week later he informed
Lamington of a subsequent visit to the Commons chamber: "Such
a different place! You cannot imagine it." [119]

But the parliamentary veteran, a patrician by nature if not by
birth, felt more uncomfortable in the corridors at Westminster
than he cared to admit to an Anglo-Indian of Tory extraction. He
complained to his private secretary that "when he walked about
the lobbies, he hardly knew the H. of C.—so changed were its
whole appearance, tone, and manners." [120] An admirer of professional politicians on both sides of the house, he resented those
M.P.s who trespassed beyond the bounds of gentlemanly opposition. "John Morley," as Churchill affectionately described him,
"was a Victorian. . . . This was the British Antonine Age. Those
who were its children could not understand why it had not begun
earlier or why it should ever stop." [121] At the same time, Morley
was a good deal less intimidated by the ideology of these recent
arrivals than his critics have alleged. He depended upon the sanc-
tity of Westminster and the hidden resources of the British character to sober any impetuous backbenchers. "I have sat five and
twenty years in the House of Commons," he reminded Minto,

> and for more than two-thirds of that period it was a Tory or
> Unionist assembly. From personal experience, therefore, I
> have no good reason to worship the wisdom and virtue of the
> House of Commons. Nobody is more familiar than I am—for
> I've been a pretty close observer of the creature—with its
> weaknesses. They are only superficial, believe me; and so far

118. Morley to Lamington, March 2, 1906, Lamington Papers.
119. Morley to Lamington, March 9, 1906, Lamington Papers.
120. F. A. Hirtzel's Diary, May 24, 1906, *1*, 47.
121. Churchill, *Great Contemporaries*, p. 77.

as they affect political opinion and action, these weaknesses only reflect those of the country at large, sometimes in a Tory mood, sometimes in a Liberal.[122]

Nor was Morley daunted by the emergence of a new party on the political left. After all, trade union leaders had been receptive to Home Rule and had strenuously opposed the Boer War. Keir Hardie, on one occasion, had offered him his allegiance.[123] "The Labour Party has now at last assumed definite shape," Morley reported to the Viceroy. "The wonder is that it did not come sooner. . . . There will be some wild-cat talk, but I represented workmen in Newcastle for a dozen years, and always felt that the British workmen are essentially *bourgeois,* without a bit of the French Red about them." [124] Convinced that "John Bull would take his socialism in very small doses," [125] he urged Minto to discount fears

that Socialism, in any deep or definable sense, will go far with our working men. I had many chances of knowing them well. They are most emphatically Individualist in practice and aim, and only Socialist in the sense—and a grand sense—of being stirred by sympathy and pity for their comrades.[126]

Along with his perceptive prophecy of long-run Labour Party attitudes, Morley provided an astute forecast of his own party's fate. In a penetrating review of L. T. Hobhouse's treatise, *Democracy and Reaction,* he disputed the author's confident assertion that "the breach of principle between" liberalism and socialism "is much smaller than might appear upon the surface." [127] The latter, he gloomily predicted, "will split the Liberal Party and probably be the means of uniting the other party." [128]

The augmented force of left-wing M.P.s clashed with more than

122. Morley to Minto, June 17, 1908, Minto Papers.

123. A. J. P. Taylor, "The Man in the Cloth Cap," *Politics in Wartime* (London, 1964), p. 47. At the height of the Boer War, Sidney Webb vigorously attacked those Socialist leaders who "out-Morleyed Mr. Morley in their utterances on the burning topics of the day." "Lord Rosebery's Escape from Houndsditch," *Nineteenth Century and After, 50* (1901), 374.

124. Morley to Minto, January 16, 1906, Minto Papers.

125. F. A. Hirtzel's Diary, March 10, 1908, 3, 28.

126. Morley to Minto, January 24, 1908, Minto Papers.

127. Morley, "Democracy and Reaction," *Nineteenth Century and After, 62* (1905), 540.

128. Morley to Minto, August 15, 1907, Minto Papers.

Morley's refined esthetic tastes. Among their ranks was an amorphous contingent whose avid interest in Indian affairs brought them into frequent conflict with the Secretary of State. "There are at least five new men in the House of Commons who will be likely to raise Indian questions," Morley calculated in the wake of the general election.[129] Within a few months, he revised his cautious estimate, though he continued to belittle this potential threat:

> The Indian Committee in the House of Commons numbers, as I learn, about 150 members—of course all Radicals and Liberals. They are of all sorts of political temperament, and as Dilke, who is one of them, assures me, they don't agree about anything and have no leading mind among them. You see, therefore, that with moderate common-sense on my part, I have no serious difficulties to fear.[130]

Recruited primarily from among retired Anglo-Indians and disgruntled politicians, the parliamentary allies of Indian nationalism were informally led by Sir Henry Cotton. In the early weeks of the new Parliament, the Indophiles tipped their hand for the first time, and Morley remained singularly unimpressed. "The Indians in the House of Commons made their debut last Monday," he informed Lord Minto.

> Cotton was the very reverse of effective and he created no prejudice in his favour by speaking for 58 minutes without saying a word that was either new or impressive old. Five others discharged maiden speeches, but with none of the grace and freshness poetically associated with maidens.[131]

Morley felt sufficiently well versed to reply to the carping criticisms of the so-called Cottonites, and sufficiently well esteemed to shrug off their insidious remarks about his personal integrity. Early in 1908, he replied to Dr. V. H. Rutherford's allegations before a packed House:

> My hon. friend and others who sometimes favour me with criticisms . . . seem to suggest that I am a false brother, that I do not know what Liberalism is. I think I do, and I must even say that I do not think that I have anything to learn of

129. Morley to Minto, January 25, 1906, Minto Papers.
130. Morley to Minto, June 22, 1906 [copy], Morley Papers.
131. Morley to Minto, March 2, 1906, Minto Papers.

the principles or maxims or the practice of Liberal doctrines even from my hon. friend.[132]

There was more than circumstantial evidence to confirm Morley's suspicions that the Cottonites contributed to his official headaches. "I may ride out the storm," he warned Asquith, "but not if Mackarness, Rutherford, Swift MacNeill and Co. are to share the bridge with me." [133] C. J. O'Donnell, an obstreperous Radical M.P., instructed one Indian politician to "keep agitating and do so effectively," because "a Whig does nothing unless pressed." [134] Amused by charges of Whiggery made by critics too young to recall the genuine article, Morley nonetheless regretted the effects of such rhetoric upon less sophisticated minds. The restoration of India's respect for the governing authorities was a prerequisite for the success of any reform scheme. By fomenting Indian national aspirations which the Imperial Government could not fulfill, the Cottonites, he insisted, were crippling many less ambitious, more constructive policies; worst of all, they convinced Indian leaders that constitutional agitation was futile. The "White Babus" in the Commons, as they were picturesquely labeled by one Indian journalist, shattered the vestiges of patient optimism within the Congress movement by relentlessly proclaiming "the hypocrisy of the only statesman in England who has hitherto been known to the people as an 'honest' politician." [135]

The hypersensitive bureaucrats in India required little excuse to reinforce their prejudices against parliamentary surveillance, and, after 1906, their hostility increased in direct proportion to the severity of the censures they received. "I never realized till I came home," the retired lieutenant-governor of the United Provinces wrote to Minto, "how democratic the present House of Com-

132. Speech of January 31, 1908, Morley, *Indian Speeches* (London, 1909), pp. 54-55. On other occasions, Radical taunts proved less easy to swallow; after the release of Lala Lajpat Rai, when Rutherford praised him for being "more like your old self," Morley fumed to his private secretary: "It makes me sick." A similar note was received from Frederic Mackarness, another Radical assailant. F. A. Hirtzel's Diary, November 14, 1907, 2, 97.

133. Morley to Asquith, December 14, 1908, Asquith Papers.

134. O'Donnell prescribed "mass-meetings by the dozen in every district—indoors and out of doors. Morley will not yield." O'Donnell to Surendranath Banerjea, March 2, 1906, Minto Papers. Banerjea forwarded this letter to Sir Lancelot Hare, Lieutenant-Governor of Eastern Bengal and Assam, who delivered it to Lord Minto's private secretary, Sir J. R. Dunlop Smith, who delivered it to Morley.

135. P. C. Ray, "Editorial Reflections," *Indian World* (August 1907), p. 186.

mons is. The rank and file of the Radical Party, encouraged by the disappointed Anglo-Indians in the House, are quite prepared to stigmatise the Indian Government as reactionary and unsympathetic." [136] Morley, too, realized the inherent dangers of the situation, though he philosophically dismissed them as minor flaws in the best of all possible governmental systems. "The House of Commons elected at the beginning of 1906," he subsequently admitted, "represented the high-water mark of all the opinions, leanings, principles, sentiments, convictions, that would naturally be most jealous, critical and suspicious of any system necessarily worked upon non-democratic principles." But Morley, whose faith in parliamentary instituitions vastly exceeded his distrust of individual parliamentarians, did not fall prey to the morbid fears that gripped the Viceroy and top-ranking Indian administrators. By and large, his seniority, his Irish experience, and his political agility saw him through. In retrospect, he discounted the delicate task he had adeptly performed:

> The Indian questions in Parliament since 1906, to any Minister who should happen to have undergone the wearing and sometimes ferocious ordeal of Irish questions—not seldom, in troubled times, forty, fifty, sixty, in an afternoon, almost as many as Indian questions in a Session—have been child's play.[137]

Unlike Lord Minto, Morley correctly gauged the featherweight consistency of his adversaries, though their taunts occasionally filled him with indignation. "The fatuity of some schools of English Liberalism about Oriental things is bottomless," he exclaimed to Frederic Harrison.[138] To his intense satisfaction, however, he found that with a few honeyed words, he could usually persuade a Radical opponent to defer a resolution or to temper an inflammatory public declaration. In the spring of 1908, he prevailed upon Rutherford to shelve a motion deprecating the Government of India's restrictions upon the native press. "I dealt with him in tones of fraternal good nature," he triumphantly related to Minto, "urged him to remember that we must show our intention to keep

136. J. P. Hewett to Minto, July 31, 1906, Minto Papers.
137. Morley, "British Democracy and Indian Government," *Nineteenth Century and After, 69* (1911), 202-03.
138. Morley to Harrison, August 7, 1909, Harrison Papers.

order as a condition of reform; and he was melted almost to tears as he left me." [139]

The accusations of parliamentary assailants made substantially less of an impression upon either Morley's doctrines or his decisions than the Radicals hoped and the Indian bureaucrats feared. At the same time, they taxed his depleted physical powers to a greater extent than either realized. Yet Morley was exhilarated by the process that wore him out. "My faith in our democracy is unshaken," he assured Minto after confronting his opponents in a Commons debate, "and I don't wonder that the German Emperor should have wished that his men of their kidney were half as sensible." [140] Morley had waited too long for the revival of an effective parliamentary opposition to entertain more than passing regrets that his Indian policies often bore the brunt of its attacks. This was a far healthier situation, he consoled himself, than that which had prevailed during the previous decade. As for his adversaries, Morley usually found a way to excuse politicians who had been led astray by lofty ideals; his critics' "only fault," he told Lord Lamington, "is that they feel rather than think." [141] Regardless of their defects, he insisted that the Cottonites deserved the consideration that befitted Members of Parliament: Morley "always said," his private secretary recorded, "that the House—even *this* House—was all right if you dealt straightly with it. Randolph Churchill said the same." [142] Fortunately Morley's twentieth-century adversaries lacked either skills or perseverance, and he was permitted to bask a while longer in the deceptive afterglow of his Gladstonian optimism.

139. Morley to Minto, June 4, 1908, Minto Papers.
140. Morley to Minto, January 31, 1908, Minto Papers.
141. Morley to Lamington, March 9, 1906, Lamington Papers.
142. F. A. Hirtzel's Diary, November 8, 1906, *1*, 95.

4   Personalities or Principles?

The personal antipathy between John Morley and the fourth Earl of Minto, the tired Radical and the tiresome Whig, has been magnified beyond all reasonable purpose and proportion at the expense of the cardinal principles upon which their collaboration in fact foundered. The recriminations and petty jealousies that punctuate their voluminous correspondence more significantly reflect the irreconcilable disparities in intellectual tastes, social backgrounds, and, above all, in the attitudes and policies which each antagonist embodied.

The two statesmen met for the first time in Ottawa at the close of 1904, neither suspecting their imminent affiliation and each believing that his lengthy political career was approaching its end. Minto was serving his final days as Governor-General of Canada, and Morley had crossed the border during a private tour of the United States to visit Goldwin Smith, with whom he had studied at Oxford. The following autumn, Minto's Unionist chiefs hurriedly dispatched him to India. He had scarcely time to accustom himself to the change in climate when his party was evicted from office and John Morley was appointed Secretary of State for India in a Liberal Government.

A year after their brief encounter, Morley graciously recalled that he had departed from the Canadian capital firmly convinced "that we speak the same political language, even though we may not always say the same things." [1] Yet it is wholly doubtful whether five years of intimate correspondence, any more than their single face-to-face conversation, allayed either party's profound suspicions of the other. Minto continued to regard Morley as the repository of such vices as Little Englandism, Home Rule, and aggressive designs upon such sacred institutions as the Established Church and the House of Lords; he feared that his partner

1. Morley to Minto, December 14, 1905, Minto Papers.

might apply to Indian problems the Gladstonian formula he had vainly advocated for Ireland. Even after Morley had proved himself a tame lion, politicians of Minto's stamp continued to quake at faint echoes of his Radical roar. By the end of 1909, the Viceroy had "seen enough to be quite certain of what he [Morley] really is—a most dangerous man. I was also warned as to him from home." [2]

Morley, in turn, recalled more tangible grievances. The course of his political career had been largely determined by his fidelity to the cause of Irish Home Rule, of which Minto had been a vigorous opponent. Morley could hardly have forgotten that two decades earlier, Minto belonged to the Whig contingent that had hastily withdrawn from the Liberal camp for precisely the same reason that he had gratefully enlisted as a full-fledged member: Gladstone's declaration of adherence to Home Rule. More recently, while Morley had ardently condemned the South African war, Minto had been instrumental in persuading the reluctant Canadians to comply with Joseph Chamberlain's request for a contribution to the military effort.[3]

The Morley-Minto partnership lacked the measure of mutual respect that is an essential ingredient for sustained cooperation. The Secretary of State consigned his collaborator to an inferior rung on his intellectual ladder. In a conversation with Lord Esher, he identified Minto "as a gentleman. Not *clever*, but the highest type of the old governing class." [4] To Sir Edward Grey, in whom he reposed greater confidence, Morley expressed disappointment that "he had not got someone out there who was 'less stupid.' " [5] Lord Minto and his wife viewed Morley with a mixture of trepidation and disdain; though they mocked his reputed vanity, their animosity can, to a considerable extent, be attributed to their own unsatisfied appetites for personal recognition.

Lady Minto, particularly, entertained distinct notions of the deference that was due a Viceroy, and she acutely resented the fact that Morley usurped her husband's share of the headlines. In nine extravagant volumes, replete with carefully mounted photographs, she provided an elaborate account of the amateur theatricals and

2. Minto to Lansdowne, November 3, 1909, Minto Papers.
3. J. L. Garvin, *Life of Chamberlain*, 3, 531-32.
4. Journal, January 11, 1908, *Journals and Letters*, ed. Brett, 2, 275.
5. F. A. Hirtzel's Diary, June 15, 1908, 3, 56.

tiger hunts that rendered viceregal life palatable. These journals are well seasoned with assertions of Morley's devious intrigues to eclipse her "Rolly" in the political limelight. Independently the Mintos expressed their suspicions that Morley was abetting either Lord Curzon or, more surprisingly, Lord Kitchener, in schemes to impugn the Viceroy's qualifications and accomplishments.[6]

For his part Morley discounted reports of this antagonism, sliding over them in his *Recollections*. The Curzon-Kitchener controversy, in which "two men of great powers and exalted public station [had taken] one another by the throat before all the world," [7] was uppermost in his mind. Morley clearly perceived that his frequent disagreements with the Viceroy were, in large part, inherent in their official relationship and in the Janus-like administrative structure over which they jointly presided. "It is a terribly cumbrous and artificial sort of system," he complained, "and I am not certain that it will last for ever, or even for many years to come." [8]

By the time it was formally liquidated, the Morley-Minto alliance had degenerated into an implacable enmity. "So our Secretary of State has resigned," Minto, the last to give up his Indian post, gloated to Lord Kitchener. "He has been the same to the last! It may be uncharitable, but I wish my successor had had a few months of my experiences!" [9] The Viceroy's wish was granted, though with hardly the repercussions he had anticipated. Morley returned to the India Office in March 1911 to relieve his ailing successor, Lord Crewe; despite Minto's dire prognostication, the interim Secretary of State enjoyed cordial relations with Lord Hardinge, who owed his viceregal appointment to Morley's mach-

6. See Lady Minto's Indian Journals, September 4, 1907, *1907-ii*, 223; also F. A. Hirtzel's Diary, March 12, 1908, *3*, 29; Minto to Sir Arthur Bigge, January 5 and 8, 1908, Minto Papers. Lord Minto ultimately accused Morley of attempting to extract his resignation on grounds of ill-health (Minto to Dunlop Smith, March 23, 1910, Minto Papers), and Lady Minto suspected that Morley was exerting influence to deprive the retired Viceroy of a Garter. Lady Minto's Indian Journals, December 19, 1910, *1910-ii*, 566.

7. Morley to Lamington, March 2, 1906, Lamington Papers; Morley subsequently labeled it a "terrific heresy" when Minto threatened to append an official protest to his decree for the release of political deportees: "Pray don't forget the severe condemnation passed by public opinion both in India and at Home upon Brodrick, Curzon and the Cabinet of that day for publishing dispatches about the Curzon v. Kitchener quarrel, and so exposing the skeletons in our Imperial cupboard to the Indians and other unfriendly persons." Morley to Minto, November 25, 1909, Minto Papers.

8. Morley to Minto, October 19, 1910, Minto Papers.

9. Minto to Kitchener, November 6, 1910, Minto Papers.

inations. "You almost tempt me to wish that I were going on as S.S. to such a G.G.," Morley confided to Hardinge,[10] who, after Morley's death, returned the compliment by stating "that it would be impossible to find an easier Secretary of State to deal with." [11]

Though they differed in their political allegiances and in their approaches to various issues, Morley and Hardinge operated within the same constitutional framework. The new Viceroy realized that the dissension between Minto and Morley had represented considerably more than a clash of two egos: "Everybody knows," he acknowledged to his gratified benefactor, "that the Secretary of State has the last word and it would be wrong if it were not so, since he represents the British Government. Otherwise, the Government of India would be like an alien Government." [12] Though Minto only dimly perceived the fact, and Morley lacked the respect for his cohort to offer a patient explanation, the Morley-Minto tug-of-war was a subordinate skirmish in the battle over constitutional principles, which reached its climax in the summer of 1911 with the passage of the Parliament Act. This was, Morley was aware, a period "when . . . singular anxiety prevail[ed] to find new doctrines and new devices for giving the House of Commons the slip." [13] In his hassles with the Viceroy, Morley was doing his share to defend the supremacy of the elected chamber.

It is an absurd oversimplification to assert that Morley promulgated doctrines in order to amplify the modest powers he had inherited. The composer of a paean to the memory of Oliver Cromwell, he was a House of Commons man all his life, even after age, infirmity, and political circumstances compelled him to seek refuge from its hectic proceedings in the humiliating calm of the House of Lords. "I am one of those," he had once proclaimed to his fellow M.P.s,

> who do not shrink from any reform in procedure that would add to the authority and dignity, the majesty, I may say, of this House. I would like to see it enlarged by every method;

10. Morley to Hardinge, April 19, 1911, Morley Papers.

11. Lord Hardinge of Penshurst, *My Indian Years* (London, 1948), pp. 21-22; with dubious justification, Lord Curzon speculated to Morley in 1908 "how splendidly you and I would have got on as S. of S. and Viceroy." F. A. Hirtzel's Diary, March 17, 1908, *3, 30.*

12. Hardinge to Morley, March 16, 1911, Morley Papers.

13. Morley "British Democracy and Indian Government," *Nineteenth Century and After, 69* (1911), 193.

because if we do not have collectively any of that dignity which doth hedge a King, at least do not let us forget that we are the heirs of the noblest traditions in the history of freedom, that we are the possessors of vast and boundless powers for good and evil, and that we are the chosen repositories of the confidence of the people of this realm.[14]

Despite his transfer to "another place" in the spring of 1908, Morley continued to champion the claims of the lower house. Appropriately enough, it ultimately fell to him to shepherd the meager flock of Liberal peers in their assault against their house's few remaining prerogatives.

Morley was a relentless advocate of the view that imperial affairs required the constant surveillance of parliamentarians in order to temper at least the abuses of despotism in those colonial areas which, according to his rigid Gladstonian criteria, were unsuited for democratic institutions. "However decorously veiled," Morley insisted,

pretensions to oust the House of Commons from part and lot in Indian affairs—and this is what the tone now in fashion on one side of the controversy really comes to—must lead in logic, as in fact, to the surprising result of placing what is technically called the Government of India in a position of absolute irresponsibility to the governed.[15]

His extensive Irish experience had made Morley wary of alien bureaucrats who were left to their own devices. "Justice and Clemency," he instructed his undersecretary, were "two words that the rulers of men, especially if irresponsible, like the G[overnment] of I[ndia], are slow to learn." [16] Indian affairs had averted parliamentary scrutiny in recent years, ostensibly because of the distance that separated them from Westminster, but largely because of the virtual indifference of M.P.s and successive Cabinets. As a result, the Government of India had had frequent recourse to those practices which aroused fiercest indignation in Morley's breast: military aggression, overexpenditure, and arbitrary rule.

Morley's arguments did not, however, reflect an altruistic con-

14. *Parliamentary Debates,* 3d ser., 322, col. 657 (February 16, 1888) .
15. Morley "British Democracy and Indian Government," pp. 198-99.
16. Morley to Godley, April 14, 1906, Kilbracken Papers (I.O.L.) .

cern for subject peoples so much as a desire to uphold the or-
dained privileges of the Mother of Parliaments. During his long
and distinguished public career—his apprenticeship to John Stuart Mill, his brush with Positivism, his conversion to Gladstonianism—Morley had consistently defended the House of Commons
against critics who grew steadily more vocal. Alarmed by the
emergence of new political forces, by the threats posed to Britain's industrial, naval, and imperial hegemonies by parvenu
powers, prominent national figures waxed impatient with traditional methods of government. This disaffection was further aggravated late in 1905 by the installation in office of a Liberal
ministry which contained such potential firebrands as John Burns,
Winston Churchill, and David Lloyd George. The Liberal triumph was anathema particularly to Indian administrators, who
had been well insulated against recent trends in their homeland.
Lord Ampthill, who had learned to distrust "Radicals" as private
secretary to a sadder and wiser Joseph Chamberlain, had a difficult
time deciding whether he most despised the Indian agitators or the
British Liberals: "In judging Indians, we must always ask ourselves whether they are any worse than the Englishmen they imi-
tate. Is Gokhale more dishonest as a politician than Sir Henry
Campbell-Bannerman or Lord Rosebery? I should hesitate to say
that he was." [17] Morley was thus thrust into contact with entrenched diehards who were predisposed to resist and resent his
influence.

Despite his lifelong reputation as an ideologue, the principles
which Morley applied at the India Office had not been culled from
textbooks. At the loss of a friendship, he had vehemently denounced Lord Lytton's Indian policies and the Disraeli Government's failure to restrain its impetuous Viceroy. "About Indian
matters," he had written to Joseph Chamberlain in 1876, before
either of them entered Parliament, "I don't see how it is to be governed under our parliamentary system without decisive power
being left to the Indian Secretary." [18] The distribution of powers
between Simla and Whitehall had long provided a topic for debate

17. Ampthill to Brodrick, November 27, 1905, Ampthill Papers. "I do not
know Mr. Morley personally," Ampthill revealed, "and there are many of his ideas
with which I cannot sympathize." Ampthill to Brodrick, December 14, 1905, Ampthill Papers.
18. Morley to Chamberlain, March 18, 1876, Chamberlain Papers.

among members of Morley's Radical coterie. Sir Charles Dilke, for one, had been convinced that:

> If India is to be governed by the British race at all, it must be governed from Great Britain. The general conditions of our rule must be dictated at London by the English people, and nothing but the execution of our decrees, the collection of evidence, and the framing of mere rules, left to our subordinates in the East.[19]

Morley was able to display such self-confidence during his Indian secretaryship because he had already examined both sides of the constitutional coin and had decided which he preferred. For a long time his ideas had remained nebulous; his vacillations reflected an attempt to discern and to follow Gladstone's tenuous golden thread. Before he entered Parliament, he had wondered whether backbenchers were competent to intervene in Indian disputes:

> An Indian subject, unless it happens to have been chosen for a party debate, empties the House of Commons, and it is not the least unreasonable that this should be so; for what does the ordinary member of Parliament know of the deciding considerations of the most important branches of Indian polity and administration?[20]

Lord Randolph Churchill's proposal in 1885 for a Royal Commission on Indian affairs elicited strong objections from Morley, who

19. Sir Charles Dilke, *Greater Britain* (2 vols. London, 1868), 2, 368-69. John Buchan (*Lord Minto*, p. 281) irrelevantly argues that Morley repudiated John Stuart Mill's dictum that "The executive Government of India must be seated in India itself." Mill's argument was lifted out of context from his *Memorandum of the Improvements in the Administration of India during the Last Thirty Years, and the Petition of the East India Company to Parliament* (London, 1858), p. 127.

20. [Morley], "A Political Epilogue," *Fortnightly Review*, n.s., 26 (1879), 330. Morley's analysis was an obvious reworking of Gladstone's arguments in a rival journal a year earlier:

> At home, still less provision is made for the adequate discharge of a gigantic duty. It depends upon a Cabinet, which dreads nothing so much as the mention of an Indian question at its meetings; on a minister, who knows that the less his colleagues hear of his proceedings, the better they will be pleased . . . and on a Parliament, supreme over them all, which cannot in its two Houses jointly muster one single score of persons who have either a practical experience in the government of India, or a tolerable knowledge of its people or its history.

Gladstone, "England's Mission," *Nineteenth Century, 4* (1878), 578.

feared that Indian issues would be exploited for purposes of party politics. Perhaps he entertained optimistic expectations of Lord Dufferin who, after all, was a Gladstonian appointee to the viceroyalty. Yet Morley was never among those who trusted the Government of India to tidy its own house. In the columns of the *Pall Mall Gazette*, he had acknowledged the need for constructive action and had groped in vain for a more direct method to constrain Britain's imperial auxiliaries.[21] Three years later, he acknowledged a change in his position in a letter to Sir William Harcourt, to whom he reported an after-dinner conversation with Charles Bradlaugh and Sir William Hunter, two M.P.s with little in common besides their friendship with Morley and their desire "to talk India." Bradlaugh, he related,

> will pretty certainly bring on a motion for a Royal Commission to rove about India—next session. When Randolph mooted this in '85, I opposed him stoutly. But we shall have to do something, and I am for my part in favour of our moving for a parliamentary committee early in the session.[22]

As the years passed, Morley grew increasingly convinced that a thorough review of imperial situations could be conducted only under parliamentary auspices. This view was influenced more by events in Ireland and South Africa than by the fact that, after 1905, Morley found himself responsible to Parliament for Indian affairs. Though he continued to oppose attempts to wield parliamentary committees as party or factional weapons,[23] he was receptive to proposals for discreet parliamentary inquests conducted, as the 1896 South African Committee had been, along strict bipartisan lines. At the close of his first year at the India Office, he advised his private secretary that a full-scale parliamentary review— not a Royal Commission—was "the only way out of the present difficulty." A select committee, he explained, "would gain time, which was important; it would probably last two years and he

---

21. See particularly October 7, 1885, p. 3.

22. Morley to Harcourt, December 30, 1888, Harcourt Papers. Harcourt accorded Morley's suggestion the Gladstonian seal of approval: "I know the G.O.M. was of opinion that there ought to be periodic reviews by Parlt. of [India's] condition and that the interval has long . . . expired since there had been such an investigation. In point of principle, no doubt, this inquiry should be by a Parlt. Committee." Harcourt to Morley, December 31, 1888, Harcourt Papers.

23. Morley to Minto August 23, 1906, Minto Papers.

thought of taking the chair himself. I asked what the terms of reference would be, and he said 'pretty wide.' " [24] This proposal was stultified by viceregal opposition, but Morley continued to search for methods to insure that Indian problems would not, like those in Ireland and Africa, escape parliamentary surveillance.

Though the sincerity of Morley's Irish sympathies cannot be doubted, his devotion to Home Rule was in part an attempt to re-habilitate the House of Commons, which had been paralyzed by the obstructionist techniques of the Irish nationalists in its ranks. "The more I think of it," he had written to Gladstone, "the more convinced I am of the folly of allowing 103, or even 40, or any other number of Irish Members, to come swooping down on our Parliament, fitfully and at their own pleasure or caprice, to spoil our business." [25] Morley had occasion to complain of this griev-ance two decades later when, as Secretary of State for India, he had to contend with a belligerent Irish faction: "It might perhaps have been a bit of heaven's mercy," he chided Lord Minto,

> if Mr. Gladstone and I had been allowed to have our way, and the Irish Members had been relieved of the duty of atten-dance at Westminster. It may be all right that, as you Union-ists say, England should govern Ireland, but as it unhappily turns out, Irishmen very often govern England.[26]

To surmount these Gaelic hurdles, the House had resorted to a closure process which Morley found equally odious. "I would rather bestow a new constitution on Ireland," he told an audience at Chelmsford in 1886, "than I would destroy the old constitution of Great Britain." [27] He assured his Unionist critics that Home Rule would, in fact, strengthen the hand of the Parliament at Westminster: "a strong central government" in Dublin "would not fritter away authority, and would not, as your proposals would, multiply the centres of resistance to, and attacks on, the Imperial Parliament." [28] There was not a single line in Glad-

24. F. A. Hirtzel's Diary, December 4, 1906, *1*, 102.

25. Morley to Gladstone, April 13, 1886, Gladstone Papers, Add. MSS. 44,255, fols. 42-43.

26. Morley to Minto, February 16, 1910, Minto Papers.

27. Speech at Chelmsford, January 7, 1886, *The Times* (January 8, 1886) , p. 6.

28. *Parliamentary Debates,* 3d ser., *308,* cols. 360-61 (August 23, 1886) .

stone's proposals, he insisted, "which impairs or restricts the supremacy as constituted by the Act of Union." [29]

Home Rule had been designed to restore not only Parliament's self-respect, but also parliamentary powers which had been appropriated to ad hoc agencies. Parliament, under both Liberal and Conservative Governments, had legislated coercive measures which were implemented by irresponsible bodies. Morley condemned the futility of these schemes and the folly of his colleagues:

> When these Acts, with all the exceptional and stringent powers contained in them, were brought before the House the argument was—"We need have no fear or jealousy in passing these provisions, because the House itself will be able to supervise their administration and the way they are carried out after they are passed." But after they were passed, the very same argument was used against supervision by this House . . . namely, that we are the most unfit Body in the world to be a court of appeal.[30]

But his protests were complacently disregarded during the ensuing years, which were marked by wholesale abdications of parliamentary authority along a barren route which stretched past Khartoum and Fashoda into the ultimate blind alley of the Boer War.

Morley's so-called Little Englandism was by no means, as critics spuriously alleged, an unmitigated aversion to the glories of empire. Like Gladstone, he was prepared to sanction imperial ventures that neither bankrupted the British pocketbook nor corrupted the national character. But the reticence of party leaders, Morley contended, allowed justifiable imperial projects to become acts of wanton jingoism. Early in 1899, he warned his countrymen against the implications of their impending move into the Sudan:

> When you annex this great territory you must recognize the fact that you cannot set up a Parliament. . . . You must govern it by a ruler practically despotic, though I hope with pretty firm and stiff instructions and supervision from this

29. *Parliamentary Debates*, 4th ser., *12*, col. 404 (May 8, 1893).
30. *Parliamentary Debates*, 3d ser., *322*, col. 652 (February 16, 1888).

country. But however all this may be, by the step that you have taken, depending as it does upon despotic rule, calling as it does for enormous expenditure, involving as it does the use of troops which are not British, you are unconsciously—and history will mark us as having done it—transforming the faces and conditions of your Empire.[31]

His melancholy forebodings were soon proved true by the arbitrary powers allotted to Lord Kitchener of Khartoum, the conqueror and administrator of the new protectorate. Soon afterward, the British nation "stumbled into war" in South Africa. The reasons were numerous and complex, but the most important, Morley later reminded his Scottish constituents, was that "there had been a steady and persistent attempt to depose the House of Commons from its august position as a high deliberative assembly." [32]

Britain's ignominy had deepened Morley's hostility not to an empire, but to an empire in which investors, militarists, and autonomous bureaucrats dictated policy. The Boer War had jolted British sensibilities, but it failed to alert politicians to their imperial obligations; nor did it settle the perpetual dispute whether Westminster should call the tune as well as pay the imperial piper. In the spring of 1904 Morley enumerated "the perils to which we are exposed by frontier agents when they are not vigilantly watched from home." He cited the case of Somaliland to a gathering at Manchester:

> Yesterday we were told that this campaign against the "Mad Mullah"—he is not the maddest of all, I think—cost us £2,370,000. By a curious coincidence, the same afternoon the Secretary of State for India admitted that the "peace mission" to Thibet was now to be advanced to Lhasa.[33]

The South African holocaust, which Morley cited as conclusive proof of his thesis, was viewed differently by statesmen of other political persuasions. The Milnerites and Chamberlainites deprecated Campbell-Bannerman's peace formula as a sellout that denied British troops and taxpayers the fruits of their hard-won

31. *Parliamentary Debates*, 4th ser., 67, cols. 459, 468 (February 24, 1899) .
32. Speech at Arbroath, October 23, 1905, *The Times* (October 24, 1905) , p. 6.
33. Speech at Manchester, May 13, 1904, Morley, *The Issues at Stake* (London, 1904) , p. 11.

victories. Sir Alfred (later Lord) Milner, according to his most recent biographer, returned from South Africa in 1905 imbued with the belief "that the parliamentary system, based upon the necessities of party and the whims of a 'rotten public opinion,' was totally unfitted for the rule of a great Empire." [34] India and Morley came perilously close to having this magnet for malcontents as Curzon's successor; but after rebuffs from Milner, A. J. Balfour settled for Lord Minto, whose views on the limitations of parliamentary authority were considerably less articulate, but only slightly more compromising.

It is impossible to ascertain the precise degree to which Minto was consciously implementing theories of imperialism, but the Viceroy left no doubt that in his view, "The great difficulty in governing India is the existence of the House of Commons." [35] His fellow Unionists took care to remind him of the vital issues at stake. "Whenever my opinion is asked about any Indian question," a young Neville Chamberlain cockily professed, "I always say I am sure 'the man on the spot' knows the right thing to be done, and does it, regardless of our wretched Parliamentarians." [36] And Sir Arthur Bigge, Minto's friend at Court, assured him that he was participating in a global struggle against overweening parliamentary pretensions:

> Oh dear! What a pity it is that the S. of S. will try and govern India—and not trouble the Viceroy who, on the spot, must know best and is moreover not influenced by H. of Commons opinions! . . .
>
> But it is the same thing in Egypt: there is a regular Egyptian party in the H. of C. who corresponds with the "Nationalist Party" in Cairo and consequently the difficulty of governing the Soudan is seriously increased.[37]

Unionist journalists added their strident voices to the din. "Democracy can only control an Empire when it is willing to delegate its control," the *Spectator* preached.[38] Sir Valentine Chirol instructed his readers that the Governor-General of India "is the

34. A. M. Gollin, *Proconsul in Politics* (London, 1964), p. 45.
35. Minto to Sir E. Clouston, April 5, 1909, Minto Papers.
36. Neville Chamberlain to Minto, December 12, 1906, Minto Papers.
37. Bigge to Minto, September 24, 1908, Minto Papers.
38. *Spectator* (July 28, 1906), p. 120.

direct and personal representative of the King-Emperor," [39] and
therefore did not owe obeisance to Parliament. An anonymous
Cassandra in the *Quarterly Review* deplored "fussy interference
. . . with the policy of proconsuls in distant parts of the empire,"
a danger "nowhere more real than in India." [40]

Morley, too, perceived the significance of his constitutional
position. He had frequently bemoaned the fact that Whitehall had
possessed neither the talents nor the inclination to balance the
scale of Indian authority. Early in 1898, he proffered an indignant
retort to Joseph Chamberlain's proposal to allow the Government
of India to persevere with its border campaigns without parliamentary meddling:

> [Chamberlain] expressed what I cannot but call a novel opin-
> ion, a pernicious opinion, a highly dangerous opinion, and it
> is this: . . . "Would you trust the observations made by our-
> selves who have to learn everything within a few months or a
> few years from documents and papers, or would you trust
> those who, like the Indian Government, have been engaged
> for years and years in studying this question, and the military
> experts whose business it is to understand and study the mili-
> tary aspects of the case?" . . . I say nothing against the
> military advisers in their own field, but I think it was my
> right hon. friend himself who said the soldier was like fire—he
> is a good servant, but a bad master. [41]

After the Boer War ended, India appeared to Morley to be among
the few remaining citadels of military and bureaucratic absolut-
ism. Lord Kitchener, often the victim of Morley's bitter denunciations, was engaged in a well-publicized struggle with Lord Curzon
who, by default, received Morley's cautious sympathy. Morley laid
the blame squarely on St. John Brodrick, the Secretary of State,
whose failure to rebuke the Commander-in-Chief violated a fundamental British practice: "Since the days when Charles I lost his

39. Chirol's arguments first appeared in *The Times,* then in his *Indian Unrest*
(London, 1910). Morley replied with a review of the latter in which he insisted
"that the Cabinet are just as much masters over the Governor-General, as they
are over any other servants of the Crown." "British Democracy and Indian
Government," *Nineteenth Century and After, 69* (1911), 189-210.

40. "A Tesselated Ministry," *Quarterly Review, 206* (1907), 278.

41. Speech at Stirling, January 27, 1898, *The Times* (January 28, 1898), p. 4.

head, it had always been agreed that the civil power should prevail over the military power." [42]

Incensed by his predecessor's inertia, Morley arrived at the India Office in December 1905 with few concrete proposals, but with a fierce determination to impede the one-way swing of the constitutional pendulum. "You seem to think," he chastised one prominent Indian administrator, "that . . . if your excellent persons in India make your demands loud enough and 'stern' enough, then the H. of C. will politely abdicate, and allow *you* to dictate. This view will never do." [43] It remained a "great riddle how a parliamentary democracy is to govern India," but Morley nonetheless insisted that "the experiment has got to be tried somehow, and perhaps the next three or four years will have a good deal to do with it." [44] In any event, he assured Sir George Clarke (later Lord Sydenham), then Governor of Bombay, "it is idle to quarrel with the political sytem that we are bound to work. After all, I don't know any better system. Do you?" [45]

Morley tactfully notified Minto that neither he nor his Liberal colleagues would have any truck with critics who denied the supreme authority of a duly-elected parliamentary majority; this pertained as much to the Government of India as to the entrenched interests in the House of Lords. "The Cabinet would certainly take fright," he warned,

> at any language or acts of ours pointing in the Curzonian direction, by seeming to set up . . . the Government of India as a sort of a great power on its own account. I don't believe there is a trace of such a thought in your own mind, but it may well be that the intoxicating fumes of the late regime may still hang about your Council Chamber.[46]

42. Speech at Arbroath, October 23, 1905, *The Times* (October 24, 1905), p. 6. "What a disgraceful sort of mess is the Curzon v. Brodrick v. Kitchener affair!" Morley exclaimed to Lord Spencer. "On the broad merits, I incline to Curzon. Perhaps I'm wrong." Morley to Spencer, August 23, 1905, Spencer Papers. After he had investigated the problem, Morley informed Brodrick, "I would not have stood from Curzon for two months what you have stood for two years." Morley to Brodrick, January, 1906 [n.d.], cited in the Earl of Midleton, *Records and Reactions* (London, 1939), p. 208.
43. Morley to Lamington, May 24, 1907, Lamington Papers.
44. Morley to Minto, October 8, 1907, Minto Papers.
45. Morley to Clarke, August 19, 1908, Morley Papers.
46. Morley to Minto, February 9, 1906, Minto Papers.

Consequently, he rejected Minto's request for a voice in the framing of the 1907 Anglo-Russian agreement.

Morley's relative inexperience in Indian affairs and the unsuspected intricacies of the problems he inherited made it impossible for him to stipulate the precise adjustments in administrative responsibilities that he favored. At a bleak moment in 1898, when he had surrendered any hope of assuming office, let alone the Indian secretaryship, he had proclaimed:

> Control by the central authorities ought not to be so minute or detailed as to fetter and to cripple those who are the agents and representatives of this country in difficult conditions abroad. At the same time it is the House of Commons at Westminster, it is the Cabinet in Downing Street, that is ultimately responsible.[47]

As Secretary of State for India, he discovered that militarism and arbitrary rule were more firmly established in imperial affairs than he had initially supposed, and he exerted his influence accordingly.

Morley's critics, who have grown more numerous and less persuasive as time passes, have argued that he assumed more powers than necessary to restore a constitutional balance; this might have been the case, but if so it was inadvertent. Morley, who harbored secret doubts whether the British Raj could survive on any basis, was convinced that parliamentary control afforded the single conceivable and creditable chance. Infuriated by a particularly flagrant display of bureaucratic injustice, he protested: "This is the sort of temper, not Keir Hardie, that will one day lose India." [48] Yet he remained primarily concerned with British society and British institutions. By keeping a tight rein on Indian affairs, he endeavored to guard against a recrudescence of the runaway jingoism that had shattered British equanimity and Liberal solidarity during the previous decade.

47. Speech at Stirling, January 27, 1898, *The Times* (January 28, 1898), p. 4.
48. Morley to Hardinge, May 17, 1911, Morley Papers.

5 The War Against the Bureaucrats

It made little difference to John Morley whether the Governor-General or the Secretary of State for India exercised preeminence in Indian affairs, so long as decisions were subordinated to Cabinet policy, expenditures drastically reduced, and military forces taken in tow. It would have been ideal had both positions been occupied by men of the same political outlook—such as when he and Lord Spencer had jointly presided over Irish affairs—but this possibility had been ruled out by A. J. Balfour's determination to present his successors with a replacement for Lord Curzon. Besides, such a combination had rarely been the case in the administrative history of British India, even when both officials were of the same political extraction.

On numerous occasions, Minto's inability to resist Anglo-Indian agitation impelled his senior partner to force the viceregal hand.[1] Had Lord Minto proved a more dynamic administrator, better able to withstand the wheedling and prodding of his bureaucrats, Morley would have been content to hold aloof from administrative problems as he had intended when he first arrived at the India Office. Morley's frequent interventions reflected not so much a Bismarckian strain, but his reluctant recognition of the fact that, under normal circumstances, men on the spot will ultimately prevail.

1. Sir Arthur Godley, who retired from the India Office in 1909 with a peerage and an implacable grudge against Morley, described the Morley-Minto rivalry to Austen Chamberlain: "When you have the following combination . . . a very able, but very vain, impulsive, and ambitious Secretary of State, extremely anxious to leave his mark on the history of India, and nurtured in the principles of the French Revolution . . . an exceptionally weak Council . . . a ditto Viceroy—you know what to expect." Kilbracken to Chamberlain, May 13, 1917, Austen Chamberlain Papers. At the close of 1910, after both administrators had severed their official ties with Indian affairs, *The Times* delivered its verdict that the powers of the Indian secretaryship had merely expanded to fill the vacuum created by Minto's weaknesses (November 4, 1910), p. 11.

Morley did not underestimate either the power or the prestige of the viceroyalty, but concluded that Minto failed to take advantage of either. When Lord Lytton was appointed viceroy three decades earlier, Morley had told Joseph Chamberlain that this was "exactly the post in which I should like to see you: it is the greatest administrative post in the realm or out of it." [2] His esteem for the viceroyalty had not diminished by the close of 1908, when he received a birthday message from Sir Dighton Probyn, Keeper of the Privy Purse, wishing that Morley was a quarter century younger and Viceroy of India: "Yes, that's what I ought to be, of course," Morley mused.[3] But Morley was not Viceroy of India and he could not exert viceregal powers. As a result, he was forced to promote parliamentary claims by less direct, often less decorous methods.

It was with reference to problems of Irish administration that Morley first decried the division of authority between imperial officials and ministers of the Crown. Shortly before his first Irish secretaryship, he had advocated a reorganization which would shift the preponderance of power to Whitehall: "Had the Viceroyalty been disestablished and the executive business of the office handed over to the Chief Secretary, many troubles which have since occurred would have been averted." [4] His brief residence at Dublin Castle in 1886 confirmed Morley's view that a consolidation of power and responsibility was necessary, though he momentarily proposed a shift in the opposite direction:

> The Imperial authority must be represented by a big man on the spot. A Sec'y. of State at Whitehall would be a farce. You must have a Ld. Lt. in Dublin, seeing the men, hearing the incidents hot and fresh. There ought not to be an Irish Secretary. The Ld. Lt. ought to correspond with the H. O. or the Ld. President or anybody you please, to whom Irish business should be *incidental* and not an exclusive concern.[5]

This change of emphasis, but not of principle, was partly the result of Morley's confidence in Lord Spencer, and partly the result

2. Morley to Chamberlain, January 7, 1876, Chamberlain Papers.

3. F. A. Hirtzel's Diary, December 21, 1908, 3, 110.

4. [Morley], "Home and Foreign Affairs," *Fortnightly Review*, n.s., 37 (1885), 582.

5. Morley to Harcourt, January 18, 1887, Harcourt Papers.

of his belief that a simplified bureaucracy would facilitate the transition to Home Rule. As Secretary of State for India, Morley was neither as impressed with the abilities of his partner nor as sympathetic to the aspirations of native politicians.

Morley arrived at the India Office in 1905 with a distrust of imperial functionaries which was inveterate, but never irrational. He regarded them, not without considerable justification, as emigrants from liberal thought and society who had resourcefully averted Cobdenite clutches by fleeing to the outer reaches of the British Empire; there, in the name of white man's burden, they beat their protectionist drums, exercised despotic powers, and lamented the decline of their aristocratic traditions. It was this atavistic breed which had involved Great Britain in perilous adventures in Africa and the Far East, and which now threatened to provoke a major crisis in India.

Though he acknowledged the need to impede the centralization of administrative powers which threatened to paralyze the Government of India, Morley hesitated to take any step that might strengthen the semiautonomous potentates in each provincial capital. "On the point of centralisation, I sometimes feel myself in a paradox," he admitted to Minto. "Do I want to transfer power from you to Lawley or Lamington?" [6] He confessed an inability to appreciate the common "superstition about local governments being allowed to gang their own gaits, without energetic supervision," [7] and his official pronouncements on the matter revealed his inability to implement John Bright's recommendations for a wider distribution of administrative authority.

To Morley's mind, events in Ireland and other parts of the Empire had conclusively demonstrated the necessity to discount the urgings of men on the spot, who were often inclined to operate less out of conviction than out of a desire to safeguard their prerogatives. He did not subscribe to the notion that direct exposure to Indian conditions automatically conferred a comprehension of the issues at stake; there were some individuals whose biases and limited intellects precluded an understanding of the situation with which they came into daily contact. Anglo-Indians, regardless of rank or profession, appeared unable to discern, for instance, the

6. Morley to Minto, June 21, 1907, Minto Papers.

7. Morley to Sir Guy Fleetwood Wilson, January 13, 1909, Fleetwood Wilson Papers (India Office Library, London).

difference between seditious activity and social agitation, and they invariably presumed the former to be the case. Morley had observed precisely the same tendency among Anglo-Irishmen a quarter century earlier:

> We have all got into the habit of using too high-sounding words for Irish turbulence. The Irish passion for exaggeration infects their English masters where Irish riot is concerned. The newspapers make mountains out of molehills. A fray between a crowd of viragos and a bailiff is called a battle; and if a mob throws stones at a troop of dragoons we think that we are within measurable distance of civil war.[8]

Morley counseled Lord Lamington "that an insurrectionary movement is one thing, and a street row, even a bad street row, is quite another thing." [9] To Sir George Clarke, Lamington's successor as Governor of Bombay, he revealed the reason for his much-criticized self-confidence: "Distance from secondary things, like mill-riots, perhaps leaves one more free to keep one's eye on the things that are primary, and above all to see them in their true perspective." [10]

Successive confrontations with the Indian bureaucratic machine intensified Morley's antagonism and suspicions. He discovered that the official mind was more impregnable than he had feared. "I wish the G. of I. were a trifle more elastic, and a trifle less encased in bureaucratic buckram," he complained.[11] In particular, he regretted that the celebrated man on the spot could not be persuaded that the truncheon was not the answer to India's problems. "I've had much to do with this business of Criminal Investigation in my Irish time," he reminded Minto, "and I should guess that an Indian policeman needs even closer watching than Irish ditto—which is saying a good deal." [12]

8. [Morley], "Conciliation with Ireland," *Fortnightly Review*, n.s., *30* (1881), 12-13.

9. Morley to Lamington, July 12, 1907, Lamington Papers. Two years after his return from India, Lord Minto admitted that he had "found in India in the official world a great tendency to assume all political expressions of an advanced nature to be seditious; in many cases they were very far from being so." Minto to Morley, December 23, 1913, Minto Papers.

10. Morley to Clarke, August 19, 1908, Morley Papers.

11. Morley to Clarke, October 21, 1908, Morley Papers.

12. Morley to Minto, January 6, 1909, Minto Papers. "Half the mischief of *Ireland* all these long years past," Morley told Minto, "has been done by the fuss

Morley was most incensed by the fact that Minto chose not to repudiate but to propagate bureaucratic views. If India's civil disaffection precipitated a second mutiny, and Britain was forced to expend capital and manpower to put it down, the blame would rest squarely on the shoulders of the

> over-confident and over-worked Tchinovniks who have had India in their hands for fifty years past. Heaven knows, I don't want to be censorious or presumptuous in judging; I know the huge difficulties; I recognize the devotion to duty. On the other hand, I demur, in the uplifted spirit of the Trodden Worm, to the view said to be current at Simla, that the Home Government is always a d———d fool.[13]

As much as he deprecated the irresponsible meddling of individual parliamentarians, he realized that the Indian situation would be far worse if Indian civil servants escaped parliamentary scrutiny. Lady Minto, who campaigned for "firmer administration" in the pages of her journal, postulated that:

> If there was no communication with England, very different methods would have been used long ago, but, as it is, the Government of India is hampered at every turn, as these miserable Radical Socialists make themselves obnoxious in the House and the Secretary of State's position has to be thought of.[14]

Morley was fully aware that he could not "effectively control the Government of India's action at this distance," but he cherished hopes that he could nonetheless dampen its authoritarian ardor. He agreed with his private secretary "that the mere fact of thinking that they have to satisfy the S. of S. will act as a salutary check or make them more careful in setting up a good case." [15]

The members of Minto's governing caste offered frequent testimony to their refusal to come to terms with either nationalist opinion or Cabinet policy. Sir Arthur Lawley, Governor of Madras, decried "the doctrine that administration to be sound

---

and bullying of police, etc." Morley to Minto, March 8, 1906 [copy], Morley Papers.

13. Morley to Minto, June 17, 1908, Minto Papers.

14. Lady Minto's Indian Journals, October 11, 1907, *1907-ii*, 270.

15. F. A. Hirtzel's Diary, November 30, 1908, *3*, 104.

must be *popular.*" [16] Sir George Clarke, whose liberalism steadily melted beneath the Asian sun, argued that "strong measures are not resented if it is believed that the public good is our only object, and the vast number of wobblers incline to the side of strength." Clarke informed Minto of his vain attempts to make this "clear to Lord Morley . . . [whose] mind runs on Western lines, which, coupled with bad advisers, mislead him to an appalling extent." [17] Sir Denzil Ibbetson, who had entered the Indian Civil Service in 1868 and who ultimately retired as lieutenant-governor of the Punjab, insisted that "we simply *can't afford* to give way, in any degree whatever to the agitation of the so-called politicians of Bengal." [18] In his view, shared by a vast majority of his colleagues:

> The real question at issue is whether the Bengali agitator, or the Government of India, is to run this country; and I believe the future of India to be seriously involved in the decision. . . . Our only safety is to show them that agitation does not move us.[19]

Morley was impressed neither by Ibbetson's logic nor by his attempts to implement his policy. In May 1907, Ibbetson successfully petitioned the Viceroy for permission to arrest and deport two Indian leaders, Ajit Singh and Lala Lajpat Rai, who were alleged to be implicated in a carefully contrived plot to topple the British Raj. Ibbetson's fellow bureaucrats hailed the decision of the Punjabi and central governments: "The deportation of Lajpat Rai is a most excellent move," the Governor of Bombay assured Minto. "Our [nationalist] leaders here are keeping very quiet; evidently the chance of a cheap journey to the furthest portions of the Empire has not attractions when quietly conducted." [20] According to the provisions of Regulation III of 1818, inscribed on the statute books long before telegraph cables linked Simla and Whitehall, it was not essential to inform the Secretary of State until after the step had been taken. Morley, who did not wish to embarrass the Government of India, was placed in the uncomfortable position of having to defend this odious action before an irate

16. Lawley to Minto, September 17, 1906, enclosed in Minto to Morley, September 26, 1906 [copy], Minto Papers.
17. Clarke to Minto, July 29, 1910, Minto Papers.
18. Ibbetson to Minto, June 25, 1906, Minto Papers.
19. Ibbetson to Minto, June 29, 1906, Minto Papers.
20. Lamington to Minto, May 19, 1907, Minto Papers.

House of Commons. Despite his rejoinders to left-wing assailants, he harbored private doubts about the incident and soon realized his error. Henceforth he refused to fall prey to bureaucratic anxieties, and he made certain that Indian officials did not act without recourse to the Home Government. This did not of course preclude the promulgation of stringent legislation, but it virtually guaranteed that the subtle distinction between rebellion and agitation would be recognized.

The Lajpat Rai episode confirmed the worst of Morley's fears. It revealed "that a man may be a capable sort of administrator (if Ibbetson really is that) of a province, and yet fail altogether to face the complex Indian (and Parliamentary) questions as a whole." [21] Yet this was by no means Morley's first brush with bureaucratic injustice. A year earlier, at Barisal, Sir Bampfylde Fuller had displayed an audacity which the Government of India chose neither to temper nor disclaim. As lieutenant-governor of the truncated province of Eastern Bengal and Assam, Fuller administered the hotbed of Indian disaffection; [22] his injudicious actions added to the grievances of this afflicted area and galvanized the antipartition agitation that was Lord Curzon's legacy. On April 14, 1906, Bengali politicians convened a provincial conference at Barisal. The lieutenant-governor had strictly forbidden antipartition demonstrations and, especially, the allegedly seditious chant, "Bande Mataram." Both edicts were promptly put to the test by local nationalists. Fuller, who anticipated such exigencies, was poised to swoop down upon the obliging culprits. Surendranath Banerjea was arrested and some three hundred student demonstrators were suspended from their colleges.

Morley rightly feared the incendiary repercussions of the Barisal incident upon Indian nationalism and upon his legion of critics in the Commons. "What you say of Fuller's doings is rather disquieting," he told Minto on April 19.

> The anti-partition people here are pretty sure to reopen the case in the House of Commons before long, and of course they are kept well-informed from India (with a few lies thrown in,

21. Morley to Minto, November 8, 1907, Minto Papers.
22. Fuller's demeanor had elicited hostility even before the Barisal outrages. The *Daily Hitavadi* (Calcutta) labeled him "an apt pupil of Lord Curzon who has even surpassed his ex-chief in vanity, love of power, and in the art of repression." (December 4, 1905). Cited in *Bengal Native Newspaper Reports, 1905* (India Office Library, London).

I daresay), and if Fuller by excess or folly is making a substance for their case, he should be removed. A subordinate
who won't take his cue from responsible superiors is a nuisance.[23]

As the facts of the case were revealed, Morley became increasingly
exasperated by viceregal reticence no less than by bureaucratic
audacity. "I am rather perplexed about the Barisal affair, and also
as to the high-handed proceedings as to Banerjea," he complained
to Minto. *"Prima facie* they strike me as all wrong. . . . The
British Raj must be a poor sorry affair, if it trembles before a pack
of unruly collegians." [24] A week later, he concluded that the prohibition of "Bande Mataram" constituted "a complete misconstruction" of a recent High Court decision against seditious activity.[25] He doubted the prudence of Fuller's policy no less than
its equity, and Hirtzel noted that Morley's "Irish experience (to
which he constantly referred) told him that the local authorities
were wrong in not allowing the agitators to 'let off steam'; and
whether they had acted illegally or not, he was convinced that
their action was impolitic." [26]

Although he refused to placate his parliamentary critics by formally repudiating the Barisal policy, Morley applied persistent
pressure to obtain the acquittal of Banerjea, the reinstatement of
the youthful offenders, and the removal of Fuller.[27] He confided
to the Governor of Bombay that

> I am in this particular case . . . altogether on their [the
> Indians'] side. . . . I am no sentimentalist about these
> things and would be as firm about "law and order" as any
> body. But I don't forget that "law and order" without com
> mon sense and sense of proportion, are responsible for most of
> the worst villainies in history.[28]

23. Morley to Minto, April 19, 1906, Minto Papers.
24. Morley to Minto, April 25, 1906, Minto Papers.
25. Morley to Minto, May 3, 1906, Minto Papers.
26. F. A. Hirtzel's Diary, December 12, 1905, *I*, 6.
27. See particularly Morley to Minto, May 6 and 7, June 27, 1906 [telegrams],
Morley Papers.
28. Morley to Lamington, May 18, 1906, Lamington Papers; two months later
he lamented to Lamington "that unwise administration has played the game of
the enemies of Partition to perfection. . . . The Lt. Gov. of E. Bengal took a
cannon to blow an insect to pieces." Morley to Lamington, July 13, 1906, Lamington
Papers.

Morley repeatedly exhorted Minto to disown Fuller, whose "temperament . . . is really a misfortune that crowns the original blunders." Sir Alfred Lyall, a mutual friend, intervened on the lieutenant-governor's behalf, but Morley refused to mollify his views and informed Minto that "every word [Lyall] uses shows that Fuller is exactly the man worst fitted for such a post." [29]

Lord Minto was inclined to share Morley's misgivings about the episode, as well as his distrust of Fuller's capabilities; yet he hesitated to yield either to Whitehall or Indian opinion. Instead he attempted to convince Morley that "direct action of the Viceroy in present case would appear to over-rule executive authority of the Local Government, and might encourage agitators here and at home." [30] The passing weeks brought indications that Minto was gradually coming round to Morley's view of the situation: "I have expressed strongly to you grave objections to change of Lieutenant-Governor in face of agitation," he telegaphed on July 21, "but it now becomes daily more evident that administration of new Province is unreliable and may lead us into further difficulties." [31]

The matter was finally resolved at the end of July, with little credit to the Viceroy, who knew what had to be done, but who shrank from constructive action. Fuller launched another campaign against Bengali schoolboys which Minto refused to sanction. When the lieutenant-governor hastily offered his resignation, it was snatched up by a grateful Viceroy, who subsequently explained to Sir Valentine Chirol of *The Times* that

> the question . . . was . . . how in the world to get a dangerous man away from a position, his retention of which would quite certainly have produced a conflagration in Eastern Bengal. He was hysterical and absolutely unsuited for a position full of risk and requiring absolute tact. I never was so relieved in my life as when he resigned.[32]

Morley shared Minto's intense satisfaction, but he could not ignore the fact that only Fuller's fortuitous renunciation of power had permitted the Government of India to dispense with his inju-

29. Morley to Minto, May 3, 1906, Minto Papers.
30. Minto to Morley, May 12, 1906 [telegram], Morley Papers; also Minto to Morley, June 30, 1906 [telegram], Morley Papers.
31. Minto to Morley, July 21, 1906 [telegram], Morley Papers.
32. Minto to Chirol, May 18, 1910, Minto Papers.

rious services. Moreover, the Barisal affair had attested to the solidarity of bureaucratic ranks: "These men, even the best of them," Morley discovered, "seem to think much more of their own dignity, and convenience, and personal friendships, and advancement than they think of the Supreme Government. Well, the only way of meeting this spirit is by resolutely overruling them." [33] No less disturbing to Morley was the discovery that the Viceroy lacked both the resources and the volition to discipline his errant civil servants. On July 2, his private secretary found him "in a bad humour . . . quite unlike himself," and furious with Minto, "who had no political experience, had tried to 'checkmate' him in regard to Aden and Tibet, and was now putting difficulties in the way of Fuller's removal. He thought the G. of I. wanted to be 'taught a lesson.' " [34] Though he realized that this was neither the best nor the most harmonious solution, Morley resolved to compensate personally for Minto's deficiencies and to avail himself of the powers which his partner hesitated to employ. He did so not so much to protect himself against his Radical adversaries nor to protect Indian nationalists against bureaucratic repression, but primarily to protect the Government of India against its agents.

In order to implement his policies and to secure an adequate flow of information to Whitehall, Morley entered into private communication with several Indian administrators. Minto took umbrage at the use of these surreptitious channels, and argued that they defied time-honored constitutional practices. Morley countered with protests against Minto's private correspondence with politicians at home. This protracted controversy often attained the frenzy and ludicrous intricacy of contemporary French farce: each antagonist professed his innocence and hypocritically exonerated the other; [35] neither was capable of literary self-restraint. Morley claimed personal exemption from the unwritten rule that a Cabinet member should not confer directly with subordinate officials in other departments. "I concur—even vehemently—in the case of every member of H. M.'s Government, *except one*," he explained, "and that exception is the Indian Secre-

33. Morley to Minto, August 15, 1906 [copy], Morley Papers.

34. F. A. Hirtzel's Diary, July 2, 1906, *1*, 58.

35. See Morley to Minto, April 2, 1907 [telegram], and Minto to Morley, April 3, 1907 [telegram], Morley Papers; also Minto to Morley, April 25, 1907, Morley Papers; Morley to Minto, February 14, 1908, Minto Papers.

tary. He is not a fortuitous member of Government, but the head of the Indian department, responsible to Parliament for all that is done or left undone in the whole sphere of Indian administration." [36]

Because Minto disputed Morley's primacy, he also disputed his logic. He adroitly frustrated the Indian secretary's attempt to conduct a private correspondence with Lord Kitchener, but it proved immeasurably more difficult to ferret out "the backstairs advice constantly given to the Secretary of State" by adjutants at Simla.[37] Minto particularly resented Sir Guy Fleetwood Wilson, a relatively recent appointment to his Council, whom he suspected to be an accredited agent of Whitehall. "I believe him to be an archintriguer," Minto advised the Secretary of State. "He cringes to me in private (which I hate) and at the same time is fomenting discontent in other directions. . . . If you hear anything of his letters home, I only say Beware!" [38] The innocuous content of Fleetwood Wilson's confidential dispatches to the India Office was hardly worth the suspicions they engendered. Minto's attribution of significance to them undoubtedly resulted from the fact that Fleetwood Wilson occasionally preached the heretical doctrine of Whitehall's infallibility.[39] Sir Arthur Godley and Sir Frederic Hirtzel, aware of the Viceroy's resentment, assured their chief that such communications "did no good," but Morley insisted that

> they did, the system being what it was, a very bad one; either everything ought to be left to the G.G. or the S.S. ought to know everything; as it was, he had been "kept in the dark all

36. Morley to Minto, April 4, 1907, Minto Papers.

37. Minto to Clarke, July 23, 1910 [copy], Minto Papers.

38. Minto to Morley, July 5, 1909, Minto Papers. Minto initially believed that "Fleetwood Wilson would be [a] most useful appointment. Hope you will succeed in getting him." Minto to Morley, June 12, 1908 [telegram], Morley Papers. Morley anticipated that Fleetwood Wilson would inject the qualities of "Drive and Devil" into Minto's Council, and he was confident that these "will help and be valued by the G.G. in his contest with bureaucracy." Morley to Fleetwood Wilson, January 13, 1909, Fleetwood Wilson Papers. But Minto was soured by a letter he received from Lord Midleton, Morley's Tory predecessor, who offered "heartiest condolences on the appointment which Morley has made to your Finance post. Fleetwood Wilson has a good deal of ability, but he is the most disloyal servant I ever had to deal with. . . . He intrigues with everybody, usually with the intention of getting a better position or more influence for himself." Midleton to Minto, August 13, 1908, Minto Papers.

39. See Sir Guy Fleetwood Wilson's dissent appended to the Government of India's Reforms Dispatch, July 19, 1909, Fleetwood Wilson Papers.

the time." Of course, it would have been different if the G.G. had been one of his own party.[40]

Lord Minto, despite his self-righteous outrage, was himself guilty of similar indiscretions. He criticized Cabinet policy in letters to prominent members of the Opposition, several of whom campaigned vigorously against aspects of the Morley-Minto reform policy; in addition, he voiced his grievances to members of the royal family which Morley considered "an illegitimate influence" that might induce royal interference.[41] Minto also enjoyed the confidence of members of the Secretary of State's staff. Godley frequently provided him with intimate descriptions of personalities and projects at Whitehall, cautioning him to "say nothing about all this in your letters, except in answer to what you may hear from Mr. Morley." [42] Less welcome at Simla were Godley's offers of well-meaning advice:

> It would not be amiss if, in writing to Mr. Morley, you could casually make it clear that in such matters as Tibet, Aden, removal of Fuller, etc.—matters in which the wishes and opinions of your Government are not identical with his—you fully intend to accept and be guided by his policy after making any proper representations.

Minto's reaction on this occasion was scrawled in blue crayon along the lower margin of the undersecretary's letter: "Infernal ass!" [43]

Morley ascribed Minto's attitude on the issue of private correspondence to bureaucratic dogma and a narrow mind. When Hirtzel reported Lord Lamington's remark "that Minto would not have anybody write or receive letters but himself," his chief assured him that "a good many people who were 'not very clever' were like that." [44] For his own part, Morley insisted that he stood within constitutional bounds, that he did not crave wider powers, but was zealously guarding those which had been entrusted to him. He protested as strenuously when any of his Liberal associates attempted to circumvent his authority. In the autumn of 1906, he

40. F. A. Hirtzel's Diary, January 30, 1909, *4*, 9; also February 17, 1909, *4*, 14.
41. Morley to Godley, September 14, 1908, Kilbracken Papers (I.O.L.) .
42. Godley to Minto, March 23, 1906, Minto Papers.
43. Godley to Minto, June 29, 1906, Minto Papers.
44. F. A. Hirtzel's Diary, August 22, 1906, *1*, 73.

defended his "sphere of influence" against encroachments by the Chancellor of the Exchequer, who proposed the construction of a railway along the Persian Gulf: "I have stiff work in keeping in step with the Foreign Department at Simla," he complained to Asquith; "I must also keep in step with the F.O. here. . . . Now, here comes the C. of Exchequer, coercing me into step with him." [45] Even the amiable Campbell-Bannerman was rebuked for treading upon the Indian secretary's toes: after the Prime Minister conferred privately with a prominent Indian nationalist, Morley remonstrated

> that on such extremely delicate ground as India, and the relations between the Congress people and the home government, it would have been a pleasant compliment, shall I call it, if the Prime Minister had said something to the S. of S. before seeing Gokhale, or after.[46]

By far the most significant case in point was Morley's refusal to permit a private correspondence between R. B. Haldane, then Secretary for War, and Lord Kitchener, Commander-in-Chief of the Indian forces. He speculated to Minto that "if Lord Kitchener were to take up a position on some question half military and half political, in which you or I or both of us dissented from Kitchener, he might be able to use the leverage of the War Office against us." [47] On a visit to Windsor Castle in the spring of 1906, Morley uncovered evidence of a War Office "plot to invade Indian patronage," and he good-naturedly admonished Haldane "that I write this under the roof where Charles I was carried away to have his head cut off for trying the same tricks in Army affairs." [48] There was absolutely no chance that the Secretary of State for India would brook from Unionist hands usurpations which he would not tolerate from his Liberal colleagues.

What Morley could not accomplish with polite admonitions and subtle threats of retribution, he achieved by high-handed ultimatums. When Minto proved an ineffective barrier against bureaucratic pretensions, the Indian secretary remedied the situa-

45. Morley to Asquith, September 26, 1906, Morley Papers.
46. Morley to Campbell-Bannerman, August 2, 1906, Campbell-Bannerman Papers, Add. MSS. 41,223, fols. 197-98.
47. Morley to Minto, February 23, 1906, Minto Papers.
48. Morley to Haldane, June 9, 1906, Haldane Papers.

tion by issuing instructions that: "Steps, if any, about seditious speeches, meetings, or writings, should only be taken after reference to Home Government, unless, of course, sudden emergency." [49] The Government of India took advantage of this loophole to deport Lajpat Rai without informing Whitehall, and Morley consequently asserted his authority in stronger terms: "The Government of India is no absolute or independent branch of Imperial Government. It is in every respect answerable to the Cabinet as any other department is." [50] Minto's successor acknowledged the conditions which had precipitated Morley's interventions:

> The fact is there has been no Government of India during the last two years, and affairs have been allowed to drift in the two Bengals with the absurd idea that there should be no interference with the Local Government. . . . It was a theory that fairly exasperated me, and I asked those who advocated it what was the use of having a Government of India and a Governor-General in Council? I am glad to say I hear less of this theory at present and the gospel of interference with the Local Governments when they are going wrong grows stronger every day.[51]

The Morley-Minto animosity reached its ignominious climax in the summer of 1910, when Edwin Montagu, Under-Secretary of State for India, referred in a Commons debate to Lord Minto as an "agent" of India Office policy.[52] There can be little doubt that this statement faithfully reflected Morley's private sentiments; [53]

49. Morley to Minto, May 6, 1907 [telegram], Morley Papers.

50. Morley to Minto, May 14, 1909, Minto Papers; Sir Arthur Godley, who had served a succession of Indian secretaries, endorsed Morley's view that
> whatever is done in India, the S. of S. must, if challenged, be prepared either to defend . . . or to condemn . . . [it] publicly. Surely, this being so, it would be only common sense on the part of the Govt. of India to ascertain privately (or officially) his disposition with regard to any important step which they may be contemplating, if they have reason to think that it will attract attention in this country.

Godley to Sir William Lee-Warner, October 4, 1907, Lee-Warner Papers (India Office Library, London).

51. Hardinge to Morley, May 25, 1911, Morley Papers.

52. *Parliamentary Debates*, 5th ser., *19*, col. 1984 (July 26, 1910).

53. When Morley replied to questions about Partition in the Commons, he deleted Hirtzel's proposed reference to the Viceroy's "superintendence, direction and control"; this, he explained, "it did not suit him to admit." F. A. Hirtzel's Diary, November 29, 1906, *1*, 101. Hirtzel also recorded Morley's refusal to con-

but the Secretary of State, who made it an inviolable practice to conceal such controversies from public view, promptly dismissed the incident as a case of parliamentary stage fright:

> Does nobody on your Council know what a supplementary question is? An interrogation sprung upon a Minister by way of a rapid poser, which the Minister has to answer in an instant as best he can. You all seem to regard it as the result of deliberate desire and deeply laid plan to disparage the most admirable of all departments.[54]

Minto and his allies remained wholly unconvinced. Lady Minto discerned "the hand of Morley, who has never quite forgiven Rolly for having stated publicly that he was the author of the reforms." [55] And Sir J. R. Dunlop Smith, who had recently transferred his secretarial services but not his allegiance to Morley, alleged that "Montagu . . . had nothing to do with the speech except deliver it. The hands were those of Montagu, but the voice was the voice of Morley." [56]

Regardless of the authorship of Montagu's pregnant phrase, Morley's intercessions grew more obtrusive as his indignation mounted. It proved impossible to overcome the inherent conservatism of the Indian bureaucracy,[57] and Minto seemed to pride himself on his determination to withhold his assistance. Morley confessed to Sir George Clarke that he felt

> like a man in a nightmare, intent on striking out, but powerless to lift his arm. . . . The machine may be a stupid giant, but a giant it is, and who is to amend the creature Heaven only knows. No S. S. can do it by himself.[58]

Sir William Wedderburn noted Morley's fatigue during their half-hour interview on May 2, 1908, and he deduced that the Indian

sult the Government of India about the Romer Committee on finance; he labeled Indian officials "his agents 'as much as the messengers at the door.'" Ibid., March 20, 1908, *3*, 31.

54. Morley to Minto, October 5, 1910 [copy], Morley Papers.

55. Lady Minto's Indian Journals, August 9, 1910, *1910–ii*, 271-72.

56. Dunlop Smith to Lady Minto, August 23, 1910, Minto Papers; see also *Servant of India*, ed. Gilbert, pp. 244-46.

57. In June 1908, while he delivered an address at Oxford to members of the Indian Civil Service, Morley observed that "it was the youngest men who 'winced' most when he spoke of reforms, etc." F. A. Hirtzel's Diary, June 11, 1908, *3*, 55.

58. Morley to Clarke, June 18, 1909, Morley Papers.

secretary was finding "it difficult to bear up against the weight of this great bureaucracy which has had everything its own way for so long." [59]

At least, John Morley could console himself, he did as much as any Whitehall reformer could have done. His failure was inevitable, for his adversaries were too set in their ways, too jealous of their privileges, and too firmly entrenched in their positions. It would eventually take nothing less to dislodge them than the transfer of power to Indian hands.

59. Wedderburn to Gokhale, May 2, 1908, cited in Wolpert, *Tilak and Gokhale*, p. 203.

6 The War Against the Generals

His appointment to the Indian secretaryship accorded John Morley extensive powers over imperial military affairs which European rivalries and Indian circumstances jointly corroded. Nicholas Murray Butler immediately presumed

> that you are going to the particular post named because of the situation created by the rumpus of last summer between Curzon and Kitchener, and that the new Government will work for the supremacy of the civil over the military in the dependencies as well as at home.[1]

Precisely the same thought occurred to Andrew Carnegie, who reassured his friend: "India is the best of all for you—much the best. What a position: 'three hundred millions under King John.' Kitchener will be uneasy." [2] Yet time after time Morley's royal prerogatives proved largely illusory, and his victories on this strategic battlefield tended to be as hollow as his crown.

Though he remained an ardent exponent of retrenchment, Morley found it impossible to do much more than hold military outlays to their inflated 1905 proportions. "Whatever else the bombs may do," he complained to Sir George Clarke, "they have at any rate made a considerable hole in any policy of mine. I hoped for instance to get some military reductions." [3] On numerous occasions, Morley alluded wistfully to his distinguished political lineage:

> In matters of my own privy purse I am the least of a miser that ever was known, but as the guardian of public money, and particularly a public like India that cannot guard its own money, I learned from Mill, and still more in my years of

1. Butler to Morley, December 11, 1905 [copy], Butler Papers.
2. Carnegie to Morley, December 17, 1905 [copy], Morley Papers.
3. Morley to Clarke, June 12, 1908, Morley Papers.

friendship with Mr. Gladstone, to be a real dragon, with hor-
rible fangs and eyes of flame.[4]

But despite his determination, he was quickly tamed by the sheer
enormity of his problem, and the modest savings he managed to
effect were little consolation.[5]

Morley was somewhat more successful in his attempts to limit
the spiraling number of Indian troops. His motive was largely
financial, but his firsthand knowledge of western nationalisms
enabled him to perceive that any increase in the size or influence
of India's military establishment would exacerbate nationalist
feelings and thereby deprive any reform scheme of its therapeutic
powers. "Of course, I thoroughly understand you and sympathise
with you," he assured Minto, "when you say how 'strongly you
feel how dangerous any appearance of a reduction of our military
prestige in India would be.' But I hope this does not mean that
every request from the military people is to be held sacred and
inexorable."[6] He refused to countenance General Beauchamp
Duff's recommendation of an augmentation of forces to offset the
inherent dangers of any "extension of Native rights," and in-

4. "While I write this sentence," Morley continued,

> I have looked up a passage in my book on Mr. Gladstone, and as probably
> no copy of it exists at Quetta, Peshawar, Agra, New Chaman, Mile 300, or
> even in the highly enlightened regions of Simla, I take the liberty of begging
> you to accept a copy from me, and to read Vol. II, pp. 61-65, just in order that
> you may think leniently of my financial churlishness, in consideration of the
> frightful school in which I was brought up.

Morley to Minto, November 2, 1906, Minto Papers. Three years later, he chided
Minto for having averted discussions of pecuniary matters:

> I am rather horrified to think that after all this long time of correspondence
> between us, I do not recall that you have ever spoken to me about Indian
> finance. And this, too, after I actually was so incredibly generous to present
> you with my three huge volumes on Mr. Gladstone, by way of kindling the
> fires of economic zeal, or even fanaticism, in your official bosom.

Morley to Minto, September 22, 1909 [copy], Morley Papers; also Speech at
Arbroath, October 21, 1907, *The Times* (October 22, 1907) , p. 10.

5. Morley admitted the insignificance of his achievements in this important
sphere: "My passion for economising Indian revenues has taken a new form on a
most diminutive scale," he jested to Minto in a letter explaining that the British
Exchequer had agreed to defray the costs of the Nepalese premier's visit to India.
Morley to Minto, January 24, 1908 [copy], Morley Papers. Morley subsequently
reported his opposition, as a member of the Imperial Defense Committee, to
proposals to extract an Indian contribution to the defense of the Persian Gulf.
Morley to Minto, March 14, 1908 [copy], Morley Papers.

6. Morley to Minto, January 18, 1907, Minto Papers.

structed Minto: "If this idea should reach your ears, either from
K[itchener] or anybody else, I do hope you will promptly stamp
upon it." [7]

But the Governor-General proved a hesitant and often unreliable confederate in Morley's private war against rising military
expenditures and ambitions. In moments of acute distress, which
occurred with alarming frequency, Minto was highly susceptible
to those visions of an imminent Armageddon that had continually
haunted Indian bureaucrats for a half century. "It is more and
more evident every day," he reported in the spring of 1907, "that
the intention of the Extremist is to influence the Native Army by
means of the Press and the circulation of seditious pamphlets." [8] A
week later, he confirmed the identity of his source:

> Lord K[itchener] is very anxious about the Army. There is at
> present no means of controlling the circulation of seditious
> leaflets amongst the troops. . . . Unpalatable as a Press Act
> must be, the danger [of] . . . the possible corruption of the
> Army by printed matter is evident to everyone who knows
> what is going on here.[9]

Morley rightly doubted the justification for Minto's consternation,
and insisted that, in any event, press restrictions constituted neither a judicious nor an effective barrier against insurrection.[10]

Morley was equally determined to curtail the Government of
India's military authority beyond Indian frontiers. His arguments
recalled those Gladstone had employed during the 1870s. He decried Minto's pretenses to a seat at the international conference
table, especially in negotiations with Russia, which had long been
regarded at Simla as a potential threat to the Indian frontier. "I
am . . . a little frightened," he confessed to the Viceroy,

> when you say . . . that "the Government of India should be
> fully consulted before the agreement suggested is entered into
> with Russia". . . . The plain truth is . . . that this country
> cannot have two foreign policies. The Government of India
> in Curzon's day, and in days before Curzon, tried to have its

7. Morley to Minto, July 5, 1907, Minto Papers.
8. Minto to Morley, June 12, 1907, Morley Papers.
9. Minto to Morley, June 18, 1907, Morley Papers.
10. See Morley to Minto, July 8 and August 2, 1907, Minto Papers.

own foreign policy. My nervous mind sees the same spectre lurking behind the phrase about "full consultation." [11]

Morley adamantly refused to subordinate British diplomatic interests to either the anxieties or designs of Anglo-Indian strategists. "The Anglo-Russian Agreement needed much care and vigilance," he later told James Bryce. "The Government of India is always Jingo, and Grey's work, as he often over-generously says, would have been impossible if there had not happened to be over the G. of I. a Secretary of State to whom the Jingo is the devil incarnate." [12]

It was no less vital, Morley contended, to halt the territorial expansion of the British Raj. In one of his earliest letters to Minto, he enunciated his position in no uncertain terms:

> The new Parliament and the new Cabinet will be, in the highest degree, jealous both of anything that looks like expansion, extended protectorates, spheres of influence, and so forth; and of anything with the savour of militarism about it. I do not dream that the G. of I. in your hands will follow in the steps of your predecessors as to Thibet, Persia, the Amir [of Afghanistan]. But I note one or two expressions about the Persian loan . . . that seem to imply the propriety of using Indian funds for expansive designs on the frontier. Of policy of that sort I am invariably jealous, and the Cabinet will assuredly sympathise with my jealousy, and so will the House of Commons even more loudly, if the occasion arises.[13]

He subsequently berated Minto for expressing the traditional viceregal attitude toward Tibet: "When you speak of the loss of British influence in Thibet as being deplorable, you do not recognize—do you—that the present Government here, just like our predecessors, regard Curzon's Thibet policy as hugely mistaken." [14]

11. Morley to Minto, July 6, 1906, Minto Papers.

12. Morley to Bryce, January 6, 1908, Bryce Papers; in a letter to the Governor of Bombay, Morley deprecated the fact that "so many Anglo-Indians [are] unable to think of any other single thing beyond the check-mating of Russia. I am no Russian, heaven knows, but I won't put on great blinkers to prevent me from seeing anything else but Russian intrigue, mendacity, etc., etc., in the whole field of international policy." Morley to Lamington, April 12, 1906, Lamington Papers.

13. Morley to Minto, January 16, 1906, Minto Papers.

14. Morley to Minto, May 2, 1907, Minto Papers. Minto confided to his wife, who was visiting England at the time, "The news from Thibet is bad. We are

If he failed to dismantle the Empire of Swagger, Morley nonetheless managed to impede its forward march.

India's militarists and their political accomplices in England presented strenuous arguments on behalf of renewed border campaigns, which Morley, to the best of his ability, attempted to refute. Weeks after he assumed office, he admitted to Minto: "I am more and more struck with . . . the dangers to our peace of mind of that borderland of ruffians who need castigation from time to time, but whose castigation may easily drag us into positions where we do ourselves no good." [15] To a certain extent Morley falsely encouraged the militarists by lending an approbatory ear to complaints against the Zakka Khels, a belligerent tribe on India's northwestern frontier. Minto plied him with graphic accounts of tribal barbarities, interspersed with professions of unflagging devotion to peace: "I am no more eager than you to fight the Zakka Khels," he wrote on April 2, 1907, "and Lord K. has always been most opposed to it." [16] Meanwhile Minto boasted to Kitchener that he was gradually persuading Morley to endorse an attack on "Zakka Khel country, and staying there, *i.e.*, occupying such posts permanently as we thought necessary. He does not mention this particular case, but there are indications of a new view of frontier policy." [17]

Ultimately Morley sanctioned a punitive expedition against the Zakka Khels, but he affixed more strings to his acquiescence than his petitioners had anticipated. He decreed that the offensive, which finally got under way early in 1908, was to follow his specifications rather than the Commander-in-Chief's. "This is certainly not the Government," he reminded Minto, "to initiate in any shape or form, the policy of occupation or annexation advocated by Kitchener in his famous memorandum." [18] On the eve of his announcement of the venture to the Commons, Morley dined at Lord Rosebery's with the Prince of Wales. "H. R. H. said he supposed we should remain in Zakka Khel country for 2 or 3 har-

rapidly losing all the friendship and influence we had there simply because Morley has got an exaggerated idea of not allowing anyone to go there." Minto to Lady Minto, April 10, 1907, Minto Papers.

15. Morley to Minto, December 28, 1905 [copy], Morley Papers.
16. Minto to Morley, April 2, 1907, Morley Papers.
17. Minto to Kitchener, February 19, 1907 [copy], Minto Papers.
18. Morley to Minto, February 3, 1908 [telegram], Morley Papers.

vests," Sir Frederic Hirtzel recorded; Morley, less enthusiastic, replied: "Oh dear, no—a fortnight." [19]

Morley took pains to insure that Kitchener's march through Zakka Khel territory was briefer and more closely supervised than his more memorable march along the Upper Nile. "I have always fully appreciated your pacific policy," Morley assured Minto, "but when military operations once begin they tend to grow, and the zeal of military subordinates must not override policy." [20] A decade earlier, for the benefit of his sheltered constituents, Morley had outlined the five acts in Lord Curzon's comedy, "Forward Rake's Progress," which was currently being performed on Indian frontier stages to the acclaim of jingo audiences:

> First you push on into the territories where you have no business to be, and, in our case, where you promised you would not go; secondly your intrusion provokes resentment, and in these wild countries resentment means resistance; thirdly you instantly cry out that the people are rebellious and that their act is rebellion, this in spite of your own assurance that you have no intention of setting up a permanent sovereignty over them; fourthly you send a force to stamp out the rebellion; and fifthly, having spread bloodshed, confusion and anarchy, you declare, with hands uplifted to the heavens, that moral reasons force you to stay, for if you were to leave this territory would be left in a condition which no civilised power could contemplate with equanimity or with composure.[21]

In order to restrain the "Forward Rake" at the core of every Anglo-Indian official, Morley made a concentrated effort to keep the Zakka Khel enterprise within its predetermined Gladstonian bounds. Kitchener chafed at Morley's directives and at one telegram in particular "laying down that we shall not *annex* territory already ours and well within our frontiers. . . . He, of course, means that the present system of administration will not be altered after the expedition." [22] But so long as his instructions were respected, Morley did not mind the derision that they provoked. He derived ample compensation from the fact that the Zakka Khel

19. F. A. Hirtzel's Diary, February 10, 1908, 3, 20.
20. Morley to Minto, February 6, 1908 [telegram], Morley Papers.
21. Speech at Arbroath, September 28, 1897, *The Times* (September 29, 1897), p. 4.
22. Kitchener to Minto, February 3, 1908, Minto Papers.

affair was conducted exactly as he had prescribed. It had been, he soon boasted to Sir George Clarke,

> not only a piece of effective military work, but the triumph of sensible policy. As you may easily guess, there were certain high people in India who would fain have made the thing the first move in "rolling the tribes up to the Durand Line," etc., etc. I was resolute against going a single inch in that direction.[23]

Years later, Morley could look back and "exult that I never sat for an hour in a war cabinet, . . . [though] I was once responsible for a frontier war with a tribe of Indian wild-cats, but it only lasted a fortnight, and only cost £ 35,000." [24]

Lord Kitchener's imposing presence at the helm of the Indian military machine intensified Morley's reforming zeal. In 1899, Morley was among the most prominent of fifty-one M.P.s who opposed a grant to Kitchener in recognition of his valor in the Sudan.[25] The passing years had neither tempered Morley's wrath nor lessened its justification. When Kitchener failed to reply to a query in 1907, Morley concluded that "the Soudan *was* rather a bad school of manners, *e.g.,* the Mahdi's head." [26] To retaliate for the disquieting decades during which Kitchener and men of his breed had trampled upon alien soil and Gladstonian sensibilities, Morley kept a tight rein on military affairs. To be sure, he relished the opportunity as a "democrat to be put in charge of the great Military Bureaucracy of the world." [27]

But Kitchener frequently added fresh insults to past injuries. He impressed Morley as an opponent of reform, an advocate of stringent repression and, to make matters worse, a participant in political intrigues. Morley was furious when the Commander-in-Chief criticized the provisions of the Anglo-Russian Convention to "an important journalist here," exhorting him to publish these objections in the British press, and when he "complained to his journalistic friend that the Home Government had refused him a

23. Morley to Clarke, March 5, 1908, Morley Papers.
24. Morley to Carnegie, March 6, 1916, Morley-Carnegie Correspondence.
25. See *Parliamentary Debates,* 4th ser., *62,* cols. 337 ff. (June 5, 1899) . Kitchener, who heard Morley's attack from the Peers' Gallery, labeled it "ludicrous and puerile." Sir Philip Magnus, *Kitchener* (London, 1958) , p. 137.
26. Morley to Minto, May 31, 1907, Minto Papers.
27. Morley to Butler, January 29, 1906, Butler Papers.

prison law which he had told them he considered essential to the safety of the Army. I wish," Morley fulminated, "he would have the courage and straightforwardness to get somebody to raise this in the H. of C. I would give him a trouncing that would astonish him." [28] Morley did not, however, have to risk another encounter with pro-Kitchener forces on the floor of the House of Commons in order to strike back at his antagonist.

Morley's most valiant, and undoubtedly most significant assault against military influence was his successful effort to bar Kitchener's open path to the viceregal throne. The search for a successor to Lord Minto began in earnest during the spring of 1909, while nearly twenty months remained of the current Viceroy's five-year term. Kitchener at once appeared the foremost contender: his candidacy was enhanced by his outstanding record of imperial service, by his resourceful campaign for the coveted position, and by the King's personal endorsement. Much to Morley's dismay, the field seemed exceedingly narrow. Haldane and Lewis Harcourt were both sounded out, but neither responded with enthusiasm. Asquith, anxious to divest himself of the Home Secretary he had inherited, proposed Herbert Gladstone, but the mere thought of "the greatest failure of this Government" made Morley's "blood run cold," and he "begged Mr. A. not to think of it." [29]

Morley's preference rested with Sir Charles Hardinge, an accomplished diplomat, whom he fastened upon primarily because Hardinge seemed the single alternative to Kitchener who might enjoy royal favor. But in the summer of 1909, he learned that the King had pledged his support to Kitchener. "The last time I heard of H. M.'s views," he wrote to Minto on July 22, "they turned towards Charles Hardinge of the F. O. to be G. G. Yesterday, he thought that C. H. was cut out for the Paris Embassy." Morley remained confident that a suitable candidate would be chosen without his assistance: "I fondly hope," he advised Minto, "that this business will not need my attention, nor do I think it very likely." [30] To more intimate correspondents, he revealed doubts whether

28. Morley to Minto, October 3, 1907, Minto Papers.

29. F. A. Hirtzel's Diary, June 24, 1909, *4*, 51. Morley found cause to lament Gladstone's inefficiency when Sir William Curzon-Wyllie, his political aide-de-camp, was assassinated by an Indian student in London: "The Home Office," he told Minto, "which is by no means the most energetic department in its present hands, will have to bestir itself." Morley to Minto, July 8, 1909, Minto Papers.

30. Morley to Minto, July 22, 1909, Minto Papers.

he would remain at the India Office long enough to take a hand in the selection of Minto's successor.[31]

When the matter came to a head nearly a year later, Morley was still wielding his ministerial powers, and his opposition to Kitchener's appointment remained indomitable. To an extent, his prejudice against the Commander-in-Chief had been tempered by Lord Minto's frequent intercessions, which played a decisive role in the succession drama. The Viceroy solemnly assured the skeptical Secretary of State that Kitchener "is not at all the blood and thunder soldier the man in the street assumes him to be." [32] At times, Minto appears to have nearly succeeded in his attempts to convince Morley, who admitted early in 1907: "You are slowly winning me over to believe in [Kitchener] as a peculiarly moderating force among your civilian advisers." [33]

Though the eventual choice of Hardinge over Kitchener has often been ascribed to Morley's distrust of the military mind and to his malice toward the hero of Fashoda,[34] Lord Minto not only echoed, but nourished many of Morley's apprehensions. The commendations the Viceroy accorded the Commander-in-Chief were often unusually backhanded: "K[itchener], with whom constitutional reforms, Indian members and the like go somewhat against the grain, has been very loyal and helpful," he reported on March 11, 1909.[35] The passing months brought only dubious support from Minto for Kitchener's candidacy. His misgivings about his friend's qualifications were sincere and justifiable; he appraised Kitchener as "a big man in many ways," who would undoubtedly "give confidence in certain quarters—at home at least —but I hear Gokhale said the other day his appointment 'would look like punishing a naughty schoolboy.' " [36] Though he discounted fears of Kitchener's potential high-handedness, Minto shared Morley's view that the promotion of a military leader would create an unfortunate impression upon Indian opinion. "What you say about the possible appointment of K.," he wrote in early April 1910,

31. Morley to Haldane, July 22, 1909, Haldane Papers.
32. Minto to Morley, February 24, 1910 [copy], Minto Papers.
33. Morley to Minto, January 2, 1907, Minto Papers.
34. See Magnus, *Kitchener*, pp. 247 ff.
35. Minto to Morley, March 11, 1909, Minto Papers.
36. Minto to Dunlop Smith, March 24, 1910, Minto Papers.

viz., that it "would be to plant our Indian system on a military basis" is no doubt true as regards the view the Indian public would take of the appointment, and the English public, too; and one cannot disregard the immediate effects of such views.[37]

And a month later, he patiently counseled that

K. possesses great caution and administrative ability, but the reasons for his appointment would be understood in England and in India in one sense only, and its effects, though due to quite mistaken conclusions, cannot be disregarded.[38]

When news of Hardinge's selection reached Simla, Minto cabled his enthusiastic approval: "Great relief to hear of successor. Appointment seems to be excellent."[39]

On April 29, 1910, a week before his death, King Edward VII made a final attempt "to persuade Morley to send Kitchener to rule India with a strong hand."[40] Such appeals were doomed to fall upon deaf ears, as had previous royal remonstrances to defer or to dilute portions of the reform scheme. By this date, Morley had proclaimed that his retention of the India Office was contingent upon the rejection of Kitchener's bid. His determination had been reinforced by conversations with the aspirant, who had recently returned to England to wage a vigorous campaign for the viceroyalty. Morley was admittedly impressed by evidence of Kitchener's hitherto untapped liberality,[41] but his Gladstonian qualms ultimately prevailed. He confessed to Lord Minto that "an unkind suspicion crossed my mind" when Kitchener professed a surprising readiness to amend the partition of Bengal; this smacked too much

37. Minto to Morley, April 7, 1910 [copy], Minto Papers.

38. Minto to Morley, May 19, 1910 [copy], Minto Papers. Minto also cited certain personal deficiencies in his bachelor friend: "I have no particular individual in my eye at all," he insisted to Morley, adding that " 'Her Excellency' too will always have a big part to play and must be reckoned with." Minto to Morley, June 3, 1909, Minto Papers.

39. Minto to Morley, June 11, 1910 [telegram], Morley Papers.

40. Sir Philip Magnus, *King Edward the Seventh* (London, 1964), p. 455.

41. Morley notified the Viceroy that Kitchener had "talked about the Partition of Bengal in a way that rather made me open my eyes; for, although he hardly went so far as to favour reversal, he was persuaded that we must do something in bringing the people of the two severed portions into some species of unity." Morley to Minto, April 29, 1910, Minto Papers.

of a conscious maneuver to ingratiate himself with "the ingenuous person to whom he was talking and with whom very naturally he wished to stand well." [42]

His interview with the retired Commander-in-Chief, to whatever degree it lessened his personal enmity, left Morley firmly convinced that India could ill afford the implicit dangers of Kitchener's appointment. In a memorandum to Minto, he enumerated his considerations:

> To put our biggest soldier in the post of G. G. would be to set up the sword as the symbol of our rule over India, and the basis of it; it would be construed as a sign that our policy of the last four years was a failure, or that we at all events were afraid that it would turn out a failure; it would shake the confidence of the Moderate Indian politicians in the stability, consistency, and good faith of British statesmen; while shaking the Moderates, it would in the same proportion furnish new arguments to the enemy.[43]

In an account of the same conversation which he furnished to Haldane, Morley interjected a few less professional observations: "Last Monday I had 1½ hours with K.—my cards frankly on the table. I liked him very well, but he is not *clever*. I think rather clumsy." [44]

On May 25, Morley advised Minto of the virtual certainty "that *Hardinge* will be our man. He is in age, health, knowledge of great affairs, and other qualities, extremely fitted. I will say more about him when the deed is done." [45] It remained for him to procure the Prime Minister's assent and to submit his recommendation for the formality of royal approval. In mid-June, he broached the subject with Asquith, stressing that his "last word" and his explicit response to its possible rejection were equally unconditional: "If I am not fortunate enough to carry you with me," he stated, "you will of course decide the thing for yourself. If, on the other hand, you do not take this responsibility, you will then, I have no doubt, support my view with H. M." [46] The task of persuading the new

42. Morley to Minto, May 5, 1910 [copy], Morley Papers.
43. Memorandum by Lord Morley, May 6, 1910, Minto Papers.
44. Morley to Haldane, May 5, 1910, Haldane Papers.
45. Morley to Minto, May 25, 1910, Minto Papers.
46. Morley to Asquith, June 15, 1910, Asquith Papers.

monarch, which had threatened to be a difficult one, was lightened considerably by Lord Minto's active cooperation.

A postscript was added to this story at the outbreak of the First World War, when the two antagonists exchanged positions on the rotating wheel of political fortune. On the evening of July 29, 1914, Morley sponsored a dinner in Kitchener's honor at the United Services Club.[47] "Within ten days," he later recalled, "Kitchener was installed in my chair in the Cabinet!" [48] But Morley could console himself that four years before the violent jolt of August 2, he had checkmated Kitchener's steady advance. It is perhaps for this accomplishment, more than any other, that he deserves India's gratitude.

47. Morley himself marveled at the strange bedfellows that political life brought together: "Milner joined me in presenting Lord K[itchener] to the H. of L. on Wednesday," he reported to Lord Hardinge. "Considering the strong language that he uses about K., I was surprised; but then I too have used strong language about *both* K. and M." Morley to Hardinge, April 28, 1911, Morley Papers.

48. Morley, *Memorandum on Resignation*, (London, 1928) , pp. 8–9.

7 Race, History, and Empire

There was substantially less ideological difference between John Morley and India's moderate politicians than the former cared to admit or the latter would permit him to forget. Both had been nourished by the ideas of nineteenth-century liberalism, and both had been deceived by its implicit promises. At the close of 1905, Congress leaders welcomed to the India Office a brother under the skin; but to the new Secretary of State, the color of that skin mattered considerably more than the common heritage it sheathed. In this respect, he shared the fundamental preconceptions of most late-Victorian intellectuals, and his policies were consequently bound by those limitations.

Morley's attitude was grounded upon historical precedent rather than anthropological theory. Since the Treaty of Paris in 1763, when colonial territories inhabited by alien populations were first acquired by the British Crown, it had been assumed that non-British peoples within the Empire deserved institutions suited to their traditions and temperaments. The Quebec Act of 1774 and the concession of a biracial legislative assembly to the conquered colony of Grenada had each been attempts to implement this policy. In the century that followed, social and political philosophy supported this principle with complex intellectual arguments, and by the time Morley arrived at the India Office, British respect for the distinctions of her subject peoples was no longer an expedient but a dogma.

Two of the philosophers most responsible for this transformation were Auguste Comte and Herbert Spencer who, despite fundamental disagreements, shared what Richard Hofstadter has described as "the monistic assumption that the laws of the universe at large are also applicable to human societies"; [1] this, in essence,

1. Richard Hofstadter, *Social Darwinism in American Thought* (Boston, 1965), p. 67; Gertrude Himmelfarb provides an illuminating commentary upon the "Varieties of Social Darwinism" in *Victorian Minds* (New York, 1968), pp. 314-32.

was the premise of social Darwinism. Both Comte and Spencer exerted a direct influence upon Morley's thought: the former through his writings and his Positivist disciples, the latter during frequent conversations at his home at St. John's Wood. Yet it would be an oversimplification to ascribe Morley's faith in the inevitability of progress to either influence or both. This was a popular faith among nineteenth-century intellectuals, particularly historians, who tended to equate history with the evolutionary process and evolution with progress, which Morley reflected had in his lifetime "become the basis of social thought, and [had] even taken the place of a religion as the inspiring, guiding and testing power over social action." [2] Unlike Sir Henry Maine, who employed theories of evolution in his attempt to explain history, Morley employed historical arguments to explain his theories of evolution.

However much Morley might disdain the Whig view of politics, with its emphasis upon class, he—like most historians of his age—subscribed to the basic tenets of the Whig view of history, with its confident belief in the moral progress of mankind in general and Englishmen in particular. Though he denied that his country's imperial mission "springs . . . from the pride of a dominating race," he did not dispute the fact that "race counts." [3] By virtue of their institutions and environment, the English people seemed to him capable of proceeding a good deal faster than other peoples along the path to ultimate perfection. He rebuked the high priest of Whig history, Thomas Babington Macaulay, for neglecting to take cultural disparities into account in his prediction that Ireland would respond as Scotland had done to English "justice and wisdom," and that thirty-five years of English education would rid India of idolaters.[4] Yet he shared Macaulay's optimism, expressed in the latter's 1835 Minute on Education, that the peoples of India might eventually become "English in taste, in opinions, in morals, and in intellect." Certainly Macaulay had underestimated the time it would take to effect this transformation, and the mutiny had since proved the dangers of rushing things along; but Morley saw no generic reason why it could not be done.

2. *Recollections, 1,* 27.

3. Speech at Forfar, November 4, 1901, *Two Years of War—and After* (London, 1901) , p. 16.

4. Ibid., p. 181; see Morley's essay on Macaulay in *Critical Miscellanies, 1* (London, 1904) .

Though Morley's views on cultural evolution might amuse or even affront liberals of subsequent generations, they made political sense in the context of early twentieth-century India. In no way did he attempt to justify either the abuse or exploitation of colonial populations. Though he confessed a reluctance on esthetic grounds to "submit to be governed by a man of colour," [5] he championed the right of qualified Indians to take a greater hand in imperial affairs. In 1888, when Dadabhai Naoroji had contested a seat at Central Finsbury and was labeled "a black man" by Lord Salisbury, it was Morley who first deplored the epithet and welcomed Naoroji to the Liberal ranks.[6] Almost two decades later, he joined with Naoroji [7] in deprecating Lord Curzon's tactless remark "that the highest ideal of truth is to a large extent a western conception." [8] He considered it doubtful whether "veracity, in its deeper sense, is universal among us Occidentals any more than among Orientals," [9] and he condemned as a "fundamental error" his countrymen's "over-weening pretension as to the superiority at every point and in all their aspects, of any Western Civilisation over every Eastern." [10]

Yet Morley suffered spasmodic seizures of that arrogant intolerance he deplored in Curzon. His review of M. E. Grant Duff's *Notes of an Indian Journey*, contributed to an early number of the *Fortnightly Review*, is Curzonian in logic if not in spirit.[11] A few years later, he made it clear to T. H. Huxley that he opposed African ventures "as business, as common sense," and without any "particular love for black skins." [12] During the course of his Indian secretaryship, he revealed scarcely more affection for the yellow race, to which, for the sake of convenience, he consigned the population of India. He inveighed against Lord Lansdowne's 1902

5. Conversation of March 15, 1907, cited in Chamberlain, *Politics from Inside* (London, 1936) , pp. 59-60.

6. See R. P. Masani, *Dadabhai Naoroji: the Grand Old Man of India* (London, 1939) , p. 265.

7. Presidential address, Twenty-second Indian National Congress, Calcutta, 1906, Naoroji, *Speeches and Writings* (Madras, 1915?) , pp. 68 ff.

8. Convocation address, Calcutta University, February 11, 1905, *Lord Curzon in India*, ed. Sir Thomas Raleigh (London, 1906) , p. 491.

9. Morley to Godley, December 6, 1907, Kilbracken Papers, Add. MSS. 44,902, fol. 125.

10. Morley, "British Democracy and Indian Government," *Nineteenth Century and After, 69* (1911) , 207.

11. "Some Recent Travels," *Fortnightly Review*, n.s., *19* (1876) , 754.

12. Morley to Huxley, March 16, 1879, Huxley Papers.

treaty with "the Jap," whom he described as "the enemy—unscrupulous, perfidious and violent," and privately sympathized with Sir Wilfrid Laurier's attempt to discourage Oriental immigration to Canada, confiding to Minto his suspicions "that if you and I were not Indians for the moment, we should be exclusionists." [13]

Until World War I cast the slogans of nineteenth-century empire into disrepute, theories of social and biological evolution were as much food for thought as the basic staple of the imperial diet. Morley was neither oblivious nor immune to the preoccupation of his times. "Who can measure the influence on our contemporary policies of Darwin and the other literature of Survival of the Fittest?" he asked an audience at Victoria University, Manchester, in the summer of 1912.[14] Darwinian arguments were particularly fashionable among those who, regardless of their political proclivities, took an interest in Indian affairs; in fact, their dependence upon a common rhetoric marked, in most cases, the single affinity between the British allies of Indian nationalism and the officials who thwarted their efforts. Keir Hardie and Annie Besant embraced their Indian brethren as fruit of the common Aryan family tree.[15] Sir Henry Cotton, another self-commissioned lieutenant in the crusade for Indian constitutional reform, justified his efforts with an intricate timetable for political evolution.[16] Members of the Anglo-Indian bureaucracy—from the Viceroy downward—were no less proficient in pseudo-Darwinian theory.[17]

13. Morley to Minto, March 26, 1908, Minto Papers.

14. Morley, *Notes on Politics and History* (London, 1913), p. 36. On the same occasion, he commended Charles H. Pearson's neglected study, *National Life and Character* (London, 1893), as a work which "opens, collects, expounds, and illustrates, vast issues in the evolution of States and races." Ibid., p. 84.

15. Besant, *Speeches and Writings* (Madras, 1921), pp. 267-68; Hardie told Englishmen "that the Indian people are of the same Aryan stock as ourselves. Take a gathering of Indians. Remove their graceful, picturesque costumes and clothe them in coat and trousers, wash the sun out of their skins, and then a stranger suddenly let down into the midst of them would have a difficulty saying whether he was in Manchester or Madras." Hardie, *India, Impressions and Suggestions* (London, 1909), p. 102.

16. H. J. S. Cotton, *England and India* (London, 1883), p. 4.

17. Anglo-Indians were obsessed with the desire to demonstrate the survival of the fittest; the Governor of Madras urged Minto to prohibit interracial showings of the "cinematographs" of a prize fight in which a Negro contender defeated his white opponent (Lawley to Minto, July 13, 1910, Minto Papers), and Lady Minto noted widespread resentment in the white community when an Indian team won the Beresford polo tournament. (Lady Minto's Indian Journals, June 16, 1907, *1907-i*, 171).

Ideologically as well as politically, Morley occupied the middle ground between these two camps.

An apostle of John Stuart Mill, an ally of the Positivists, the biographer of Burke and a number of the principal philosophes, Morley was the repository of many of the theories of evolution that infused nineteenth-century thought. Proud of his intellectual lineage, he was quick to take offense when Indians cited the writings of "Mill or Burke, or Macaulay, or that splendid man Bright" to substantiate their claim to democratic institutions.[18] There are, he realized, more than one set of conclusions to be inferred from the writings of any individual,[19] and the particular inferences that he drew from the lives he probed reveal a good deal about his personality and concerns. His portrait of Oliver Cromwell was a celebration of the House of Commons and a subtle tract on the Irish problem; his forays into the Enlightenment were—no less than his biographies of Cobden and Gladstone—deliberate attempts to propagate specific Liberal doctrines. It is therefore significant that among the diverse biographical studies Morley wrote, questions of social evolution figure so prominently.

Morley's comparatively sympathetic evaluation of Jean-Jacques Rousseau, published in 1873, provides a case in point. Although Philip Mason, in his valuable *Essay on Racial Tension*,[20] traces the arguments of nineteenth-century racists to Rousseau's concept of the noble savage, Morley dismissed Rousseau as a hopeless romantic on the subject. He found particular fault with Rousseau's *Discours sur l'inégalité*, which posits that "the mode of advance into a social state has always been one and the same, a single and uniform process, marked by precisely the same set of several stages, following one another in precisely the same order." To the contrary, Morley protested,

> evidence goes to show that civilisation varies in origin and process with race and other things. . . . There is no sign that Rousseau . . . ever reflected whether the capacity for advance into the state of civil society in any highly developed form is universal throughout the species, or whether there are

18. Speech at Arbroath, October 21, 1907, *The Times* (October 22, 1907), p. 10.
19. "Talk of History as being a science as loudly as ever we like," Morley contended, "the writer of it will continue to approach his chest of archives with the bunch of keys in his hand." Cited in Algernon Cecil, "Mr. Morley," *Monthly Review*, 23 (1906), 14.
20. London, 1954, p. 50.

not races eternally incapable of advance beyond the savage
state, just as there are many individuals constitutionally incapable of being fitted for the performance of any but the
lowest functions in the social state.[21]

There is much of Morley's India Office attitude foreshadowed in
his early pronouncement that "such pretension as that every man
could be made equally fit for every function . . . —this is most
illusory and most disastrous." [22]

His opinions on the relativity of political and social systems are
no less explicit in his biography of Edmund Burke, written a half
dozen years earlier. It is here, in his first full-scale work, that he
first expressed grave doubts whether British rule in India could
possibly succeed; [23] yet, like Burke, he paused in his tirade against
imperial excesses to recognize the British Raj as a fait accompli
which conferred heavy moral responsibilities as well as an opportunity for capital gain. Aware that his subject's motives in the
Warren Hastings affair were not entirely creditable, Morley nonetheless praised Burke for acting "upon the pardonable hypothesis
that Europeans ought not only to have been less tyrannical,
perfidious, and destructive than barbarous rajahs, but not to have
been tyrannical and perfidious at all." [24] Like Burke, who had
articulated the theory of imperial trusteeship, Morley believed
that the British had intervened in India "to implant—slowly,
prudently, judiciously—those ideas of justice, law, humanity,
which are the foundation of our own civilisation." [25]

Neither his reverence for Burke nor his comparative inexperience had prevented Morley from detecting flaws in Burke's arguments; these too were self-revealing. The eighteenth-century statesman, a Dubliner by birth, was taken to task for having failed to
perceive "that Irish evolution had moved in an independent
course. To assume its identity with general Western development
is as extravagant as such an assumption would be in the case of
Jamaica or the Cape of Good Hope." [26] And, Morley pointed out,

21. Morley, *Rousseau* (2 vols. London, 1873) , *1*, 182-83.
22. Ibid., p. 187.
23. Morley, *Edmund Burke: A Historical Study* (London, 1867) , pp. 196-97.
24. Ibid., pp. 214, 216; also see Morley's conversation with Gladstone on Burke,
cited in Morley, *Life of Gladstone, 3*, 469.
25. Morley to Minto, October 7, 1908, Minto Papers.
26. Morley, *Edmund Burke*, p. 128.

"Burke forgot his own favourite doctrine of the relativity of all political systems, quite as fully as his adversaries did," by proposing, during a fit of eloquent passion, "the English scheme of government . . . as a remedy for the disorders and misfortunes of France." [27] But Morley, not without considerable justification, preferred to regard as characteristic of Burke his prolonged attack upon Hastings' venality rather than his distraught polemic against the French regicides; in the former, Burke maintained a cultural empathy which Morley found wanting in both eighteenth-century philosophy and nineteenth-century politics, and which he attempted to emulate during his later career.

It is imperative to remember, as his latter-day critics did not, that Morley was extremely selective in the ideas he culled from each of the great minds he probed. He applauded Rousseau's exaltation of the human conscience, but scorned his romantic depiction of primitive societies; in equal measure, he praised Burke for recognizing the social responsibilities of government, but deprecated his political opportunism. And nowhere is Morley's subjectivity more apparent than in his celebrated relationship with John Stuart Mill.[28]

As decades passed, Morley was joined in his adulation of Mill by the graduates of Indian universities. Yet it is obvious that Mill's Eastern disciples and their Secretary of State imbibed antithetical lessons from their common master. Despite allegations that he had "shelved . . . the principles of a lifetime," [29] it is obvious that Morley remained faithful to what he considered the cardinal tenets of Millite philosophy.

Morley could well have issued his self-defense in Mill's own words, penned in 1859:

> To suppose that the same international customs and the same rules of international morality can obtain between one civilised nation and another, and between civilised nations and barbarians, is a grave error, and one which no statesman can

27. Ibid., p. 276.

28. "A young disciple's reverence, gratitude, and admiration," Morley observed, "was pretty sure to grow stronger as the days went by, though even young disciples do not always lose the rudiments of a mind of their own, and nobody would have been more displeased than Mill himself had it been otherwise." *Recollections, 1,* 52-53.

29. Morley replied to these taunts in his address at Arbroath, October 21, 1907, *The Times* (October 22, 1907) , p. 10.

fall into, however it may be with those who, from a safe and unresponsible position, criticise statesmen.[30]

For Mill, like his protégé a half century later, distinguished between those nations "capable of, and ripe for representative government," and "others, like India, . . . still a great distance from that state"; [31] and he, too, considered the latter the product of social and environmental conditions.[32] Though Mill cited "independence and nationality" as the twin factors in "the due growth and development of a people further advanced in improvement," he cautioned that these could easily prove "impediments" to less sophisticated races.[33] Confident that the "ideally best form of government will be found in some one or other variety of the Representative System," Mill was no more prepared than Morley to stipulate

> a theorem of the circumstances in which that form of government may be wisely introduced; and also to judge . . . what inferior forms of polity will best carry . . . [immature] communities through the intermediate stages which they must traverse before they can become fit for the best form of government.[34]

Morley never forgot what many of his Indian critics found inconvenient to recall, that nineteenth-century liberalism contained no provisions for its export beyond the confines of western society. "One thing is certain," he assured Goldwin Smith, "that I should be guilty of criminal folly if I were to feel bound to apply the catch-words of our European liberalism as principles fit for an Asiatic congeries like India." [35]

Morley's assailants also failed to realize that his problem was not a deviation from past principles, but in fact a rigid adherence to them. While Sir Charles Dilke presided at London meetings of the

30. John Stuart Mill, "A Few Words on Non-Intervention," *Dissertations and Discussions, 3,* (London, 1867) , 167.

31. Mill, *Considerations on Representative Government* (London, 1861) , pp. 313-14.

32. See Mill's discussion on Indian attitudes to criminal justice, *Memorandum on the Improvements in the Administration of India* (London, 1858) , p. 40.

33. Mill, "A Few Words on Non-Intervention," *Dissertations, 3,* 167.

34. Mill, *Considerations on Representative Government,* pp. 43-44.

35. Morley to Smith, January 2, 1907, Smith Papers (Cornell University Library, Ithaca) .

Indian League, and Frederic Harrison criticized the inadequacy of the Morley-Minto proposals,[36] Morley continued to uphold precisely those mid-Victorian doctrines which his two longtime friends had formulated and since discarded.

In 1868, after a world tour, Dilke submitted his blueprint for a *Greater Britain* which "combined a fervent English nationalism with radical sentiments and incorporated Gobineau's idea of racial inequality along with Darwin's biological principle of natural selection." [37] His arguments profoundly influenced Morley, whom he later helped to enter Parliament, no less than his other Radical colleague, Joseph Chamberlain. It is evident that Dilke found India difficult to fit into the context of his imperial scheme: "For a score of centuries," he explained, "the Hindoos have bribed and taken bribes, and corruption has eaten into the national character so deeply, that those who are the best of judges declare that it can never be washed out." [38] Dilke recognized the fact that India was little more than a geographical convenience, an immense area inhabited by heterogeneous races among whom the British alone maintained order.[39] He conceded that if, at some remote date, "India has passed through the present transition stage from a country of many peoples to a country of only one," it would be folly for Britain to "continue to rule . . . [without] the consent of the majority of [India's] inhabitants." [40] Morley, for one, concurred wholeheartedly with this policy, but whereas Dilke argued that Indian development had reached this stage by the early twentieth century, Morley maintained that it was still a long way off.

The influence exerted by Positivist thinkers upon Morley's Indian policies is more difficult to gauge, though no less apparent. Despite his repeated denials of any affiliation with the Positivist sect, Morley was a close friend of many self-proclaimed members, and he featured their contributions in the *Fortnightly Review*. Ironically, he proved in the long run a more orthodox exponent of the Comtist doctrines of social Darwinism than such full-fledged believers as Frederic Harrison and E. S. Beesly. It was Positivist influence, Warren Staebler has explained, which led Morley to "a

36. *Indian Review, 10* (1909), 3.
37. Richard Koebner and H. D. Schmidt, *Imperialism* (Cambridge, 1964), p. 87.
38. Sir Charles W. Dilke, *Greater Britain*, (2 vols. London, 1868), 2, 381.
39. Ibid., pp. 366-67.
40. Ibid., pp. 257-58.

definition of 'the historic conception' as 'a reference of every state of society to a particular stage in the evolution of its general conditions.' " [41] Though most Positivists regretted Britain's presence as a territorial power in India, few had advocated an unconditional withdrawal.[42] The Sepoy Mutiny had confirmed in their minds both the immediate obligations and the ultimate futility of the British Raj, and it cast a long shadow across the pages of *International Policy,* a provocative compendium of Positivist arguments which appeared in 1866. Frederic Harrison took pains to explain that he was "not foolishly dressing up this Bengal rebellion into a war of nationalities," and that he knew "well that there is no Indian nation, and that their savage instincts are no result of patriotism." [43] The atrocities of 1857 prompted leading Positivists to exhort their countrymen to exercise in India "the full meaning of our pre-eminence" as a European civilization; [44] though they continued to deny the "alleged incapacity for progress" among nonwestern peoples,[45] they were forced to acknowledge the "disturbing and irritating fact" that only "from the activity of the West" could there come "some modifications in the general management of human affairs as are to be wished or expected." [46]

Although the Morley-Minto reform scheme incorporated several Positivist recommendations—most notably E. H. Pember's demand for Indian representation on the Viceroy's Executive Council [47]—it elicited indignant denuciations from Harrison and Beesly. Political responsibilities had accelerated Morley's drift from his Comtist associates, but the gulf between them remained essentially philosophical. In 1909, Morley told Frederic Harrison's son, Austin, that he considered it "useless to attempt 'sudden reformation' " as Comte had prescribed; the latter, he explained, "had sought to impose a system of culture without taking sufficient account of human nature." [48] No one during the first decade of the

41. Warren Staebler, *The Liberal Mind of John Morley* (Princeton, 1943), p. 40.

42. See E. H. Pember, "England in India," *International Policy* (London, 1866), p. 315; the notable exception was Richard Congreve, whose *India* (London, 1857) antedated the mutiny.

43. Frederic Harrison, *Autobiographic Memoirs* (2 vols. London, 1911), *1*, 173.

44. Pember, "England and India," *International Policy,* p. 225.

45. H. D. Hutton, "England and the Uncivilised Communities," ibid., p. 564.

46. R. Congreve, "The West," ibid., p. 12.

47. Pember, "England and India," ibid., p. 296. By 1909, these ideas were common property and could by no means be classified positivist arguments.

48. Austin Harrison, *Frederic Harrison: Thoughts and Memories* (London, 1926),

twentieth century could have seriously charged Morley with the same offense.

In addition to the writings of eighteenth-century philosophers and statesmen, Mill, the Radicals, and the Positivists, there was another important pre-Gladstonian influence upon Morley's theories of cultural relativism. A handful of Anglo-Indian officials—among them Sir Alfred Lyall, Sir Henry Maine, M. E. Grant Duff, and Sir William Hunter—had contributed their talents to the *Fortnightly Review* and the benefits of their experience to its editor. By far the most prominent member of this group was Lyall, who later served as a backstairs adviser during Morley's tenure at the India Office. Morley accorded him his highest tribute, the title "friend of a lifetime," and designated him "the one man to whom I must look for counsel in decisions of real moment." [49] Yet Lyall's contribution to the 1909 reforms should not be exaggerated: Morley made it clear that his old friend "is hardly my idea of a born reformer." [50] Lyall exerted his most profound influence upon Morley during the 1870s and '80s, and he did so by underscoring the philosophic lessons that Morley learned elsewhere.

Lyall illustrated his theories with copious references to his years of experience as an Indian administrator. "Empire," he wrote, "is a necessity . . . at certain stages of civilisation and the world's progress . . . and an empire well administered is the best available instrument for promoting civilisation and good order among backward races." [51] Here was a definition which would satisfy even an inveterate Little Englander. Lyall cautioned his countrymen that "the germs of representative institutions" would take a long time to do their work "among a people that has for centuries been governed by irresponsible officials, and in a country where

---

p. 177. Morley's polemics against Comte's philosophy are legion; see particularly "The Life of James Mill," *Fortnightly Review*, n.s., *31* (1882), 503-04; *Recollections*, 1, 69; Morley to T. H. Huxley, January 13, 1869, Huxley Papers.

49. Morley to Minto, January 21, 1909, Minto Papers. Morley publicly expressed indebtedness to Lyall, "whose own insight, imagination and genius have made him the most instructive and luminous of the writers that Indian experience has produced." "British Democracy and Indian Government," *Nineteenth Century and After, 69* (1911), 190.

50. Morley to Godley, March 27, 1907, Kilbracken Papers (I.O.L.). Morley's disappointment with Lyall's conservatism is also reflected in F. A. Hirtzel's Diary, December 6, 1906, *1*, 103.

51. Lyall, "Race and Religion," *Fortnightly Review*, n.s., 72 (1902), 941-42.

local liberties and habits of self-government have long been oblit-
erated or have never existed." [52] It was dangerous, he warned, to
apply western concepts to India,

> an empire of the antique pattern, quite different from the
> western nationalities, a country where complexities of race
> and creed meet us at every turn in the course of our adminis-
> tration. . . . In India these distinctions are far deeper than
> they were under the Roman Empire, and so far as one can
> judge, they are ineffaceable.[53]

The theories which Lyall and men of his stamp propounded were
neither eloquent nor profound; but coming from men of known
integrity and proved administrative ability, they lent weight to the
teachings of more abstract thinkers.

The final contributor to Morley's racial views was undoubtedly
the most important. Left to his own devices, Morley would presumably have modified his judgments, as many other members of
his generation had done. But his long affiliation with Gladstone
ossified his views, and taught him how to mold a collection of
vague sentiments into a coherent imperial policy.

Accumulated at various stages in his long public career, those
theories of evolution which exerted an influence upon John Morley's Indian policies were essentially those which Gladstone had either instilled or reinforced. Like Gladstone, who denied to primitive Natal the political concessions he willingly bestowed upon
Cape Colony or French-speaking Canada,[54] Morley devised an intricate system of cultural weights and measures. He deprecated the
"very dangerous and gross fallacy" that all mankind—because of
natural law or any other abstract proposition [55]—was fitted for
identical institutions; this was as absurd, he told his Scottish con-

52. [Lyall], "Government of the Indian Empire," *Edinburgh Review, 159* (1884),
15.

53. Lyall, "Race and Religion," *Fortnightly Review*, n.s., 72 (1902), 939.

54. Paul Knaplund, *Gladstone and Britain's Imperial Policy* (New York, 1927),
p. 102.

55. "No right is worth straw apart from the good that it brings," Morley insisted to Chamberlain in 1885; "and all claims to rights must depend—not upon
nature—but upon the good that the said rights are calculated to bring to the
greatest number. General ability, public expediency, the greatest happiness of the
greatest number—these are the tests and standards of a right; not the dictate of
nature." Morley to Chamberlain, January 6, 1885, Chamberlain Papers.

stituents, as the argument that "because a fur coat in Canada at certain times of the year is a most comfortable garment, therefore a fur coat in the Deccan of India is a sort of handy garment which you might be very happy to wear." [56] The prudence of Morléy's analogy may be seriously questioned, but it is more difficult to question its validity.

For purely intellectual reasons, Morley fastened upon Christianity, which was Gladstone's standard, as his own cultural yardstick. Gladstone, in his sixteenth address to the electors of Midlothian, had condemned "the exercise of despotism over [the] Christian and civilised people" of Cyprus, at the same time that he had sanctioned virtually the same policy for the people of Singapore.[57] Though Morley was not religious, he was nonetheless intensely theological, and this quality had endeared him to his mentor. "Whatever faith we may profess," he wrote to Lord Lamington, "or if we profess neither Crescent nor Cross, how much the most interesting thing in the world Religion is, to say nothing of aspects of it beyond mere interest." [58] Convinced that the masses of any society could ill afford to dispense—as he could—with religious restraints, he concluded that Christian ethics were, on the whole, least incompatible with democratic processes. His criteria were sufficiently flexible to accommodate the Irish Catholics, the Boers,[59] and, most surprisingly, the Egyptians. "Egypt was," he reasoned, "to all intents and purposes, not in India or Asia, but in Europe; it had an important European population; it had active European interests with strong governments at their back." [60]

But however generous Morley's standards, Hindus and Muslims

56. Speech at Arbroath, October 21, 1907, *The Times* (October 22, 1907), p. 10; a number of Indian politicians were disappointed, he knew. "Why? Because I have not been able to give them the moon. I have got no moon, and if I had I would not give them the moon. I will give the moon when I know who lives there, and what kind of conditions prevail there."

57. Speech at Penicuik, March 25, 1880, Gladstone, *Political Speeches in Scotland, 2,* 287-89.

58. Morley to Lamington, December 31, 1906, Lamington Papers.

59. Morley's attitude toward the Boers was constant: "The Transvaal Government," he wrote in 1879, "was a government of Europeans, and not a kingdom of barbarians." Morley, "The Plain Story of the Zulu War," *Fortnightly Review,* n.s., 25 (1879), 330. More than two decades later, he told his Scottish constituents that British pretensions to racial superiority over the Boers were as "intolerable" as English disdain for the Scots. Speech at Forfar, November 4, 1901, *Two Years of War,* p. 23.

60. *Parliamentary Debates,* 3d ser., 274, col. 1033 (February 15, 1884).

of any national variety were categorically excluded from the ranks of the politically sophisticated. He took it for granted that the Young Turk movement would "come to grief," [61] and, as late as 1912, he saw no evidence "on any marked scale" that Islam had the "capability to adapt itself to all the modern requirements of a civilised state"; [62] he debated this point at length with Lord Cromer, who agreed that there was little hope of reforming Muslim society "on a Koranic basis." [63] Like Gladstone, in his eloquent denunciation of the 1876 Bulgarian Horrors, he considered the religion of the Unspeakable Turk inimical to "Christian liberty and reconstruction." [64]

Gladstone, Morley recalled, had attributed the 1857 Mutiny to the East India Company's "lack of effort to convert India to Christianity." [65] Morley was convinced that without such a conversion neither British rule nor British institutions could survive in India, and that progress—which was by no means "a universal law, for all times, all states, all societies" [66]—would continue to elude the grasp of Indians. In his mind, two facts were unqualified and interdependent: that "there was no progress in the East and that progress was bound up with Christianity." [67]

Though he conceded every Christian's right to responsible government, Morley believed that this delicate plant, perfected in English hothouses, thrived best in Anglo-Saxon soil. He attributed the remarkable success of American democracy to the fact that "four-fifths of the white people" in the United States could "trace their pedigree to English forefathers." The Latin American republics, he pointed out, were blessed with fertile land, mineral wealth, and political sovereignty, but had belied the "dream that to endow a community with freedom is of itself enough to make sure either of progress or order." Borrowing an argument from Darwin, he assured an audience at the Carnegie Institute in Pitts-

61. F. A. Hirtzel's Diary, April 14, 1909, *4*, 30; also Morley to Harrison, August 7, 1909, Harrison Papers.

62. Morley, *Notes on Politics and History*, (London, 1913), p. 91.

63. Cromer to Morley, March 8, 1913, also Morley to Cromer, March 7 and 9, 1913, Cromer Papers, PRO/FO 633/23.

64. Gladstone thought the same of Disraeli's religious heritage; see Gladstone to the Duke of Argyll, August [?], 1876, cited in Morley, *Life of Gladstone*, 2, 551-52.

65. F. A. Hirtzel's Diary, November 13, 1906, *1*, 96.

66. Morley, *Notes on Politics and History*, p. 83.

67. F. A. Hirtzel's Diary, May 26, 1907, 2, 30.

burgh that South American history would be appreciably different, "if the region of the Plata had become British and a large
British immigration had followed." [68]

Morley's affection for the peoples of Britain's white dominions
and for the American nation which in 1776 had converted English
"thought into actual polity" [69] was abundantly evident. These
communities, he insisted, were bound more closely to Great Britain by an inherent devotion to individual liberties than they could
be by any artificial scheme for Imperial Preference. Yet he grew
increasingly afraid that the two leading Anglo-Saxon states, the
United States and Great Britain, were imperiling their respective
constitutional achievements by engaging in reckless imperial campaigns. The Boer War left Britain a legacy of social disorder and
political fragmentation. James Bryce reported from the British
Embassy in Washington that his American hosts, who had recently
wielded their proverbial "big stick" against Spaniards, Orientals,
and Latin Americans, were beset with "corruption, legislative
and other." [70] And French democracy was in notoriously difficult
straits at this time.

The prospects of American democracy in particular, and of
democratic societies in general, were also dimmed, Morley believed, by the rapid proliferation of colored peoples in their ranks.
During the 1890s, he had opposed annexation of African territory
which threatened to upset the racial balance of the British Empire, for this would implicitly upset the constitutional balance as
well. Long before it became fashionable, he perceived the racial
problem in its international context, and he was especially concerned with the "serious, suggestive, and apparently insoluble
problem" of the American Negro [71] which he expected to exert
an unhealthy influence upon the subjugated peoples of Africa and
the East. On a visit in 1910 to Skibo, Andrew Carnegie's Scottish
retreat, he discussed this problem with Booker T. Washington, to
whom he was first introduced six years earlier. "The future of the
Negro in the United States of America has always interested me, as
well it might," he wrote to Lord Minto.

68. Speech at Carnegie Institute, Pittsburgh, November 3, 1904, *The New York
Times* (November 27, 1904), p. 8.
69. Ibid.
70. F. A. Hirtzel's Diary, January 22, 1908, 3, 14.
71. Speech at Brechin, January 18, 1905, *The Times* (January 19, 1905), p. 6.

What will the numbers amount to, twenty or fifty years hence? Terrible to think of! ! Talk of India and other "insoluble problems" of great States. I declare the American Negro often strikes me as the hardest of them all.[72]

Pessimistic whether even the strongest democratic fibers could withstand twentieth-century stresses and strains—social, communal, and economic—Morley had little faith that Asian apprentices, to whom such institutions were alien by nature, could survive the impending onslaught. He told his private secretary that he "was not in favour of setting up parliamentary governments everywhere, and did not regard parliamentary government as the highest ideal" in every situation.[73] He agreed with L. T. Hobhouse that in a variety of circumstances, responsible government could prove more a curse than a blessing: "It is at best an instrument with which men who hold by the ideal of social justice and human progress can work, but when those ideals grow cold, it may, like other instruments, be turned to baser uses." [74]

By the time he reached the India Office, Morley had grown "cool and sceptical about *political* change." Successive Irish failures had been sufficient "to quench any futile ambition to play the part of constitution monger," [75] and had instilled doubts whether institutions imposed from above could prove either durable or effective. Ireland, at least under Parnell's tutelage, had revealed itself a viable political unit with an aptitude for representative government; yet even the Irish, to whom he remained a steadfast ally, often exasperated Morley by their petty jealousies and rival allegiances. Lord Rosebery recalled that, as Chief Secretary, Morley's private dictum had been that "Ireland would not be a difficult country to govern—were it not that all the people were intractable and all the problems insoluble." [76] During a hiatus in the struggle for Home Rule, Morley complained to Sir William Harcourt: "I wish to heaven our allies were Englishmen, with English habits of business." [77]

Despite his sincere devotion to the cause of Irish reform, Morley

72. Morley to Minto, September 1, 1910, Minto Papers.

73. F. A. Hirtzel's Diary, July 5, 1906, *1*, 59.

74. Morley, "Democracy and Reaction," *Nineteenth Century and After, 62* (1905), 366.

75. Morley to Minto, March 26, 1908, Minto Papers.

76. Cited in James, *Rosebery*, p. 200.

77. Morley to Harcourt, November 30, 1887, Harcourt Papers.

cherished no illusions that the Irish people shared the political genius of his fellow Englishmen. Though he had campaigned for
Radical franchise reforms in Britain, he remained convinced that
"One Man, One Vote [was] rather too narrow" a theory for application in Ireland.[78] After enumerating to a predominantly Tory
House of Commons the profound differences between social conditions on both sides of St. George's Channel, he concluded that
"the most misleading proposition that any statesman can advance"
was "that an institution which is good for Great Britain is therefore good for Ireland." [79]

Even as defined by its most ardent advocates, Home Rule was
not an attempt to outfit Irish fledglings with man-sized English
hand-me-downs. The proposals of 1886 and 1893, which Morley
helped to formulate and defend, guaranteed the continued supremacy in Irish affairs of the Imperial Parliament at Westminster. Home Rule was designed to enable Irishmen, subject to ultimate British approval, to evolve a representative system suited to
their national requirements and temperament; nothing less than
this, Morley contended, would satisfy Ireland's "crying need" for a
"strong government," equipped to cope with the social and political disorders of that island.[80] Moreover, he was confident that a
regime at Dublin with which they could identify would stimulate
a respect for law and order among cantankerous Irishmen. Long
before he devised his Irish formula, he had asked Joseph Chamberlain whether "by conceding some sort of Home Rule, we might be
developing in the Irish a new sort of sense of responsibility." [81]

Home Rule, then, was less a recognition than a hopeful anticipation of latent Irish capabilities. Irish emigrants, who had obtained first-class citizenship as Americans, Canadians, or Austral-
ians, proved as law-abiding as Englishmen or Scots, thereby
demonstrating to Morley's satisfaction that "the Irish will be a
loyal people when you give them institutions which are worth
being loyal to." [82] In 1868, during his unsuccessful campaign for a
seat at his native Blackburn, Morley—whose Irish policy remained

78. Morley to Gladstone, December 31, 1890, Gladstone Papers, Add. MSS.
44,256, fol. 103.
79. Parliamentary Debates, 3d ser., 308, cols. 360-61 (August 23, 1886).
80. Morley, Three Policies for Ireland: Coercion, Compromise, Conciliation
(London, 1886), p. 2.
81. Morley to Chamberlain, October 10, 1877, Chamberlain Papers.
82. Parliamentary Debates, 3d ser., 322, cols. 662-63 (February 16, 1888); also
"Conciliation with Ireland," Fortnightly Review, n.s., 30 (1881), 17.

amorphous and whose knowledge of Indian affairs remained
imperfect—contrasted Britain's sins in Ireland with the dubious
virtues of her Indian rule: democratic institutions were denied,
with greater justification, to India, where Britain compensated
with "a steady and unshaken respect for the wishes of the people." [83] The Lytton viceroyalty soon dispelled his illusions about
British paternalism in India, but he continued to doubt whether
it was either wise or feasible to attempt, among the multifarious
races of the India subcontinent, the constitutional experiment he
advocated for Christian Ireland.

India was the perpetual riddle of the British Empire. Even
nineteenth-century Liberals, who confidently devised policies for
virtually every situation, failed to produce a scheme for the future
of Britain's eastern dependency. This may, in large measure, be attributed to the fact that Indian problems had not yet claimed serious attention at Westminster; but the fault also lay with the
Liberal politicians themselves, who were reluctant to adjust their
utilitarian slide rules to Asian specifications.

As Secretary of State for India, Morley exhibited in full measure
that "relative and historic standpoint" that he had found wanting
in the controversial second book of James Mill's *History of India.*
"It is odd," he reflected in 1882, that "a thinker of Mill's calibre
and philosophical training" had not sought "some explanation of
[India's] superstitious beliefs, grovelling customs, and backward
institutions, in the facts of human nature, history, and surrounding circumstances." [84] Convinced throughout his life that "the
original and most solemn duty" of any government was "to do its
best for the happiness of all the people who come under its influence," he had deemed it imperative for the Irish Government,
which was alien, "not to measure that happiness by its own views
of what a nation ought to wish for, but simply and solely by the
views and actual wishes of a decisive majority of the people." [85]
But in India's case, Morley knew of no way to gauge public opinion, and he refused to accept the crisp British accents of Congress

83. Speech at Blackburn, May 28, 1868, *Ireland's Rights and England's Duties*
(Blackburn, 1868?), p. 6. This analogy reflects the influence of Mill who, in the
same year, asserted that "India is now governed, if with a large share of the
ordinary imperfections of rulers, yet with a full perception and recognition of
its differences from England." *England and Ireland* (Dublin, 1918), pp. 27-28.

84. "The Life of James Mill," *Fortnightly Review*, n.s., *31* (1882), 501.

85. Speech at Blackburn, May 28, 1868, *Ireland's Rights,* p. 6.

spokesmen as the accredited voice of the inarticulate multitudes; instead he relied upon his own definition of Indian welfare and imperial responsibility.

Like Gladstone, Morley drew a sharp distinction between Indian well-being and revolutionary political change; in his mind, the two appeared inimical. The introduction of representative institutions without the prior existence of a responsible mass electorate would impede genuine political growth: "Over three hundred different constitutions were promulgated in Europe between 1800 and 1880," he calculated, "so slow have men been in discovering that the forms of government are much less important than the forces behind them." [86] And no amount of supplication or agitation was sufficient to persuade him that the natives of India, after centuries of exploitation by potentates and Brahmins, were qualified to exercise those liberties that freeborn Englishmen had won at the expense of a reformation and a monarch's head. His public and private pronouncements were ambiguous on the crucial point of whether Indians would ever fully qualify, chiefly because he took for granted that the question would remain academic well beyond his lifetime.

Yet Morley was not reluctant to share with hungry Indians those crumbs from the English constitutional table which could be easily digested. Like Gladstone, he was convinced that while "you may not give to Indians an unbounded freedom," it was nonetheless possible to confer "certain freedom, certain franchises, privileges at any rate." [87] He told Lord Minto that his fundamental opposition to Indian political reform constituted "no reason why we should not see whether experience has taught some lessons worth learning or not." [88] But like the Grand Old Man, he deplored any "attempt to force English institutions on the colonies." [89] Even in the heyday of his radicalism, Morley had warned that:

> To insist on a whole community being made at once to submit to the reign of new practices and new ideas, which have

86. Morley, "Democracy and Reaction," p. 538.

87. Speech at Davidson's Mains, March 19, 1880, Gladstone, *Political Speeches in Scotland, 2,* 96.

88. Morley to Minto, March 26, 1908, Minto Papers.

89. Speech at Chester, November 12, 1855, Gladstone, *Our Colonies* (London, 1855) , p. 20.

just begun to commend themselves to the most advanced speculative intelligence of the time,—this, even if it were a practical process, would do much to make life impracticable and to hurry on social dissolution.[90]

He had since grown increasingly wary of those "simple ideas and absolute principles" which were "the passion of modern society," [91] and he remained convinced that democracy would not transform Indian conditions so much as Indian conditions would pervert the essence of democracy.

The debility of prewar western democracies intensified Morley's belief that it was futile to undertake constitutional experiments in the East. The underpinnings of Indian society, he reasoned, could not support the burdens of democratic institutions, which were proving too heavy a load for most European states; India's social structure would crumble, plunging millions into chaos and communal violence. The mass hysteria of 1947, which many have alleged to be the product of Morley's imperial design, was, in fact, the unwelcome confirmation of his grim prediction.

90. Morley, *On Compromise* (London, 1910) , p. 203.
91. Morley, "British Democracy and Indian Government," p. 200.

8 The Communal Question

Because the Morley-Minto reforms are often regarded first and foremost as an exercise in divide and rule, it is necessary to pay special attention to the issue of communal electorates. A disproportionate amount of scholarship has already been lavished upon this controversy, imparting to it a significance which it lacked during both Morley's secretaryship and his lifetime.[1] Without attempting to absolve two centuries of British rule in India of its divide and rule stigma, one may confidently assert that during the first decade of the twentieth century, neither the Viceroy nor the Secretary of State consciously implemented the pernicious theories which allegedly produced two warring nations within the bosom of Mother India.

No one could have been more aware than an intrepid Home Ruler of the inevitable consequences of a fragmented nationalist movement. The threat of impending Irish civil conflict—as much the legacy of Parnell's fall as the product of Unionist intrigues—revived any faded memories during Morley's India Office years. During the interval between two Gladstonian Home Rule bills, he had professed that "from the Irish point of view, I'd far rather see a Parnellite Ireland than a divided Ireland."[2] There was nothing in Gladstone's formula, he insisted, inimical to Irish unity, not even a proposal for a "legislative body in Dublin for the representation of the Protestant and propertied minority" which, he ex-

1. Most recently, M. N. Das (*India Under Morley and Minto*, London, 1964) has stretched the elastic material in the Morley and Minto collections—his only sources—over a prefabricated ideological structure. He portrays Minto as a Machiavellian schemer, who introduced communal electorates in a deliberate attempt to disrupt the forces of Indian nationalism and thereby perpetuate the British Raj, and he assumes that Morley—who chose the Florentine statesman as the subject of his 1897 Romanes Lecture—was unable to recognize a twentieth-century facsimile.

2. Morley to Spencer, January 21, 1891, Spencer Papers. Morley added that "From an English point of view, our position appeared to me to be very bad in either."

plained, had been inserted "to appease the misgivings and mistrust of our critics, [rather] than . . . to satisfy any misgivings of our own." [3] Least of all had the Gladstonians sought to encourage a separatist spirit in Ulster, and Morley was dismayed when such a spirit ultimately appeared. While a third Home Rule measure remained deadlocked in Parliament, he predicted "hard times if Home Rule starts in an Ireland savagely divided," [4] and he maintained that "Ulstermen shall not be treated differently from other religions of the United Kingdom." [5]

There is no conceivable reason for Morley to have wished to introduce to India conditions which he had spent a political lifetime trying to avert in Ireland and elsewhere. He had condemned any South African policy which might "[sow] the seeds of division between the Dutch and English in Cape Colony"; the outcome, he warned, "will be Ireland all over again, with what is called a loyalist district, and outside of that an enormous territory . . . saturated with sullen disaffection." [6] But it was equally evident to him that in areas where communal divisions were deeply ingrained, they could not be discounted; and in such circumstances, he considered it Britain's obligation to protect the interests and security of minority populations. "I believe I don't underrate the elements of division" in Canada, he told Goldwin Smith, "but both in Canada and Ireland, I'm a sort of friend of the R[oman] C[atholic]s." [7] Essentially the same considerations prompted Morley to safeguard the rights of India's Muslim community. Important, too, was the fact that the Muslims constituted a conservative element in early-twentieth-century Indian politics. Yet Morley had no ambition to widen or perpetuate the Hindu-Muslim rift.

Morley conceived of India's Muslim problem in its international context, an approach he shared with the majority of contemporary Muslim spokesmen. Reflecting the traditional British assumption (which he himself had criticized) that "we . . . know how to deal with Mahometans," [8] he confided to Lady

3. Speech at Newcastle, April 21, 1886, Morley, *Mr. Gladstone's Irish Policy* (Newcastle, 1886?), pp. 16-17.

4. Morley to Carnegie, November 28, 1913, Morley-Carnegie Correspondence; see also Jenkins, *Asquith*, p. 293.

5. Morley to Austen Chamberlain, December 11, 1913, Chamberlain Papers.

6. Speech at Arbroath, September 5, 1899, *The Times* (September 6, 1899), p. 8.

7. Morley to Smith, April 28, 1905, Smith Papers.

8. [Morley], "A Political Epilogue," *Fortnightly Review*, n.s., 24 (1878), 329.

Minto that he was "an Occidental, not an Oriental," and that, so far as he could tell, he "like[d] Mahometans, but . . . [could not] go much further than that in the easterly direction." [9] Sir Valentine Chirol, Indian correspondent for *The Times,* professed that Morley favored Muslims "for their virility, their superiority of character, and also their greater propinquity of religious thought to that of the Christian West." [10] In a halfhearted effort to convince the Aga Khan that there was no truth to rumors that "like all other English Radicals, I had a hatred of Islam," Morley asserted that "if I were to have a label, I should be called a Positivist, and in the Positivist Calendar . . . Mohamed is one of the leading saints and has the high honour of giving his name to a week." [11] Yet there is no reason—not even the provisions for communal representation in the Morley-Minto reforms—to consider these philosophical musings the promulgation of an imperial policy.

A confirmed agnostic, Morley had always resented attempts to wield religion as a weapon in political combat. He distrusted statesmen of any faith who did so, and considered Amir Ali, who led a Muslim deputation to the India Office on January 27, 1909, "a vain creature, with a certain gift of length, [whom] I believe . . . I could convert . . . from the Crescent to the Cross, if I would only make him a K.C.S.I." [12] Long after Morley had supposedly embarked on the straight and narrow path of divide and rule, he joined Lord Hardinge in condemning proposals for separate educational institutions for each religious community: "I strongly agree with your dislike of these denominational schemes." [13] Though he has been portrayed as either the dupe or accomplice of policies that favored India's Muslim minority, Morley admitted to intimate friends that it defied "the wit of man

9. "Don't betray this fatal secret," Morley added with mock solemnity, "or I shall be ruined." Morley to Lady Minto, June 29, 1906, Minto Papers; see also Morley to Bryce, August 27, 1906, Bryce Papers.

10. Chirol to Sir Herbert Risley, n.d. [copy], given by Risley to Lady Minto, June 2, 1907, Minto Papers.

11. Morley to Minto, February 18, 1909, Minto Papers. This facetious oath of allegiance to Mohammed, which Morley repeated to numerous correspondents, contains more literary merit than historical truth, and is quite meaningless in the light of his frequent disclaimers of any affiliation with the Comtist sect; nevertheless, it has been cited as an espousal of the Muslim cause.

12. Morley to Minto, January 28, 1909, Minto Papers.

13. Morley to Hardinge, March 31, 1911, Morley Papers.

to frame plans that will please Hindus without offending Mahometans, and we shall be lucky if we don't offend both." [14] He instructed Minto "to take care that in picking up the Mussulman, we don't drop our Hindu parcels," and to guard against disclosing "the full length to which we are or may be ready to go in the Moslem direction." [15]

The Morley-Minto policy encountered its major difficulties precisely because Minto failed to take the elementary precautions that his partner retrospectively prescribed. On October 1, 1906, Minto received a deputation of Muslim petitioners at Simla, and he offered wholesale assurances that

> I am as firmly convinced, as I believe you to be, that any electoral representation in India would be doomed to mischievous failure which aimed at granting a personal enfranchisement regardless of the traditions of the communities composing the population of this continent.[16]

There were immediate protests from Hindu nationalists, who viewed both the Muslim appeal and the viceregal reply as stratagems to wean politically conscious Muslims from the Congress ranks.[17] Yet, as S. R. Wasti convincingly demonstrates, neither this confrontation nor the subsequent birth of the Muslim League were marionette shows for which the Government of India pulled the strings.[18]

Morley had no prior knowledge of the vague promises that Minto intended to concede. There exists, however, no indication that the Viceroy attributed to this portion of his address the significance that it attained in the light of future events.[19] In the later, less cordial years of their collaboration, Morley frequently rebuked Minto for having revealed his hand before the opening card had been played. Early in 1909, he recalled that the Viceroy's

14. Morley to Harrison, November 4, 1909, Harrison Papers.

15. Morley to Minto, January 28, 1909, Minto Papers.

16. Cited in Minto to Morley, October 4, 1906, Morley Papers.

17. L. Hare, Lieutenant-Governor of Eastern Bengal and Assam, to Minto, October 20, 1906, Minto Papers.

18. Wasti, *Lord Minto and the Indian Nationalist Movement* (Oxford, 1964), pp. 59 ff; it is as an account of incipient Muslim political forces that this study makes its most valuable contribution.

19. See Minto to Morley, September 10, 1906, Morley Papers; Minto eventually felt duty-bound to carry out the "pledges I had given to the Mahommedans" on this occasion. Minto to Lansdowne, January 21, 1909 [copy], Minto Papers.

"language to the Islamites about their 'just claim to something more than numerical strength' was perhaps a trifle less guarded than it might have been." [20] As the months passed and accusations of divide and rule began to reverberate, Morley ungallantly notified Minto that he had no intention of helping to shoulder the blame: "I respectfully remind you once more that it was *your* speech about their extra claims that first started the Mahometan hare. I am convinced my decision was best." [21]

Morley's proposed solution to the vexing problem of minority representation was a blueprint for electoral colleges through which members of the reformed legislative councils would be indirectly elected in direct proportion to the numerical strength of their respective communities; this was in essence an extension of the principle by which certain municipal bodies and interest groups had elected their representatives to provincial councils. The hypothetical case with which Morley attempted to illustrate this electoral procedure attested to its staggering complexity: in a province of twenty million inhabitants, fifteen million Hindu and five million Muslim, a twelve-man provincial council was to be elected consisting of nine Hindu members and three Muslim; the province would be divided into three electoral districts, each of which would have an electoral college of one hundred members elected at large, seventy-five of whom would be Hindu and twenty-five Muslim; each of the three colleges would then return three Hindus and one Muslim to the provincial council.[22]

Morley's scheme had the backing of his makeshift reforms committee at Whitehall, but received little encouragement from more respected quarters. Gokhale, who did not agree with Minto that electoral colleges would deprive the Muslim community of its due influence upon public affairs, nonetheless deferred to Minto's political judgment in order to "avoid any bone of contention." [23] Sir Alfred Lyall counseled Morley that it was worthwhile "to make any concession to [the Muslims] on this question that may be profitable." [24] Minto waged a relentless campaign by mail and

20. Morley to Minto, January 21, 1909, Minto Papers.
21. Morley to Minto, December 6, 1909, Minto Papers.
22. Dispatch of Secretary of State, November 27, 1908, Morley Papers.
23. Cited in Minto to Morley, January 15, 1909 [telegram], Morley Papers.
24. See Lyall to Morley, February 4, 1909, Morley Papers; also Lyall to Morley, February 15, 1909, Morley Papers.

telegraph to convince Morley that Muslim interests required and deserved constitutional protection, and that India was politically too immature for the relatively sophisticated electoral college experiment. And, of course, Muslim spokesmen left no doubt that they preferred the Viceroy's proposals.[25] Under pressure from all sides, and faced with the disturbing prospect of a parliamentary insurrection,[26] Morley's resistance ebbed. He took refuge behind the myth that he had merely suggested electoral colleges as food for thought, an impression which Minto was only too pleased to foster.

Morley's belated conversion to the policy of communal representation reflected neither inexperience nor fatigue so much as political expediency. It was imperative, he reasoned, to leave no loose ends in the reform measure which might be tugged at by parliamentary opportunists. Above all, he felt justly confident that accusations of divide and rule were groundless: Minto had rejoiced when a group of prominent Hindus and Muslims offered a demonstration of biracial accord in March 1907,[27] and a few months later, he had anticipated a gradual eradication of "caste and religious differences." [28] By no means did the Viceroy wish Muslims to retire into political isolation; rather he preferred to guarantee an adequate representation of minority interests, while Muslim candidates competed simultaneously in open constituencies. "My view has always been," Minto told Lord Kitchener, "that, whilst they [the Muslims] certainly must have a certain number of seats guaranteed as a community, it would be suicidal for their political future to be rated on a lower standard than Hindus and to be completely debarred from competing with them." [29]

Notwithstanding a strong personal preference for an integrated electorate, Morley did not find it too difficult to subscribe to the

25. Morley received a delegation of Muslim leaders on January 27, 1909; his noncommittal remarks to them are included among his *Indian Speeches*. Amid vehement attacks by Muslim spokesmen, Morley solicited the assistance of Sir William Lee-Warner, a respected India Office official, to "help me to make my peace with the Mahometans, when the time comes." Morley to Lee-Warner, January 4, 1909, Lee-Warner Papers.

26. Morley to Minto, October 21, 1909 [telegram], Morley Papers.

27. After receiving this deputation, Minto assured Morley that "of all the wonderful things that have happened since I was in India, this to my mind was the most wonderful." Minto to Morley, March 19, 1907, Morley Papers.

28. Minto to Morley, June 5, 1907, Morley Papers.

29. Minto to Kitchener, June 28, 1909 [copy], Minto Papers.

Viceroy's proposals for communal representation. Unable to discern either the existence of a unified Indian nationalism or the boundaries of a viable Indian nation, he—no less than Minto—sought the best means to recognize the status quo. He deplored communal divisions, but he recognized that no imperial statesman could afford to ignore them. Class and professional interests had long been safeguarded under the preexisting council structure; there seemed little reason to deny similar considerations to a religious minority. Both administrators were aware that separate electorates, like the concession of privileges to the high-born and the well-bred, were incompatible with the cardinal tenets of democracy, but both agreed that democratic institutions for India were out of the question. It would be irrelevant to accuse the authors of the 1909 reforms of defying the spirit of theories of which they had explicitly defied the letter.

Considering any electoral procedure peripheral to their overall design, Morley and Minto were equally surprised by the attention lavished upon these regulations, and would have been horrified to have heard the accusations which were engendered during subsequent decades by a widening Hindu-Muslim divergence. If either had an ambition to divide and rule, it was—as initial critics observed [30]—in an attempt to impose a constitutional barrier between wavering moderates and intractable extremists. Yet divide and rule ultimately acquired a religious connotation which has persisted to the present day.

G. K. Gokhale, who had once appealed for a token from the Government "to show that they do not look on Mohammedans as their pets," [31] defended the communal electorate scheme in the face of mounting nationalist abuse. In a speech before the Imperial Legislative Council on March 29, 1909, he appealed to his compatriots for patience and tolerance, two commodities that years of eager anticipation had virtually exhausted:

> it has been urged by some of my countrymen that any special separate treatment of minorities militates against the idea of

30. In a letter to the editor of the *Spectator* (April 25, 1908, p. 666), the Reverend N. Macnicol of Poona argued that concessions designed to prevent the restoration of Congress unity were based "on the cowardly principle of *Divide et Impera*." Bipin Chandra Pal, a militant Extremist, issued the identical charge in his *Nationality and Empire* (Calcutta, 1916), pp. 274-75.

31. Cited in Dunlop Smith to Morley, October 29, 1907; enclosed in Minto to Morley, October 29, 1907, Morley Papers.

the union of all communities in public matters. Such union is no doubt the goal towards which we have to strive, but it cannot be denied that it does not exist in the country today, and it is no use proceeding as though it existed when in reality it does not. . . . Unless the feeling of soreness in the minds of minorities is removed by special separate supplementary treatment such as is proposed by the Government of India, the advance towards a real union will be retarded rather than promoted.[32]

But Gokhale, on whom Morley and Minto relied for information as well as support, grossly underestimated both the durability of racial tensions and the depths of nationalist despair.[33] Neither his personal injunctions nor his machinations behind the scenes at Lahore prevented the twenty-fourth annual Congress from recording "its strong sense of disapproval of the creation of separate electorates on the basis of religion." Surendranath Banerjea moved a resolution, which the Congress carried unanimously, objecting in no uncertain terms to

the excessive and unfairly preponderant share of representation given to the followers of one particular religion; the unjust, invidious, and humiliating distinctions made between Muslim and non-Muslim subjects of His Majesty in the matter of the electorates, the franchise, and the qualifications of candidates; the wide, arbitrary and unreasonable disqualifications and restrictions for candidates seeking election to the Councils; the general distrust of the educated classes that runs through the whole course of the regulations; and the unsatisfactory composition of non-official majorities in Provincial Councils, rendering them ineffective and unreal for all practical purposes.[34]

Morley, who had anticipated grumblings among more militant congressmen, consoled himself with the knowledge that "we did

32. Gokhale, *Speeches*, p. 209.

33. Wasti (pp. 169-70) paints a foreshortened picture of nationalist opinion by contending that despite the "many Hindus . . . [who] expressed nervousness at . . . the principle of separate representation," there were "a few enlightened ones amongst them [who] did not much resent it."

34. *Proceedings of the Twenty-fourth Indian National Congress*, p. 47. Wasti (pp. 217-18), in his cursory account of the 1909 Congress proceedings, omits any mention of the resolution condemning communal electorates.

not leave an indecent quantity of fur in the traps." [35] He remained optimistic that the imminent restoration of civil peace and political stability would distract Indian critics from their local and religious grievances. A parliamentarian first and foremost, Morley could afford to be "very sure of one thing, and this is that if we had not satisfied the Mahometans, we should have had opinion here— which is now with us—dead against us. Nothing has been sacrificed for their sake that is of real importance." [36]

As nationalist cries grew steadily more truculent and threatened to drown out the polite applause for their reforms, Morley reminded Minto "that it was you who set the troublesome ball rolling in a famous speech which I have heard so often quoted in debate that I know every word of it by heart." [37] The taunt was unkind, for though he had looked upon communal electorates with marked disfavor, his opposition had been neither constructive nor sustained. Though his approach to the problem had been the more idealistic, he shared his partner's tragic inability to devise an electoral formula which would satisfy both short-term requirements and long-term goals. It was as much the insoluble riddle of imperial India as bureaucratic intransigence which thwarted Morley. Like E. M. Forster's well-intentioned Dr. Aziz, planning a picnic menu that would at once appease the appetites and satisfy the dietary observances of his guests, Christian, Hindu, and Muslim, "Trouble after trouble encountered him, because he had challenged the spirit of the Indian earth, which tries to keep men in compartments."

35. Morley to Minto, April 28, 1909, Minto Papers.
36. Morley to Minto, November 18, 1909, Minto Papers.
37. Morley to Minto, April 28, 1909, Minto Papers.

9 The Mailed Fist and the Open Palm

Despite persistent allegations during the first decade of the twentieth century that he financed his residency at the India Office by shamelessly mortgaging his "principles of a lifetime," there is no evidence that either racial prejudice, political advantage, or the heightened impatience of advanced years made John Morley any more predisposed to high-handed practices than he had been in his prime. Much has been said of his subconscious yearning to emulate history's men on horseback; [1] but if, in any sense, he joined the lesser ranks of Machiavellian statesmen during his Indian secretaryship, it was less the fulfillment of a grown-up schoolboy's dream than a response to administrative exigencies. A succession of Indian outrages left him no choice but to resort to coercive measures in order to protect life, limb, and the dwindling chances for a successful reform policy in India.

It cannot be overemphasized that Morley succumbed to neither the intimidations of his surroundings nor the pressures of his colleagues. When he decided to sanction stringent legislation, he did so pragmatically and rarely in the strength or quantity that the Government of India had recommended. His policies were determined exclusively by his assessment of the available facts, though, by unfortunate necessity, he often had to rely upon anxious bureaucrats for his information. Above all, he approved coercive measures because he sincerely believed, as he had for decades, that prudent applications of repression were often the prerequisite to responsible political growth.

Morley was heralded as a rabid anticoercionist, a reputation he neither courted nor deserved, but one which carried numerous political advantages; less fortunately, it gave rise to overconfident expectations that "the statesman that won his spurs in Ireland will

1. See particularly Austen Chamberlain, *Politics from Inside* (London, 1936), p. 87; also J. H. Morgan, "More Light on Lord Morley," *North American Review, 221* (1925), 489.

not tarnish them or have them hacked from his heels in India." [2]
Although he had consistently opposed the harsh legislation that
W. E. Forster and A. J. Balfour had promulgated during the
1880s, he never believed that Ireland could be effectively governed without recourse to certain artificial restraints: "Nobody
but a madman would have undertaken to keep order [in Ireland]
without a Crimes Act," he wrote to Gladstone from Dublin Castle.[3] Morley reserved his condemnations for those policies which
relied too heavily on coercion, "that standard medicine that has always left the malady where it was, unless it made it worse." [4] Arrests and prosecutions, he pointed out, were useful only when
accompanied by constructive measures; they would not themselves
deter violence or agitation, but instead would draw attention to
the causes of disaffection and arouse sympathy not for the Government, but for its victims. Undiluted repression would, in addition,
"undermine respect for Law" and "deepen and widen popular resentment against the very institutions" which the Government
had "professed [an] ambition to cherish and preserve." [5] But
though he disparaged the use of coercion as a means in itself, he
conceded that it might prove beneficial so long as it was used spar-
ingly, judiciously, and without prejudice. There was a world of
difference, he reflected, between Lord Spencer's coercive policy,
which was "at least law," and that of W. E. Forster, which was "as
unconstitutional in theory as it was inflated in policy and calami-
tous in result." [6]

No one could possibly have been more aware than Morley of the
fact that continued disturbances would be seized upon by appre-
hensive Englishmen as a pretext for shelving conciliatory measures; [7] and no one proved more determined to persevere with
reforms despite bomb explosions. He charted the vicious cycle in a
letter to Minto: "Shortcomings in government lead to outbreaks;

2. *India* (December 15, 1905) , p. 277.
3. Morley to Gladstone, June 19, 1893, Gladstone Papers, Add. MSS. 44,257,
fol. 114.
4. Morley, *Recollections, I,* 173.
5. *Parliamentary Debates,* 3d ser., 327, cols. 1167 ff., 1148 ff. (June 25, 1888) and
322, cols. 182-83 (February 10, 1888) .
6. Morley, *Life of Gladstone, 3,* 71.
7. *The Times,* during the turbulent summer of 1908, expressed the popular
view that "the morrow of a carnival of bomb-throwing is not a convenient occasion for proclaiming concessions." July 1, 1908, p. 13.

outbreaks have to be put down; reformers have to bear the blame, and their reforms are scotched; reaction triumphs; and mischief goes on as before, only worse." [8] Two decades earlier, as a member of Gladstone's short-lived third Government, Morley had argued that recurrent Irish violence rendered Home Rule more imperative and no less practicable:

> the more you prove to me [that] there is disorder and lawlessness in Ireland, the better evidence there is that you need our policy,—the better evidence there is that you cannot revert to the policy which has produced that barbarous state of mind, temper, and habit which leads to these detestable crimes. [9]

He had assured his political opponents that Home Rule did not denote a sell out to Irish rebels, but an attempt to strengthen the hand of moderate Irishmen: "If you reject our proposal, and you dismiss us from office," he warned, "you will be doing exactly what these violent extremists most ardently wish for." [10] As Chief Secretary for Ireland, he had considered reform and repression two complementary agents of British policy. Later, at the India Office, his attitude remained essentially the same: "at the same time" that political concessions were on the anvil, "we must use language to convince people that we mean to stand no nonsense and that disorder will extinguish the chances of reform." [11]

Despite a variety of striking similarities, Morley realized that early-twentieth-century Indian problems differed considerably from those he had encountered in Ireland. [12] India posed an in-

8. Morley to Minto, May 3, 1907, Minto Papers.

9. Speech to the Eighty Club, London, June 8, 1886, Morley, *The Irish Question* (London, 1887?), p. 16.

10. *Parliamentary Debates*, 3d ser., *204*, col. 1266 (April 9, 1886); on a subsequent occasion, he told critics of Home Rule that "The dynamiters and assassins will be delighted if you reject the Bill." Ibid., 3d ser., *205*, col. 926 (May 13, 1886).

11. Morley to Minto, April 26, 1907, Minto Papers.

12. "Reference has been made," Morley told his fellow M.P.s,

> to my having resisted the Irish Crimes Act, as if there were a scandalous inconsistency between opposing the policy of that Act, and imposing this policy on the natives of India. . . . This inconsistency can only be established by anyone who takes up the position that Ireland, a part of the United Kingdom, is exactly on the same footing as those 300,000,000 people—composite, heterogeneous, with different histories, of different races, different faiths. Does anyone contend that any political principle is capable of application in any sort of circumstance without reference to conditions?

Parliamentary Debates, 4th ser., *175*, cols. 879–80 (June 6, 1907).

finitely greater challenge to imperial statesmanship, for by this time British politicians were aware of what had to be done in Ireland even if they hesitated to do it. He was inhibited by the fact that he not only lacked firsthand knowledge of Indian conditions, but was continually reminded of this deficiency; he might reason that this hardly mattered, but he convinced relatively few critics. "Good friends of mine in this Office," he told Minto, "often say: 'Ah, you don't know India,' which is true; but then they proceed to impress upon my innocent mind principles of government that would justify Trepoff at Petersburg, or the Orange Ascendancy, who have made such a detestable mess in Ireland." [13] Proconsuls who had returned from "the spot" conspired with those who remained on duty to acquaint him with the facts of imperial life. "Natives always attribute leniency to fear," Lord Roberts professed to Lady Minto, and he assumed it his mission "to bring this home to Lord Morley." [14]

To contemporaries these not-so-subtle thrusts might have appeared to dictate Morley's decisions. In moments of acute exasperation, he was heard to extol the virtues of Strafford and to advocate a Thorough policy for India. His five years at the India Office were punctuated by legislative assaults upon freedom of the press and the right to public assembly, and by a plethora of political deportations and arrests. At the outset of their partnership, Morley made a conscientious attempt to demonstrate to Minto that he was prepared to be as cooperative in these unsavory affairs as the Viceroy, in turn, was conscientiously attempting to be about reforms. Moreover, Morley felt duty-bound to accord the Government of India's actions his public support even when they were simultaneously the object of his scathing private censures. Lady Minto, among others, was willingly misled by the sporadic thunderclaps emitted from Whitehall; she noted that Morley's terse words to the Commons about the Lajpat Rai incident had "quite a Cromwellian ring about them," and she cordially welcomed Radical John to the august ranks of Britain's imperial trustees.[15]

Yet Morley's wholesale conversion to strong-arm methods was more apparent than real, a fact Lady Minto realized more quickly than most parliamentary Radicals, who were scandalized by his

13. Morley to Minto, May 3, 1906, Minto Papers.
14. Roberts to Lady Minto, [May 5], 1908, Minto Papers.
15. Lady Minto's Indian Journals, May 13, 1907, *1907–i*, 139.

justifications of autocratic power, and ignorant of his covert repri-mands to the Viceroy. For this reason, Morley's personal corre-spondence during his India Office years affords a more accurate representation of his views than his platform oratory, in which he consistently stressed his intention to meet force with force. In practice, he remained as staunch an opponent of purposeless coer-cion as he had ever been during his Irish Office days. The single difference was that in his former capacity, he had been more con-fident that there existed an effective alternative to iron rule.

In cases where it proved even remotely possible for Morley to exercise his authority or influence, repressive legislation was in-variably either vetoed or whittled down from the ambitious pro-posals formulated at Simla and Calcutta. But there were numerous matters which required neither the approval nor advice of the Home Government, and here he found himself unable to do more than register a retrospective protest with Minto at the same time that, for reasons of honor as well as expediency, he defended these odious actions before parliamentary critics. To some, it seemed "the irony of fate" that the veteran Home Ruler had transported "the whole armoury of Irish coercion" to Indian soil: "deporta-tion and imprisonment without trial, suppression of meetings, po-lice reports, power of district judges or resident magistrates." [16] Yet there can be no doubt that Morley, to the limits of his ability and beyond the limits of his official powers, staved off these mea-sures as long as possible and then jealously guarded against their abuse.

During the hectic course of his secretaryship, Morley grudgingly assented to two press acts which elicited fierce Radical opposition without satisfying Indian bureaucrats. Minto had begun to agitate for permission to muzzle the Indian press at an early date, but his initial petitions encountered implacable resistance at Whitehall, where the Secretary of State remained faithfully wedded to a free press despite a pronounced distaste for the excesses of Indian jour-nalism.[17] Though Morley unwittingly buoyed viceregal hopes by mentioning "that one day you may feel inclined to make a new

16. Austen Chamberlain's Diary, May 14, 1907, cited in *Politics from Inside*, p. 87; it was undoubtedly another "irony of fate" that put Chamberlain in Morley's India Office shoes eight years later.

17. See Morley to Godley, August 31, 1906, Kilbracken Papers (I.O.L.); also Morley to Minto, October 19, 1906, Minto Papers.

press law"—an occasion he trusted would not arise "in my time" [18]—he revealed himself a foe of such proposals and he strictly forbade the men on the spot to take matters into their own eager hands. [19] But in spite of his vow that "nothing can induce me to assent to a new version of poor Lytton's Act," [20] his persistent condemnations of press restrictions were seasoned with tacit promises that he would endorse a measure which carefully avoided the arbitrary and discriminatory flavor of Lytton's 1878 Vernacular Press Act: "You won't find me squeamish about a press law," he assured Minto, "and for a *general* press law there is, no doubt, only too good a case to be made out." [21] The legislation which took effect on June 8, 1908, was less the result of his capitulation to bureaucratic demands than an effort to arrest the drift to extremism which threatened to preclude further consideration of Indian reform proposals. As such, it satisfied virtually all of Morley's Gladstonian criteria and fell far short of Minto's urgent plea for "power to seize the presses." [22] He remitted his verdict on May 28, explaining that

> I do believe that our introduction of a *judicial* element at every stage is an improvement, apart from general principles of a Free Press on the one hand, and the maintenance of Law and Order on the other. . . . It will make it easier for the Moderates to resist the Extremist attack. Such an attack is sure to come, and it is our business, as I think, not to do anything that will give substance to Extremist taunts and reproaches against their Moderate opponents. Of course, our proceeding must be effective, but I do not think that any of

18. Morley to Minto, November 2, 1906, Minto Papers.

19. Morley to Minto, May 20, 1907 [telegram], Morley Papers.

20. Morley to Godley, July 30, 1907, Kilbracken Papers, Add. MSS. 44,902, fol. 119; in a letter to the Prime Minister, Morley acknowledged that there was strong royal pressure for press legislation, but he again cited Lytton's Vernacular Press Act, the utility of which had been totally eclipsed by the racial hatreds it generated. "I think only one single attempt was made to use it," Morley recalled, "and that was no brilliant success." Morley to Campbell-Bannerman, August 21, 1907, Campbell-Bannerman Papers, Add. MSS. 41,223, fol. 259.

21. Morley to Minto, August 2, 1907, Minto Papers.

22. Minto to Morley, May 14, 1908 [copy], Minto Papers; see Morley to Godley, July 30, 1907, in which Morley adamantly insists that "the assent of the *Supreme Gov't.* will have to be secured" in such cases, and that judicial authority would have to reside with "the civil power." Kilbracken Papers, Add. MSS. 44,902, fol. 119.

the modifications suggested here will at all impair your purposes.[23]

The precautions Morley took were sufficient to placate even the aged Lord Ripon, now Lord Privy Seal, who had been responsible for expurgating Lytton's Vernacular Press Act from the Indian statute book and who was "very unhappy" at rumors of its imminent restoration.[24] After a vain attempt to persuade Ripon of the imperative need for a punitive policy,[25] Morley relieved his anxieties by allowing him a glance at his May 29 telegram to the Viceroy. Aware of the strings that had been attached to Morley's assent, Ripon breathed more easily, withdrew his objections, and told Morley that:

> Your telegram is very satisfactory to me and it . . . completely changes the character of the proposed legislation from that which the G. of I. intended. . . . Your amendments are very ingenious. They completely alter the basis of the scheme and turn it from an authoritarian into a judicial proceeding.[26]

There was an equally warm endorsement for the controversial measure from Lord Cromer who, *The Times* recalled, had upheld a free press in Egypt and "was a member of Lord Ripon's Indian administration which took the regrettable step of cancelling Lord Lytton's Press Act." [27] In an interview at Whitehall, Gokhale agreed that the Government's action had been "inevitable" and he pledged "to do all he could . . . to muzzle, or at all events not to excite, his various allies in the press and the House of Commons." There was also hesitant support from Sir Henry Cotton, the de facto leader of the Indophile parliamentarians.[28]

23. Morley to Minto, May 28,1908, Minto Papers.

24. Ripon to Morley, October 17, 1907, Ripon Papers, Add. MSS. 43,541, fols. 145-49.

25. See Morley to Ripon, May 29, 1908, Ripon Papers, Add. MSS. 43,541, fols. 178-79.

26. Ripon to Morley, June 1, 1908, Ripon Papers, Add. MSS. 43,541, fol. 183.

27. *The Times* (July 1, 1908) , p. 13; the editorial concluded that "the ripening wisdom of maturer years has at last led Lord Cromer to modify his convictions."

28. Morley to Minto, June 8, 1908, Minto Papers. Not all Morley's Radical critics followed Cotton's timorous lead; Wilfrid Scawen Blunt inserted an acrimonious version of past and present events into the pages of his diary (June 14, 1908) :

> That "wretched fellow" Morley has had a new Press Law passed in India giving powers to local authorities to seize printing presses and confiscate with-

During the eighteen-month respite between press acts, continuous bureaucratic appeals for supplementary legislation attested to
the paltry nature of the 1908 measure. Again Morley initially refused to comply with these requests, and provided a stale sermon
instead of fresh repression: *"Stolidity,* which may often be a horrid
vice in affairs of Government, is, I suspect, rather a virtue in deal-
ing with seditious articles in newspapers. I wish you all had my
three or four years of administration in uneasy Ireland." [29] For
the second time an outbreak of terrorism appeared to vindicate
the Government of India's arguments and threatened to subvert
the Morley-Minto reforms. Early in 1910, Morley approved the
text of another press bill which, if nothing else, would calm bureaucratic nerves. "We worked hard on your Press Act," he informed Minto,

> and I hope the result has reached you in plenty of time. I
> daresay it is as sensible in its way as other Press Acts, or as
> Press Acts can ever be. . . . Neither I nor my Council would
> have sanctioned it if there had been no appeal in some form
> to a court of law; and you tell me that you would have had
> sharp difficulties in your own Council.[30]

The Governor of Bombay, who had set the coercive gears in motion, was disappointed by the finished product; "it does not go as
far as I hoped," he complained to the Viceroy, "and I cannot like
the principle of allowing the High Courts to upset—if they
choose—a deliberate decision of Government. No Government
can venture to risk a rebuff which would lower their prestige in
the sight of everybody." [31] Though Minto shared these misgivings, he was unable to surmount the obstacle of a Secretary of State
who believed that "a press act is not much more for Indian unrest

out trial where sedition has been published. It was this same John Morley of
whom Lytton used so bitterly to complain to me as his most violent attacker
while in India, notwithstanding their personal friendship, and on these very
points, if I remember rightly, of his Afghan campaign and his Press Law,
which is identical with this of Morley's today.
Blunt, *My Diaries* (2 vols. London, 1920), 2, 212.

29. Morley to Clarke, October 19, 1909, Morley Papers. A month earlier Morley
had notified Clarke: "You must not count on my sanctioning any moves in this
direction. If you cannot govern India without this, you won't be better able to govern with it." Morley to Clarke, September 17, 1909, Morley Papers.

30. Morley to Minto, February 3, 1910, Minto Papers.

31. Clarke to Minto, February 21, 1910, Minto Papers.

than a 'pill for earthquakes.' " [32] On February 8, 1910, the second press bill of Morley's secretaryship headed the agenda of the newly reformed Legislative Council, where Gokhale was among those who spoke in its behalf. The moderate leader, too, had reasons for profound disappointment, and his remarks provide a fitting post-mortem to India's half decade of Morley-Minto rule: "while the plans of statesmen have matured slowly, events designed by malignant fates to frustrate their purpose have moved faster." [33]

Freedom of the press was only one of the "principles of a lifetime" which Morley allegedly repudiated during his tenure at the India Office, and it was neither the first nor the one which provoked the most bitter outcry. Shortly before the promulgation of the first press act, he rose in the Commons to disclose that Lala Lajpat Rai and Ajit Singh had been deported for reasons which he was not prepared to enumerate at that time. Though he brushed aside Radical protests that the Punjabi disturbances had been caused by spontaneous opposition to proposed agrarian legislation,[34] he gave increasingly more credence to these arguments in his private remonstrances to Minto.[35]

For a brief moment, Morley was persuaded that the prosecution of Lajpat Rai had been legally justifiable, but that judicial delays would have deprived the deed of its salutary effect. Against his better judgment, he trusted that the undisclosed facts of the case would eventually vindicate this repugnant maneuver. At the same time, he was uncomfortably aware that "my Tory critics will scent an inconsistency between deporting Lajpat and my old fighting of Balfour for locking up William O'Brien and making him wear the prison garb." [36] He must also have recalled his vigorous protest in 1888 when John Dillon, an Irish M.P., had been imprisoned for preaching sedition; the Crimes Act, he had then reminded A. J. Balfour, did not add new offenses to the statute book, and the decision to deny Dillon a court hearing implied that the Irish leader was not guilty in any legal sense.[37] But Morley's critics,

32. Morley to Minto, February 3, 1910, Minto Papers.

33. Speech of February 8, 1910, Indian Legislative Council, Gokhale, *Speeches*, p. 400.

34. C. J. O'Donnell, *The Causes of Present Discontents in India* (London, 1908), pp. 93-94.

35. See Morley to Minto, May 25, 1907 [telegram], Morley Papers.

36. Morley to Minto, May 31, 1907, Minto Papers.

37. *Parliamentary Debates*, 3d ser., *327*, cols. 1148 ff. (June 25, 1888).

much to his relief, were not as relentless as he had been. A sufficient amount of his Radical glory remained untarnished to win
him either support or disapprobatory silence from the latter-day
Levelers on the Liberal back benches. "Deportation is an ugly dose
for Radicals to swallow," he later boasted to Minto; "in truth, if I
did not happen to possess a spotless character as an anti-coercionist
in Ireland, our friends would certainly have kicked a good deal." [38]

But it soon dawned upon Morley that the deportations he was
strenuously defending were as pernicious as they were unconstitutional. Though he still felt compelled to deny as much to his parliamentary assailants, he instructed Minto that further recourse to
the Regulation of 1818 would not be tolerated. Concurrently, he
pressed for Lajpat Rai's immediate release. While Minto warned
of deep-laid plots to commemorate the fiftieth anniversary of the
Sepoy Mutiny,[39] and *The Times* conjured up spine-tingling
images of an interracial bloodbath by serializing Sir Evelyn
Wood's *Revolt in Hindustan*,[40] Morley shattered "the delusion
that this country will turn a blind eye toward acts of repression.
This will be a fatal error. All such acts must be more guarded than
ever." [41]

As the facts of the Lajpat Rai case seeped out, Morley grew
painfully aware that his proclamations and Minto's policy were
equally indefensible.[42] It was "utterly abhorrent" to him that the
defendant had been denied legal counsel by his imperial cap-
tors,[43] and he made it unmistakably clear "that I would not sanction deportation except for a man of whom there was solid reason
to believe that violent disorder was the direct and deliberately
planned result of his action." [44] In the autumn of 1907, he pro-

38. Morley to Minto, May 16, 1907, Minto Papers. Morley's fear of a division in
the Commons on this issue proved happily unjustified; he reported to Minto after
his June 6 speech that "The Irish . . . told me beforehand that they would not
vote, seeing my years of friendship for them. The Labour people were sensible, as,
for that matter, they usually are. . . . If a division had come off, we should have
had not 30 men, I think, against us." Morley to Minto, June 7, 1907, Minto Papers.
39. Minto to Morley, August 14, 1907, Morley Papers.
40. The first of eighteen daily installments appeared on September 30, 1907.
41. Morley to Minto, June 13, 1907, Minto Papers.
42. When it was no longer "quite inadvisable to do so," Minto at last admitted
that he had "always had grave doubts as to the justice of Lajpat's imprisonment."
Minto to Morley, November 5, 1907, Morley Papers.
43. Morley to Minto, May 7, 1908, Minto Papers; also Minto to Lady Minto,
May 7, 1908, Minto Papers.
44. Morley to Minto, September 19, 1907, Minto Papers.

cured Lajpat Rai's release from a Burmese prison with promises
that "if Lajpat opens fire again, we shall certainly support you to
the uttermost in again putting his fire out by a douche of deportation." He left no doubt, however, that if the unfortunate occasion
presented itself, Whitehall would require ample warning and the
testimony of a more "infallible authority" than a provincial administrator.[45]

To his lasting embarrassment, Morley realized that he deserved
the taunts that obliging Radicals showered upon him. "My assent
to deportation," he remarked to Minto at the close of his second
year at the India Office, "has atoned for all youthful indiscretions
in Burke's direction, and Curzon magnanimously received me into
the bosom of the Imperialistic Church." [46] The Lajpat Rai affair
taught valuable lessons, all of which made it more difficult for the
Government of India to exercise a free hand and a strong arm. It
was essential, Morley discovered, to administer "a modest dose of
reproach" now and then in order to prevent an overreliance upon
"Reason of State . . . [which] benumbs political conscience and
obliterates the spirit of the law." [47] As a consequence, his directives on the subject of political deportation were successively more
stringent. At first he merely cautioned Minto against an "over-free
resort to 1818, however great the temptation," [48] but within the
year he announced: "I shall not be in a hurry to sanction Deportation any more, that is very certain; and . . . I should not be surprised if the Regulation of 1818 has to disappear." [49] Prevailing
tensions made it as impolitic to jettison this inherited weapon as to
employ it; instead it was left to rust in the Government of India's
armory, its point blunted by Morley's decree that it was to be han-
dled "with the utmost care and scruple—always, where the material is dubious, giving the suspected man the benefit of the
doubt." [50]

Morley did not have long to wait before his determination to
impede further use of the 1818 Regulation was put to the test.
With Lajpat Rai secure behind prison walls, the administrators of
other provinces began to clamor for permission to divest them-

45. Morley to Minto, November 8, 1907, Minto Papers.
46. Morley to Minto, December 26, 1907, Minto Papers.
47. Morley to Godley, January 15, 1908, Kilbracken Papers (I.O.L.).
48. Morley to Minto, June 13, 1907, Minto Papers.
49. Morley to Minto, April 15, 1908, Minto Papers.
50. Morley to Minto, January 13, 1909, Minto Papers.

selves of local mischief-makers. Minto diffidently appealed to Whitehall for leave to deport Bipin Chandra Pal, though he confided to his wife, who was visiting England, that "I am half afraid Morley will object." [51] His pessimism was promptly justified by a stinging riposte from Whitehall, forcing him to report sheepishly to Sir Arthur Lawley, Governor of Madras, who had initiated the request, that although he remained "in full sympathy with your wish," he hesitated to make matters more difficult for Morley, who "has backed me up well." [52] A year later, Minto accorded his approval to a petition from Sir A. H. L. Fraser, Lieutenant-Governor of Bengal, for permission to deport Aurobindo Ghose.[53] Again Morley refused his endorsement, and the Bengali Government was left to pursue the matter without success in the criminal courts.

Sir George Clarke, Governor of Bombay, with more dexterity and more tangible evidence to substantiate his case, instituted legal proceedings in July 1908 against B. G. Tilak who, at least to the satisfaction of *The Times,* was "the real protagonist of the campaign of violence in India." [54] After pleading his own defense for some twenty hours, quoting from such Brahminical texts as "Pundit" Morley's *On Compromise,*[55] Tilak was sentenced by a Parsi judge to a six-year imprisonment. Clarke, confident that his efforts had earned peace for his province and the undying gratitude of India's beleaguered moderates, [56] was amazed to witness Gokhale leading the agitation for Tilak's acquittal. Morley shared neither Clarke's complacency nor his surprise. "The conviction of Tilak fills me with anything but exultation," he told Minto.

51. Minto to Lady Minto, June 27, 1907, Minto Papers.

52. Minto to Lawley, May 31, 1907 [copy], Minto Papers.

53. Fraser assured the Viceroy that Ghose "is the ring-leader. He is able, cunning, fanatical. . . . He has been in the forefront of all, advising seditious writing and authorising murder. . . . [But] we cannot get evidence against him such as would secure his conviction in a Court." Fraser to Minto, May 26, 1908, Minto Papers. Two years later, Fraser recounted his tribulations in "Indian Unrest," *Nineteenth Century and After, 68* (1910), 747-54.

54. *The Times* (November 4, 1910), p. 10. The link between the political extremists and the bomb-throwers was a good deal more tenuous than *The Times* or, for that matter, most contemporaries took for granted. Clarke was, however, correct to assume that "The murder plots are only the natural and logical result of the movements educated men like Tilak, Savarkar . . . and Aurobindo Ghose started." Clarke to Morley, February 10, 1908, Morley Papers.

55. *The Trial of Bal Ganghadar Tilak* (Madras, 1908?) , p. 77.

56. Clarke to Morley, June 25, 1908, Morley Papers.

It is as inevitable as anything in the laws of political parties and factions can be, that the Moderates will be bound, by the necessity of the thing, to take his side against us. They may take his side vehemently, or they may take it with reserve, but they are sure to quarrel with us about it.[57]

Like the moderate congressmen, Morley understood that an extremist martyr posed a greater threat than any seditious message that Tilak could disseminate, and he doubted the value of Clarke's Pyrrhic victory in the Bombay criminal courts. Moreover, he nursed bitter regrets that no attempt had been made to obtain his counsel; "if you had done me the honour to seek my advice as well as that of your lawyers," he castigated Clarke, "I am clear that I should have been for leaving him alone." [58]

For his part, Morley would have preferred to bury the whole affair. The best solution, he jested to his private secretary, would have been to conciliate Tilak with a formal invitation to the Governor's annual garden party.[59] Singularly unimpressed by the fact that the Governor had taken pains to follow instructions by submitting his case to a recognized court of law, he reasoned that Tilak's writings were undoubtedly "bad enough to warrant a prosecution, if you want one on general political grounds; but not at all so bad as to make a prosecution inevitable, if on general political grounds you would rather have done without one." [60] Clarke offered to exculpate his administration by publishing the court's verdict against Tilak, but Morley informed him that: "The language of judges where issues of political expediency are involved seldom impresses me." [61] And Morley was no less scornful about the justice of the case in a letter to Minto: "The jury is most obviously a packed jury; it is evidently not the goddess of Chance

57. Morley to Minto, July 24, 1908, Minto Papers.

58. Morley to Clarke, July 31, 1908, Morley Papers; also Morley to Clarke, July 3, 1908, Morley Papers.

59. F. A. Hirtzel's Diary, July 24, 1908, 3, 67; this is obviously a variation upon Clarke's earlier remark: "I would infinitely prefer to have asked him to dinner, and to have it all out with him face to face; but this was not possible, as one of his friends admitted to me." Clarke to Morley, June 24, 1908, Morley Papers.

60. Morley to Minto, July 16, 1908, Minto Papers. "So far, I have heard no particulars," Minto admitted on July 23, but this did not prevent him from expressing full confidence that Tilak's indictment "will have an excellent effect." He added, "Luckily, there is in this case no appeal." Minto to Morley, July 23, 1908, Morley Papers.

61. Morley to Clarke, July 31, 1908 [telegram], Morley Papers.

that has brought about the singular result of seven Europeans and two Parsees, and *not one Hindu."* [62]

But what alarmed Morley most was the fact that Clarke had operated well within constitutional bounds and had demonstrated to attentive fellow bureaucrats the way to circumvent Whitehall's authority. The alacrity with which other administrators mastered the Governor of Bombay's lesson subjected the Morley-Minto relationship to new strains. A spate of anarchic violence in the spring of 1908 was met by severe retaliation on the part of local authorities, whose "thundering sentences" aroused Morley's "deepest concern and dismay." He complained to Minto of one case in which

> stone-throwers in Bombay are getting *twelve months!* This is really outrageous. . . . We must keep order, but excess of severity is not the path to order. On the contrary, it is the path to the bomb. It will be insupportable if you, who are a sound Whig, and I, who am an "authoritaire" Radical (so they say), go down to our graves (I first) as imitators of Eldon, Sidmouth, the Six Acts and all the other men and policies which we were both . . . brought up to abhor.[63]

Minto, however, refused to intervene in provincial legal proceedings; instead he offered assurances that due respect had been paid to the process of law, and he expressed doubts whether "a year's imprisonment for stone-throwing [was] the least too severe." [64] Morley, satisfied with neither argument, retorted that it was essential to consider Indian opinion, the stifling of which would prove disastrous. He proposed to Minto "an exhibition of Mercy towards common offenders" to demonstrate "that you are wholly free from any atom of ferocity where ordinary wrong-doers are concerned," [65] and lectured Clarke that "Governments become useless whenever the governed are voiceless. That's the very root of liberalism in its widest and deepest sense. Let us stick to that, and don't let us think the agitators (not even Tilak) all perversity and wrong." [66]

Morley's objections to the punitive measures of 1908 were both humanitarian and pragmatic. Aside from his marked distaste for

---

62. Morley to Minto, July 16, 1908, Minto Papers.
63. Morley to Minto, July 30, 1908, Minto Papers.
64. Minto to Morley, August 18, 1908, Morley Papers.
65. Morley to Minto, October 7, 1908, Minto Papers.
66. Morley to Clarke, September 18, 1908, Morley Papers.

"Russian" methods, he tended to doubt their efficacy. His Irish notebook, to which he constantly referred, reinforced this view. Twenty-seven years earlier, at the time of Parnell's internment at Kilmainham Gaol, he had agreed with Goldwin Smith that political arrests were "at best a sad and somewhat ignominious necessity," and told the readers of the *Pall Mall Gazette:* "If all the agitators are put in gaol, agitation must necessarily become extinct. But we cannot keep them in gaol for ever, and many who enter prison [as] reformers leave it as revolutionists." [67] When Lord Minto solicited special powers to imprison suspects without bail, Morley reminded him of the Irish Coercion Act of 1881, which "was a gross failure, and ended in the Phoenix Park murders of 1882." [68] And Irish precedents provided ample testimony that an overindulgence in coercion would deny reform legislation the cordial reception that was vital to its success. For this reason, above all, Morley considered it "idle for us to pretend to the Natives that we wish to understand their sentiment, and satisfy the demands of 'honest reformers,' and all the rest of our benignant talk, and yet silently acquiesce in all these violent sentences." [69]

The promulgation of the reforms in the House of Lords on December 17, 1908, failed either to abate extremist outrages or to temper the Government of India's responses. While Parliament debated the provisions of the proposed legislation, Morley endeavored to make certain that Indian bureaucrats would not defy the letter of the projected reforms as well as their spirit. "If only we do not overdo deportation," he cautioned Minto, "I trust things will mend." [70] He vetoed suggestions to deprive former deportees of their right to obtain political office under the revised system,[71] and, for the sake of that system, he unleashed an offensive to disown deportation as a disciplinary measure and to obtain the prompt release of its current victims.

Undoubtedly, as Minto never ceased to allege, parliamentary pressures weighed heavily upon his partner. Morley reported on May 5 that some 150 M.P.s had petitioned the Prime Minister against deportation: "Asquith will give them a judicious reply,"

67. *Pall Mall Gazette* (October 14, 1881) , p. 1.
68. Morley to Minto, November 19, 1908 [telegram], Morley Papers.
69. Morley to Minto, August 26, 1908, Minto Papers.
70. Morley to Minto, December 19, 1908 [telegram], Morley Papers.
71. Morley to Minto, April 19, 1909 [telegram], Morley Papers.

Minto was assured, "but you will not be able to deport any more of your suspects—that is quite clear." [72] Later that month, Morley predicted "a pretty heavy gale . . . in the H. of C. about Deportation [which] shows every sign of blowing harder as time goes." [73] Yet by June 10, it was evident that the gathering storm he had sighted on the parliamentary horizon contained more thunder than lightning. F. W. Mackarness, who had unsuccessfully attempted to tack an amendment to the previous Royal Address,[74] took advantage of a sparse House to introduce a bill against deportation. "It was," Morley informed Minto,

> carried through first reading without a division, for if the Government had divided, they might have been beaten. . . . The Government will be asked to assent to a second reading, [which is] tantamount to a vote of censure on you and me, and therefore you can be pretty sure that we shall not assent to anything of the kind.[75]

These carping attacks frightened the Indian secretary more than he cared to admit, but substantially less than the Viceroy assumed. "You are mistaken in laying all the blame on Parliament," Morley remonstrated. "If the Cabinet had gone the other way, nothing would have induced *me* to assent." [76] His primary concern remained the fate of the reform bill, whose long imminence was about to end. Gokhale, whose direct appeals to Whitehall invariably influenced Morley's mind in India's favor, impressed him with the need to preface the reforms announcement with the release of political deportees.[77] Morley took the moderate leader's

---

72. Morley to Minto, May 5, 1909, Minto Papers.

73. Morley to Minto, May 27, 1909, Minto Papers.

74. *Parliamentary Debates*, 4th ser., *1*, cols. 807 ff. (February 24, 1909) .

75. Morley to Minto, June 10, 1909, Minto Papers; see *Parliamentary Debates*, 4th ser., *6*, cols. 297 ff. (June 10, 1909) .

76. Morley to Minto, May 13, 1909, Minto Papers; also Morley to Minto, March 17, 1910, Minto Papers.

77. See Morley to Minto, October 14, 1909 and October 27, 1909 [telegram], Minto Papers. There can be no doubt that Gokhale's previous reticence on this issue had been interpreted by Morley as a tacit endorsement of Minto's arguments: "The Indian politicians make no serious clamour about Deportation, etc.," he told Frederic Harrison: "Any Indian will tell you that, when M[ackarness] put down a motion to the effect that Coercion endangered and undid Reforms, he was talking flat nonsense. Why should an English lawyer make difficulties (or try to make them) when the responsible leaders in the country concerned make none worth speaking of?" Morley to Harrison, March 14, 1909, Harrison Papers.

point that "continuous detention makes a mockery of the language that we are going to use about reforms," [78] and he argued that a magnanimous gesture would "be a mark of confidence in our policy and our position." [79] Minto, on the other hand, remained convinced that such a move would be universally interpreted as an admission of British weakness.[80]

To a less appreciable extent, Morley's intensified campaign for the release of deportees reflected an outpouring of indignation that had accumulated over a five-year period. By this time he had come to realize the futility of gentle prodding. "The sentences in India are outrageous," he angrily protested on September 22, and he proclaimed his intention "to overhaul them thoroughly and offer a strong pronouncement to you . . . unless Heaven and the House of Lords, which are by no means identical, send me into the wilderness." [81] Within a month, he made good his threat by dispatching an official request for the immediate release of deportees.[82]

Lord Minto resented this "strong order" [83] and cabled his dissent.[84] With the unanimous support of his Council, he promised to bow to any formal instructions he received from His Majesty's Government, but refused to be "held responsible for the results." [85] Conceding that Minto had presented his "case with remarkable force," [86] Morley laid the matter before the Cabinet. "I said that I should be content with the release of *two*," he recounted. "The Cabinet, however, led by Grey, were against making two bites of a cherry and were unanimous in pressing you to let out the whole

78. Morley to Minto, October 20, 1909 [telegram], Morley Papers.
79. Morley to Minto, August 20, 1909, Minto Papers.
80. Minto to Morley, September 1, 1909, Morley Papers.
81. Morley to Minto, September 22, 1909, Minto Papers.
82. Morley to Minto, October 20, 1909 [telegram], Morley Papers.
83. Minto to Sir Herbert Risley, October 21, 1909, Minto Papers.
84. Minto to Morley, October 22, 1909 [telegram], Morley Papers; also Minto to Morley, October 21, 1909, Morley Papers.
85. Minto to Morley, November 2, 1909 [telegram], Morley Papers.
86. Morley to Minto, November 9, 1909, Minto Papers. "I comfort myself, in my disquiet at differing from you," Morley professed, "by the reflection that perhaps the Spanish Viceroys in the Netherlands, the Austrian Viceroy in Venice, the Bourbon in the Two Sicilies, used reasoning not wholly dissimilar and not much less forcible. Forgive this affronting parallel. It is only the sally of a man who is himself occasionally compared to Strafford, King John, King Charles, Nero, and Tiberius."

batch, when you launch the Regulations." [87] News of the Government's decision, including the strategic reference to the Foreign Secretary, reached Minto on November 13, the day that an attempt was made to assassinate him during a visit to Ahmedabad.[88] Though he did not hestitate to announce that he "attach[ed] no political importance whatever to [the] incident," [89] it profoundly influenced his subsequent policy, especially in the light of similar outrages that followed.

A series of bomb explosions, one of which hit its human target at Nasik, convinced Minto that it was inadvisable to release the deportees on the first day of the new year, as he had previously promised.[90] Morley was "very dissatisfied" with Minto's revised timetable, and he made no effort to conceal his indignation during an interview with Sir Harvey Adamson, a member of the viceregal council; he expressed regrets "that he had not definitely insisted on release a few months ago when the Cabinet declared for it," and reiterated his determination to pinpoint a specific release date.[91] On January 22, he reminded Minto:

> You were prepared to release on 1st January when the [legislative council] elections would be over. They are now over, so that plea for delay vanishes. Then came Nasik. That was a good argument for delay, but not indefinite. I have come to the conclusion that detention cannot any longer be justified.[92]

Adamson embarked for India carrying the Secretary of State's unqualified edict for the prompt discharge of all deported political offenders. "This is the last letter that I shall inflict upon you in this matter," Morley promised, "but I cannot budge from my case,

87. Morley to Minto, October 29, 1909, Minto Papers.

88. "It is rather curious," Lady Minto reflected, "that on the very day on which Morley did his best to force Rolly to release the deportees, putting such powerful pressure as I think few men would have resisted, such as the opinion of the whole of the Cabinet, and especially Edward Grey, that the proof of the sedition that has been preached by the deportees should have resulted in this bomb outrage on ourselves." Lady Minto's Indian Journals, November 16, 1909, *1909-ii*, 328.

89. Minto to Morley, November 14, 1909 [telegram], Morley Papers.

90. Minto to Morley, December 26, 1909 [telegram], and January 1, 1910 [telegram], Morley Papers.

91. Adamson to Dunlop Smith, January 3, 1910, Minto Papers.

92. Morley to Minto, January 22, 1910 [telegram], Morley Papers.

and the clock has struck. After you have seen Adamson, please let me know whether you accede to my private request, or whether I shall be forced to official instruction."

Morley's "last letter" in this bitter debate was sufficient to convey the full implications of the affair. "The question between us two . . . may, if we don't take care, become what the Americans would call ugly," he warned.

> You had nine men locked up a year ago by *lettre de cachet*, because you believed them to be criminally connected with criminal plots, and because you expected their arrest to check these plots. For a certain time, it looked as if the *coup* were effective, and were justified by the result. In all this, I think, we were perfectly right. Then you come, by and by, upon what you regard as a great anarchist conspiracy for sedition and murder; and you warn me that you may soon apply to me for sanction of further arbitrary arrest and detention on a larger scale. I ask whether this process implies that the nine *détenus* are to be kept on under lock and key indefinitely because you have found out a murder-plot contrived not by them, but by other people. You say . . . their continued detention will frighten evil-doers generally. That's the Russian argument: by packing off train-loads of suspects to Siberia, we'll terrify the anarchists out of their wits, and all will come out right. That policy did not work out brilliantly in Russia, and did not save the lives of the Trepoffs, nor did it save Russia from a Duma, the very thing that the Trepoffs and the rest of the "offs" deprecated and detested.[93]

Morley was more incensed by viceregal procrastination than his syllogisms might suggest. He speculated to Clarke that "a personal change in the G. of I.—which cannot be very long delayed—may be the means of some good." [94] Minto too concluded that their difficulties were largely personal, but he attributed them to Morley's pathological quest for supreme powers and his lamentable inability to withstand pressures from the parliamentary left.[95]

Before the Viceroy finally submitted, he made a last effort to convince the Home Government that the Indian situation was

93. Morley to Minto, January 27, 1910, Minto Papers.
94. Morley to Clarke, February 2, 1910, Morley Papers.
95. Minto to Lansdowne, February 3, 1910 [copy], Minto Papers.

steadily deteriorating and that martial law was required. Morley replied that the mere suggestion "makes my hair stand on end," [96] and before the debate could be carried further, Minto had contradicted his own arguments.[97] On February 5, Minto notified Whitehall that the deportees would be released as soon as the 1910 press bill had cleared the legislative council, "unless something unforeseen renders it impossible." [98] Morley confessed that "the relief to me is immense." [99] With the valuable endorsement of its Indian members, the council approved the press restrictions on February 8, and within twenty-four hours, Minto fulfilled his promise by ordering the prison gates opened.

For administrative as well as personal reasons, Minto perpetrated the myth that he had taken this fateful step on his own initiative and not because his arm had been twisted. "I expect our decision to release them must have been somewhat of a surprise to you, though I felt sure it would be a pleasant surprise," he informed Morley,[100] who had previously received no less than three telegrams to the same effect.[101] Minto related his considerations in a memorandum to members of his council dated February 22, in which he stressed the highly dubious fact that his decision had been the result of solitary soul-searching; [102] he admitted, however, that he was "especially anxious . . . to avoid any appearance or any documental suggestion that the Government of India had acted under pressure." [103] Indeed, Minto appears to have been as reluctant to admit to himself as to others that his hand had been forced. To Lord Lansdowne, a former Viceroy and an intimate friend, he insisted that "Morley had nothing to do with it; as I have already told you, he was constantly pressing me to let them out, but I refused to do so before I thought it was safe. When I did

---

96. Morley to Minto, February 3, 1910, Minto Papers.

97. Minto to Morley, February 9, 1910, Morley Papers.

98. Minto to Morley, February 5, 1910 [telegram], Morley Papers.

99. Morley to Minto, February 6, 1910 [telegram], Morley Papers.

100. Minto to Morley, February 9, 1910, Morley Papers.

101. Minto to Morley, February 5, 8, and 9, 1910 [telegrams], Morley Papers.

102. If this was at all the case, Minto merely reached the conclusions which Morley had been preaching for weeks. Minto's alleged criteria were, in fact, virtual recapitulations of Morley's recent pronouncements on the matter. See Minto to Clarke, February 15, 1910 [copy], Minto Papers; also A. F. Pinhey, Minto's private secretary, to E. J. Buck, February 10, 1910 [copy], Minto Papers.

103. Memorandum to Council on the Release of Deportees, February 22, 1910, Minto Papers.

think so, I let them out on 'my own.' " [104] Yet it is inconceivable that Minto could seriously have doubted Morley's contribution to his decision; in any event, Morley suffered from no such illusion.

Encouraged by his success and eager to embellish the reforms declaration, Morley suggested the proclamation of a general amnesty on the occasion of either King Edward's funeral or the 1911 coronation.[105] But there was too little time and too much antagonism between the two statesmen for Minto to embark upon another grand design. It was the latter's declared intention not to budge until he could be certain "that India is at peace, and that the murder-clubs are done with, and that the press will be decorous and reverential." Morley could not resist deriding such an attitude, which he likened to that "of Aesop's rustic with no bridge, waiting until the river has flowed away." [106]

During the final months of their collaboration, Minto could perceive no justification for dismantling the complex, coercive machine which, he proudly pointed out, had restored order to Indian society.[107] Morley, on the other hand, was not nearly so confident that India's time of troubles had ended; nor did he believe that, in the long run, coercive techniques would prove any more successful halfway around the globe than they had across the choppy Irish straits.

104. Minto to Lansdowne, March 24, 1910 [copy], Minto Papers.
105. Morley to Minto, May 12, 1910, Minto Papers.
106. Morley to Minto, July 27, 1910, Minto Papers.
107. Early in 1910, Minto assured Morley that they had weathered the extremist storm and that future incidents, "if they occur, will be rather in the nature of thuggism than political crimes." Soon after, he furnished testimony from Gokhale, S. P. Sinha, and "in fact everyone whose opinion is worth having" that the Indian "political position is . . . very much improved." Minto to Morley, February 9 and 17, 1910, Morley Papers.

10   Reforms and Apprehensions

Reviewing the collected works of Lord Morley in 1921, a critic for the *Times Literary Supplement* was moved to recall

> a time, at which Lord Morley can afford to smile, when a Chancellor of the Exchequer compared Mr. Morley to "that atrocious young man," as Sainte-Beuve called [St. Just], and devout Tories made each other's flesh creep by the prospect of a Liberal Government in which, holding high office, he would set up a guillotine for his political opponents in Trafalgar-square.[1]

He did not exaggerate.

Yet as Morley's career entered its final phase and British politics and society became increasingly democratized, it was evident that Radical John was hardly the rabble-rousing Jacobin who had outraged mid-Victorian sensibilities by campaigning for disestablishment and secular education, championing Mazzini and Gambetta, and printing a reference to the Almighty in his journal without the conventional capital "G." His essay *On Compromise,* which had "found its unexpected way into Urdu and Gujerati"[2] as well as a dozen less exotic languages, had seemed "too full of passion" when first published in 1874, but "lost its fiery savour" by the turn of the century. [3] Yet many continued to mistake this thirty-year-old literary exercise as Morley's professional credo, not realizing that times and the author had both changed. "To say [Morley's] political career will not always stand the inflexible moral tests of his essay on Compromise is true enough," J. H. Morgan, a journalist friend, tried to explain,

1. *Times Literary Supplement* (February 10, 1921) , p. 82.
2. Morley, *Recollections, 1,* 102.
3. Augustine Birrell, "Lord Morley of Blackburn, O.M.," *Empire Review, 38* (1923) , 1363.

but it has to be remembered that he wrote that denunciation of political casuistry long before he entered politics, and, having once entered them, made no pretence of applying its precepts to a world in which, by that time, he had found that they had, and could have, little place.[4]

During the early years of the twentieth century, with the arrival at Westminster of a contingent of younger and more vociferous Radical M.P.s, the surviving giants of nineteenth-century radicalism were dwarfed by comparison. "Morley was a Radical," Lord Haldane subsequently reflected, "but he was a Radical politician with a highly critical spirit. There was a good deal of the Conservative element in him." [5] Morley, for one, would have readily seconded his friend's view. He keenly resented Andrew Carnegie's transatlantic "political massage," intended to

> [restore] me to that vigorous revolutionary youth which you suppose to have departed from me. . . . The man whose first literary task and first success was a glorification of Burke can never have been at heart a revolutionary champion. Be sure of that, and reproach me no more with being "venerable" and out of date.[6]

As proof of his levelheadedness, Morley cited his terms as Irish secretary, and asked: "Why had I not overturned Dublin Castle until not one brick remained upon another?" His answer also accounted for his self-restraint at the India Office where, to a more appreciable extent, it proved impossible to "[sweep] away the mass of vested interests guarded by Statutes, Treasury Minutes, Orders-in-Council, and all the other bulwarks and bastions of the civil service." [7]

Tory journalists and politicians, who tended to appreciate Morley's sentiments and the Government of India's impregnability,

4. "The Personality of Lord Morley," *Quarterly Review, 241* (1924), 347.

5. Haldane, *An Autobiography* (London, 1929), p. 95. Lord Lytton arrived at the same conclusion a half-century earlier, when he remarked that "the unparliamentary Radicals, who are labouring to keep alive a sentient soul in English society, are infinitely more conservative in the only worthy sense than the so-called Conservative Party, which can see nothing better to do than to serve as an awkward squad in the great Phillistine Army." Lytton to Morley, March 16, 1871, Lytton Papers.

6. Morley to Carnegie, October 9, 1909, Morley-Carnegie Correspondence.

7. Morley, *Recollections, 2,* 45-46.

were not especially alarmed when the poacher was installed as gamekeeper in 1905. The editor of the *Spectator*, confident that Morley was "eminently a cool-headed and conservative statesman," assured nervous readers that they had nothing to fear.[8] An anonymous contributor to the *Quarterly Review* performed the feat of distinguishing Morley's benign anti-imperialism from the malignant variety:

> His Little Englandism is unlike that of the more blatant adherents of that craven creed. It is negative and not positive. Never has he been known to subscribe to the washy sentimentalism which affects to believe that if the strong man would only throw away his weapons no one would spoil his goods. . . . No imperialist, we feel assured, would resist with any more dogged and unyielding resolution any invasion of British territory than the present Secretary of State for India.[9]

Contemplating the possible alternatives, St. John Brodrick hoped that Morley would follow him at the India Office: "If John Morley is my successor, I shall not have much difficulty in bringing things before him. I only hope it may not be Bryce." [10] Sir Dighton Probyn, Keeper of the Privy Purse, greeted Morley's appointment with good-natured skepticism: "Heaven only knows what he may want later," he told Lord Minto, "but *at present* I do not think he wishes to 'give up India to the Indians' !!" [11]

The fact that right-wing spokesmen gauged Morley's predilections more accurately than either Indian nationalists or their parliamentary allies implies neither duplicity nor indifference on the part of the Secretary of State, against whom time and the cumbersome machinery of Indian administration were allied. Morley lacked sufficient vigor and self-assurance to move as decisively as his impatient critics demanded. More importantly, he lacked an overall sense of purpose. As a result of these combined deficiencies, Morley, as Ramsay MacDonald observed, "introduced a gentler hand, but not a new policy." [12] Winston Churchill, whose subsequent Indian views were admittedly influenced by Morley's argu-

---

8. *Spectator* (December 9 and 16, 1905) , pp. 964, 1025.

9. "A Tesselated Ministry," *Quarterly Review*, 206 (1907) , 278-79.

10. Brodrick to Lamington, December 8, 1905, Lamington Papers.

11. Probyn to Minto, March 9, 1906, Minto Papers.

12. J. Ramsay MacDonald, *The Government of India* (London, 1919) , p. 58.

ments, "lived to see the chiefs of the Conservative Party rush in where Radical Morley feared to tread." [13]

Over the decades, Morley had resigned his honorary membership in the so-called "Perish India" sect,[14] but his countrymen's activities on the subcontinent continued to fill him with misgivings. "The more I read and think about British rule in India," he confessed to Lord Hardinge, "the more stupendous and the more glorious it appears. . . . Only let me be frank, and add, as I always do, that I am never quite sure that if Clive had been beaten at Plassey, it might have been no bad thing either for Indians or English." [15] Though he gloried in his resplendent imperial plumage, Morley remained convinced that "a foreign Protectorate throttles spontaneous improvement." [16] This he saw demonstrated in Egypt, where the presence of an alien authority made it "impossible . . . for a Native Administration to grow up with strength and confidence in its own resources." [17]

Despite his earlier tract against the evils of political compromise, Morley had long since come round to L. T. Hobhouse's view that: "The first duty of statesmen was not with general principles, but . . . to make the best of the actual situation." As Hobhouse argued,

> it might conceivably have been better for both countries that India had never been conquered, [but] there was the Indian Empire in being, a realized fact which nothing could get over, a responsibility that could no more be shaken off than the responsibility for Cornwall.[18]

Britain's honor and India's well-being jointly precluded a hasty withdrawal from Indian soil. "How should we look in the face of the civilised world," Morley asked his constituents, "if we turned our back upon our duty and upon our task? How should we bear the savage stings of our own conscience when, as assuredly we

---

13. Churchill, *Great Contemporaries*, pp. 80-81.

14. At a Guildhall banquet in the spring of 1906, Joseph Chamberlain asked Morley: "You don't belong to the 'perish India' Party?" According to Sir Frederic Hirtzel, the Indian Secretary replied: "You and I both belonged to a party which said that, but I no longer think it." F. A. Hirtzel's Diary, May 17, 1906, *I, 45*.

15. Morley to Hardinge, April 11, 1911, Morley Papers.

16. [Morley], "A Political Epilogue," *Fortnightly Review*, n.s., *24* (1878), 319.

17. *Parliamentary Debates*, 3d. ser., *284*, cols. 1031 ff. (February 15, 1884).

18. L. T. Hobhouse, *Democracy and Reaction* (New York, 1905), pp. 26-27.

should, we heard through the dark distances the roar and scream of confusion and carnage in India?" [19] By this late date, he had learned to accept the "second best" in political life.[20] "I did not choose India," he reminded Andrew Carnegie. "I have no illusions about it. I know we are walking in the dark there. But as I drew that lot when the present Government was made, I must make the best of it." [21]

As India's parliamentary guardian, Morley regarded his imperial ward with an ambivalent mixture of pride and remorse that was unmistakably Gladstonian. The Grand Old Man, his eye fixed upon rising military appropriations "which might well have been avoided," had informed Lord Ripon that "I am one of those who think that to our actual as distinguished from the reputed strength of the Empire, India adds nothing." Yet Gladstone, like his disciple a quarter century later, had seen no reason to grudge his labors merely because the situation was regrettable and the outlook dim:

> We have undertaken a most arduous but a most noble duty. We are pledged to India, I may say to mankind . . . and we have no choice but to apply ourselves to the accomplishment of the work, the redemption of the pledge, with every faculty we possess.[22]

An inexorable belief in the ultimate futility of the British Raj had discouraged the formulators of nineteenth-century Liberal doctrine from applying their talents to a practicable definition of British aims in and for India. As both the perpetrator and heir of this distinguished tradition, Morley mirrored this shortsightedness. During past decades, he had kept at arm's length from Indian controversies, with the notable exception of border aggressions. Alfred Lyall, a frequent contributor to the *Fortnightly Review* and eventually Morley's consultant at Whitehall, had regretted Morley's decision in 1894 to "remain faithful to Ireland" by refusing Lord Rosebery's offer of the Indian secretaryship: "I would it had been otherwise, for we much need some one who can stand up

19. Speech at Arbroath, October 21, 1907, *The Times* (October 22, 1907), p. 10.
20. See Morley's speech at the Carnegie Institute, Pittsburgh, November 3, 1904, *The New York Times* (November 27, 1904), p. 8.
21. Morley to Carnegie, December 29, 1908, Morley-Carnegie Correspondence.
22. Gladstone to Ripon, November 24, 1881, Ripon Papers, Add. MSS. 43,515, fols. 5-6.

effectively for India in the House of Commons." [23] Indian politicians too had earnestly solicited his assistance and had come away with heavy hearts and empty hands, unable to understand his silence on matters which appeared to satisfy his philosophic criteria. In 1889, an "agent of the India Congress people" invited Morley to endorse proposals to reform the Indian legislative councils, but he was reluctant to divert his attention from pressing Irish matters.[24] Three years later, when the India Councils Bill was debated in the House, Gladstone accorded it his warm approval, but Morley held scrupulously aloof.

When G.K. Gokhale visited England in 1897 to testify before the Welby Commission on finance, he made certain to pay a visit to Morley, of whom he professed to be "not only an admirer but a pupil." [25] But Gokhale, as he revealed to a friend, was primarily concerned with Morley the politician, not Morley the philosopher: "My object in going to see him was to enlist his sympathy on the side of our aspiration, to which he has been unaccountably cold." On May 13, the Indian leader enjoyed "about an hour's conversation" with Morley, who provided dire prophecies rather than promises of assistance:

> He spoke to me very frankly on the subject and said that somehow or other he had got an impression that a terrible catastrophe was in store for England in connection with India. It was not a conclusion reasoned out in any way, but merely a vague intuitive presentiment.[26]

Barely old enough to recollect contemporary accounts of the horrors at Delhi and Cawnpore, Morley belonged to a generation of politicians whose attitudes toward India had been molded by memories of the mutiny. The events of 1857 had registered a pro-

23. Lyall to Morley, n.d., cited in Sir Mortimer Durand, *Life of the Rt. Hon. Sir Alfred Comyn Lyall* (London, 1913), p. 359. The sincerity with which Rosebery offered the India Office may be doubted; see Morley, *Recollections*, 2, 18-20; also James, *Rosebery*, Appendix 3, p. 512; Lewis Harcourt's Journals, March 4, 1894, Harcourt Papers.

24. Morley's apathy is evident in a letter to Sir William Harcourt written the following day in which he related that Congress leaders "would be content with a Parliamentary Committee to inquire into the one demand of representation on the Legislative Councils. That is manageable, and could be done in one session." Morley to Harcourt, February 9, 1889 [copy], Harcourt Papers.

25. Gokhale to Morley, May 9, 1897 [copy], courtesy S. R. Mehrotra.

26. Gokhale to G. V. Joshi, May 14, 1897 [copy], courtesy S. R. Mehrotra.

found impression upon Gladstone, who, less than a year before his death, implored Sir Arthur Godley "to scrutinize all controversial facts in India with the utmost care, after our disgraceful miscarriage in the matter of the greased cartridges, so very old in date and yet so recently (and unblushingly) made known." [27] Richard Cobden and John Bright had each cited the mutiny as evidence of the utter hopelessness of British rule in India, and Morley filled a score of pages in his biography of the former with quotations from their correspondence on the subject. "One stands aghast and dumbfounded," Cobden told his collaborator, "at the reflection that, after a century of intercourse with us, the natives of India suddenly exhibit themselves greater savages than any of the North American Indians who have been brought into contact with the white race." [28] But Cobden, shocked even more by the severity of British reprisals, explained to Bright that

> we seem in danger of forgetting our own Christianity and descending to a level with these monsters who have startled the world with their deeds. It is terrible to see our middle-class journals and speakers calling for the destruction of Delhi and the indiscriminate massacre of prisoners.[29]

In the sanctuary of the India Office, Morley kept his wits about him and discounted frantic Anglo-Indian warnings that Indians would commemorate the fiftieth anniversary of the sepoy revolt with an interracial bloodbath.[30] He remained justly confident that India had come too far along the path of westernization to resort to the futile barbarities of 1857.[31] Nine years earlier, his fears that the centennial of the Wolfe Tone rebellion would unleash an Irish uprising had proved unfounded,[32] and he had learned from

27. Gladstone to Godley, July 9, 1897, Kilbracken Papers, Add. MSS. 44,901, fol. 97. "Thank God for the recovery of Delhi," Gladstone wrote to Sir Arthur Hamilton-Gordon on October 29, 1857, cited in Paul Knaplund, ed., *Gladstone-Gordon Correspondence* (Philadelphia, 1961), p. 28.

28. Cobden to Bright, August 24, 1857, cited in Morley, *The Life of Richard Cobden* (London, 1905), p. 672.

29. Cobden to Bright, September 22, 1857, cited in ibid., p. 676.

30. In a speech before the viceregal council, Lord Kitchener announced: "My officers tell me that it is all right, but they said the same thing in the Mutiny days till they were shot by their own men." Cited in Minto to Morley, May 16, 1907, Morley Papers.

31. *Recollections*, 2, 154.

32. Morley to Harcourt, January 6, 1898, Harcourt Papers; also Morley to Spencer, January 7, 1898, Spencer Papers.

his mistake. But Morley, whose career had been compounded of campaigns against one imperial outrage or another, accepted Cobden's view that it was criminal for Britain to expend her money, men, and principles to achieve imperial grandeur; he agreed that Englishmen could not "play the part of despot and butcher [in the Empire] without finding our character deteriorated at home." [33] The Boer War, for example, had demonstrated that national ignominy and political disorder were the inevitable consequences of unbridled jingoism. Although he was deeply concerned with the moral and legal rights of subject peoples, his preoccupation remained—throughout his career—the defense of British institutions. A series of "revolting and atrocious" executions in Egypt during the spring of 1906 elicited a typically Cobdenite protest from Morley, who "thought there was great risk of our contact with barbarous races reducing our methods to the level of theirs." [34] Wary of possible repercussions upon British morality, he attempted to refute the argument advanced by numerous Anglo-Indians that leniency would be misinterpreted as weakness by non-Europeans. "We are not Orientals," he declared;

> that is the root of the matter. . . . We English, Scotch, and Irish are in India because we are not Orientals. . . . We are representatives not of Oriental civilisation but of Western civilisation, of its methods, its principles, its practices; and I for one will not be hurried into an excessive haste for repression by the argument that Orientals do not understand this toleration.[35]

If Morley redressed a fair number of Indian grievances and encouraged the growth of an Indian national consciousness, he did so with English political and social considerations uppermost in mind. This, in large measure, was the essence of his so-called Little Englandism.

---

33. Cobden to George Combe, May 16, 1858, cited in Morley, *Cobden*, p. 680; Burke, too, "hated the arbitrary and despotic savour which clung about the English assumptions over the colonies." Morley, *Edmund Burke*, p. 146.

34. F. A. Hirtzel's Diary, June 29, 1906, *1*, 57. "Is it not just possible," Cobden had asked, "that we may become corrupted at home by the reaction of arbitrary political maxims in the East upon our domestic politics, just as Greece and Rome were demoralised by their contact with Asia?" Cobden to William Hargreaves, August 4, 1860, cited in Morley, *Life of Cobden*, p. 825.

35. Speech at Arbroath, October 21, 1907, *The Times* (October 22, 1907), p. 10.

Engaged in a concentrated effort to render the Empire safe for British democracy, Morley had little time and even less inclination to render democracy safe for Indian consumption. As one Indian critic noted, his

> vision of the future government of India seems neither wide nor clear, and lacks the wisdom of the prophet and the seer. The flight of imagination which inspired Bentinck and Macaulay to dip into the future and draw a picture of self-governing India is conspicuous by its absence in the intensely prosaic temperament of Mr. Morley.[36]

Unable to devise a creditable method to extricate Great Britain from her Indian commitments, Morley grappled with India's problems on a day-to-day basis, hoping that successive gestures of good will would compensate for the lack of a well-conceived design. He adopted as his personal motto a remark by Ferencz Deák, the Hungarian statesman: "I can answer for today; I can do pretty well for tomorrow; the day after tomorrow I leave to Providence." [37] Extremely reluctant to "loosen the bolts," he assured a much-relieved Viceroy that: "If we can hatch some plan and policy for half a generation that will be something; and if for a whole generation, that will be better." [38]

Like Cobden and Gladstone, Morley cherished no illusions that a single inoculation of liberalism would answer all India's needs and thereby guarantee the permanence of British rule. "Personally," he confided to Sir Guy Fleetwood Wilson, "I have no exorbitant faith that any political reforms whatever will carry India very far along the rough road in front of her." [39] He told Sir George Clarke:

> I don't see why the same causes that foment sedition today should not continue to foment it the day after tomorrow, and for many another long day to come. I cannot for the life of me see, so long as the general conditions remain what they are,

36. P. C. Ray, "Editorial Reflections," *Indian World* (August 1906), p. 197.

37. Morley to Minto, July 15, 1909, Minto Papers.

38. Morley to Minto, April 17, 1907, Minto Papers.

39. Morley to Fleetwood Wilson, January 13, 1909, Fleetwood Wilson Papers. In a letter to John Bright, Cobden had disclaimed any "faith in the doctrine that by any possible reforms we can govern India well, or continue to hold it permanently." Cobden to Bright, August 24, 1857, cited in Morley, *Life of Cobden*, p. 674; also Cobden to Bright, September 22, 1857, cited in ibid., p. 677.

how the unrest itself is going to vanish. The people may not hate us, but as the wisest rulers of British India have said again and again, they don't love us and they never will.[40]

The course of Irish nationalism, flowing in channels cut by previous continental varieties, had reaffirmed the universal inability of political concessions to surmount racial barriers. "Austrian administration in Lombardy was good rather than bad," Morley knew, "yet it was hated and resisted because it was Austrian and not Italian. No rational person can hold for an instant that the source of a scheme of government is immaterial to its prosperity." [41]

Lord Minto's proposed solution to the Indian problem was characteristic of the Unionist frame of mind: "we must be physically strong or go to the wall." [42] Morley, on the other hand, spurned the persistent suggestion "that we have nothing to do but to keep the sword sharp." [43] It hardly seemed worthwhile, he reasoned, to purchase temporary hegemony in the East by encouraging the forces of militarism and extraparliamentary despotism at home. He reminded the Viceroy that the "greatest and deepest fact" remained "that we are governing a population who don't love us and who will less and less patiently acquiesce in our rule." [44] The circumstances of British rule no less than a difference in pigmentation made this certain. Like Gladstone, he recognized that "no conquest ever has been permanent unless followed by an amalgamation," [45] which was out of the question in the case of India.

Yet this somber view of the Indian situation did not preclude either an attempt to reduce disaffection or a gentle nudge toward responsible institutions of a carefully circumscribed nature. Assuming that "the whole system of Indian government is a gigantic riddle," [46] Morley conscientiously endeavored to implement a conciliatory program sufficient to fulfill immediate needs without

40. Morley to Clarke, September 3, 1908, Morley Papers.
41. Morley, "Some Arguments Reconsidered," in James Bryce, ed., *Handbook of Home Rule* (London, 1887), pp. 250-51.
42. Minto to Morley, May 28, 1906, Morley Papers.
43. Morley to Minto, October 31, 1907, Minto Papers.
44. Morley to Minto, May 27, 1909, Minto Papers.
45. Note by Gladstone [1877], Gladstone Papers, Add. MSS. 44,763, fol. 96.
46. Morley to Lamington, May 11, 1906, Lamington Papers.

belying its Gladstonian origins. "We are obliged to move in a liberalising direction," he notified Lord Lamington, "whether we are particularly partial to such a move in such a country as India or not. (When I said country, I ought to have said continent.) " [47] His ultimate move, like the ideals behind it, was the product of the instincts and prejudices that he had accumulated over the decades.

Apart from his vigorous condemnation of the Government of India's frontier aggressions, Morley had done little to earn his reputation as an avowed enemy of Curzonian policy. Least of all had he taken any notice of the retributive legislation, culminating in the 1905 partition of Bengal, which had so incensed Indian opinion.

His attitude toward that capricious Viceroy had been ambivalent and, as he subsequently admitted, unduly lenient. He had been impressed by previous displays of Lord Curzon's intellectual acumen, and in 1904, when Curzon visited England between vice-regal terms, Morley had told him: "I shall count myself very unlucky if I don't shake hands with you before you go." [48] Second-hand reports of Curzon's intense rivalry with Lord Kitchener prompted Morley to idealize the Viceroy as a comrade in the battle against military encroachment upon civilian affairs, a view he modified as soon as the Indian Empire was entrusted to his care and the sordid facts of the Curzon-Kitchener controversy were laid before him. "I have seen a good deal of Lord Curzon, and he is a man who supplies plenty of topics," he reported to the Governor of Madras during his first weeks at the India Office. "It is not certain that I shall agree with all that was done in his reign and your vice-reign, but at any rate, I promise you an open mind to begin with." [49]

Further investigation weakened Morley's respect for Curzon's political judgment, as well as his support for the former Viceroy in his feud with Lord Kitchener. "Surely he is all wrong about the development or revolution in 'public opinion' in India?" he asked

47. Morley to Lamington, August 24, 1906, Lamington Papers.
48. Morley to Curzon, September 11, 1904, Curzon Papers.
49. Morley to Ampthill, January 4, 1906, Ampthill Papers. Lord Ampthill had assumed viceregal duties during Curzon's absence from India in 1904.

Sir Arthur Godley, after perusing the latter's correspondence with Curzon.[50] In a letter to Lord Minto, he attributed their common distress "to the spirit of restlessness, and energy misplaced and out of season, that was kindled throughout your [civil] service by your terrible predecessor." [51] Minto, who customarily leapt to the defense of Unionist policy and policy-makers, found it impossible to condone Curzon's high-handed measures: "If a true history of Curzon's rule is ever written," he admitted to Morley, "it will make the world wonder. Few people at home know the legacy of bitter discontent he left for his successor." [52]

Despite their repudiation of Curzonian tactics, neither Minto nor Morley could conceive of a means to revive among Indians the respect for British justice which Curzon had destroyed. Morley cherished the vain hope that time would prove an effective remedy: "My strong impression," he told Lord Lamington, "and it grows stronger as the days pass—is that the best way of finishing and dispersing the Curzon malaria is to preserve a sullen silence. Then it may possibly cease to poison the air." [53] But the passage of time made it no easier to conciliate Indian opinion so long as the grievances engendered by the previous administration remained unrectified.

Early in his secretaryship, in a hasty reply to clamorous back-benchers, Morley labeled the partition of Bengal a "settled fact"; [54] thereafter he felt obliged to maintain his position, though he came to doubt its wisdom [55] and realized that "I had only to lift my finger, and the H. of C. would have overthrown the 'settled fact' in a trice." [56] His obstinacy cannot be dismissed on grounds of sheer perversity, for he received repeated assurances that the antipartition agitation was "settling down" and "that the ultimate results of what has been done will prove generally beneficial to the

50. Morley considered this perusal "not wholly without useful admonition for a new S. of S.!" Morley to Godley, January 29, 1906, Kilbracken Papers, Add. MSS. 44,-902, fol. 99.

51. Morley to Minto, March 29, 1906, Minto Papers.

52. Minto to Morley, September 12, 1907, Morley Papers.

53. Morley to Lamington, May 25, 1906, Lamington Papers.

54. *Parliamentary Debates*, 4th ser., *152*, col. 844 (February 26, 1908).

55. Morley advised Sir Valentine Chirol "that so long as he was S. of S. it was a settled fact. There might come along another S. of S. who would be wise!" F. A. Hirtzel's Diary, March 15, 1909, *4*, 22.

56. Morley to Minto, January 24, 1907, Minto Papers.

populations concerned." [57] Indeed it has been argued that however tactlessly it had been executed, the partition of this unwieldy province was not only an administrative expedient but a genuine piece of progressive reform legislation: theoretically, relief projects, economic development, law enforcement, and the dispensation of justice would all be facilitated in eastern Bengal after it had been detached from the administration of the more populous, urbanized west.[58] And various Indian politicians, attempting to ingratiate themselves with the authorities, had crippled their cause by intimating that the revocation of partition was by no means a crucial plank in the Congress platform.[59]

A steady procession of friends and past associates—including several prominent Positivists, Sir Charles Dilke and Leonard Courtney—called upon Morley to reverse his stand. The last, recently dignified as Baron Courtney of Penwith, invested a futile hour on June 28, 1908, pleading for a fundamental reassessment of policy. Morley, according to his private secretary, "refused absolutely and said he would not now reconsider even if he could satisfy himself that the partition was wrong on its merits." [60] Later that year, Morley resisted stout Radical efforts to "sweeten the 'reforms sugar plum' by undoing partition", which would have been, he insisted, a contradiction of British intentions: "we are making reforms solely because we think they are right, not because we expect gratitude." [61] During the final months of his secretaryship, he found it a source of considerable satisfaction that he had managed to withstand the revisionist winds that blew from India and from certain parliamentary quarters. "If I go to heaven," the intrepid agnostic speculated to Sir George Clarke, "one reason will be that in spite of much pressure here, long and loudly continued, I stood firm by the Settled Fact." [62]

Yet somehow Morley conjured up illusions of redress with each

57. Minto to Morley, December 13, 1905 [copy], Minto Papers.

58. Most recently, Michael Edwardes (*High Noon of Empire,* London, 1965) has presented cogent arguments along this line.

59. See Minto to Morley, December 20, 1905 [copy], Minto Papers; also Morley to Clarke, July 3, 1908, Morley Papers; Sir J. R. Dunlop Smith to Lovat Fraser, February 14, 1909 [copy], Minto Papers.

60. F. A. Hirtzel's Diary, June 28, 1908, 3, 59.

61. Ibid., November 9, 1908, 98.

62. Morley to Clarke, April 28, 1910, Morley Papers.

sincere profession of adherence to the geographical status quo. "It is true that he took an early opportunity of announcing that the partition was a 'settled fact,' " Lovat Fraser, a self-proclaimed Curzonian, conceded, "and from that attitude he never veered a hand's breadth; but there was always some little reservation, some slight hesitancy, some implication of doubt which served to raise false hopes." [63] For one thing, Morley's reputation continually contradicted his disclaimers. One Bengali journal greeted his remark about the "settled fact" with the confident, though fallacious reminder: "Were not the Vernacular Press Act and the Jury Notification settled things, and did not he and his chief, Mr. Gladstone, 'unsettle' them?" [64] During the last week of 1906, in an address to his fellow nationalists at Calcutta, Surendranath Banerjea pointed out that Morley had failed to "adduce any justification for the Partition," and that he had gone so far as to admit that the scheme was neither technically perfect nor acceptable to the vast majority of Bengalis. Banerjea expressed confidence that if Indian nationalists administered "a persistent push from year to year," they would be able to "dislodge" Morley.[65] Others shared Banerjea's impression, if not his complacence. Lovat Fraser, for one, refused to "place any reliance in Morley's repeated assertions. He believes them and means them at the time; but, like Gladstone, he never finds any difficulty in convincing himself afresh." [66] On December 12, 1911, when the partition was at last modified by a royal proclamation at Delhi, there were those—including Sir William Wedderburn [67]—who presumed that this was the final achievement of John Morley's grand design for India.

If Morley underestimated the emotional appeal of provincial

63. Lovat Fraser, *India Under Curzon and After* (London, 1911), p. 388.

64. *Amrita Bazar Patrika*, February 20, 1906, cited in *Bengal Native Newspaper Reports, 1906.*

65. Speech at 1906 Indian National Congress, Banerjea, *Speeches and Writings*, p. 117.

66. Fraser to Dunlop Smith, February 13, 1909, Minto Papers.

67. Wedderburn, "King George and India," *Contemporary Review, 101* (1912), 163-64. Morley was, in fact, informed of the projected change by his successor at the India Office, Lord Crewe, who considered him "particularly apt to tear his hair and scatter ashes when a novel scheme is afoot." Crewe to Hardinge, September 15, 1911, cited in F. A. Eustis II and Z. H. Zaidi, "King, Viceroy and Cabinet," *History, 49* (1964), 171-84. Morley's subsequent performance belied Crewe's expectations; he relayed the details of the measure to the House of Lords, where it incurred the opposition of both Curzon and Minto.

boundaries, an error which experienced Indian politicians have since been known to commit, he nonetheless displayed an exceptional comprehension of the forces at work within the Indian nationalist movement. Like Minto, he tended to discount Congress claims and to look askance at Congress aspirations; yet he proved better able to see nationalist demands in their proper context. Most of all, he demonstrated a sympathy for the moderate politicians and an appreciation of their plight which Minto, who confused the ideals and memberships of the respective nationalist camps, tended to lack. The Viceroy's complaints about G. K. Gokhale's alleged duplicity were frequent and, in the harsh light of later events, rather pathetic. Time and again he deplored the moderate leader's failure to "come forward . . . as an advocate of constitutional reform . . . against the preaching of sedition." [68] Although Gokhale had explained "that it would be impossible for him to express moderate views in an extremist atmosphere, that it would all fall flat," Minto considered these excuses "very lame," and speculated that Gokhale is "much under the influence of wire-pullers and also no doubt is affected by mercenary considerations." [69] Minto was equally skeptical when Surendranath Banerjea refused "to publicly renounce his boycott oath" on the grounds "that by doing so the student boys, over whom he has influence, would throw him overboard as a useless leader, and would fall into the hands of the Extremists." [70]

Morley was more amused than alarmed by Minto's plaintive forebodings and by his excessive expectations of moderate cooperation. "When you say that [Gokhale] . . . is 'much under the influence of wire-pullers,' " he asked, "does this mean more than that he is a mildly revolutionary leader who does not want a revolution, but cannot abdicate nor break off from the people who do want one?" With a thorough grasp of the situation, Morley patiently explained that it served neither British interests nor Gokhale's for the latter "to come to open breach with the extreme men." There was little chance, he told Minto, that Gokhale might influence fellow nationalists, though it remained distinctly possi-

---

68. Minto to Morley, July 10, 1907, Morley Papers; also Minto to Morley, January 29, 1908, Morley Papers; Lady Minto's Indian Journals, November 1, 1907, *1907-ii*, 279.

69. Minto to Morley, November 5, 1907, Morley Papers.

70. Minto to Morley, March 10, 1910, Morley Papers.

ble that "among the Indophile Radicals in the House of Commons . . . Gokhale may, voluntarily or involuntarily, be of some possible service." [71] Morley shrugged off bureaucratic charges that Gokhale was "a crafty and sinister conspirator," though he acknowledged that the Congress leader "has used phrases about National Autonomy, Self-Governing Colony, and so forth"; these, he assured Lord Lamington, were "merely words and phrases for marking time or keeping his head above water," and he reminded Lamington that "Like all politicians, in more advanced as in backward countries, [Gokhale] has to talk a certain amount of Moonshine. That is—if I do not scandalise you too much—an unlucky necessity of most party leaders." [72]

Morley scoffed at the Viceroy's entreaties to take what Gokhale "says or writes . . . with the greatest caution," [73] citing his intimate acquaintance with "three revolutionary leaders—Mazzini, Gambetta, Parnell" [74] as proof that he was well versed in such transactions.[75] Each of these cases had demonstrated to him that "The Moderate can never afford to attack the Extremist when the latter is attacked by the Government of which they are both . . . critics." [76] This was precisely the situation he had faced in Ireland, where "even a strong man like Parnell could not . . . afford to disown the Extremist, though privately in moments of despair he spoke of 'those Papist *rats.*' " [77]

Morley, by no means satisfied with his moderate allies, was particularly apt to impugn their character and motives when his own integrity had been called into question. His first two budget speeches elicited praise and gratitude from Gokhale, but on each occasion the latter voiced serious misgivings to English friends.[78]

71. Morley to Minto, November 29, 1907, Minto Papers.

72. Morley to Lamington, June 20, 1907, Lamington Papers.

73. Minto to Morley, November 2, 1909 [telegram], Morley Papers.

74. Morley to Clarke, August 19, 1908, Morley Papers.

75. Morley to Minto, November 5, 1909, Minto Papers.

76. Morley to Clarke, October 1, 1908, Morley Papers. Morley's nineteenth-century illustrations failed to convince Clarke, who continued to bemoan the fact that "Moderates in India are like nitrogen in the air. They have no moral courage and, being timid, they are inert." Clarke to Morley, January 13, 1910, Morley Papers.

77. F. A. Hirtzel's Diary, May 23, 1907, 2, 47.

78. See Morley to Minto, July 27, 1906, Minto Papers; also Godley to Minto, July 27, 1906, Minto Papers; Morley to Minto, July 18, 1907, Minto Papers; Sir Herbert Risley to Minto, July 19, 1907, Minto Papers.

Still Morley, when his anger had abated, was able to perceive that the difficulty was not Gokhale's perfidy, but his shocking ineptitude: "I have often thought during the last twelve months," he revealed in a letter to Minto, "that Gokhale as party manager is a baby. A party manager, or for that matter any politician aspiring to be a leader, should never *whine*. Gokhale is too often whining, just like the second-rate Irishmen between Dan O'Connell and Parnell." [79] Private consultations were sufficient to dispel Morley's suspicions of Gokhale, but not his profound regret that the Indian national movement lacked a more authoritative, fully accredited spokesman with whom he could deal on a man-to-man basis. Parnell had occupied such a position among Irish nationalists during the 1880s and, as a result, British policy had been invited to be vigorous and far-seeing. But it was painfully evident to all concerned that Gokhale commanded no comparable allegiance from his Indian associates. [80]

Decades of scrupulous attention to Irish affairs had rendered Morley conscious of the benefits to be derived from energetic, responsible leadership at the helm of any nationalist movement. In his two terms as Chief Secretary, and as intermediary between Gladstone and Parnell in the interim, he had found the latter's power a cause for satisfaction, not anxiety. [81] It was imperative, he had insisted to Gladstone on November 17, 1890, "that the Irish party should continue to speak with one voice—as, I am convinced, they will do." [82] But Morley's optimism, like Irish solidarity, had vanished within days; an adverse decree in the O'Shea divorce case spelled an end to the Home Rule alliance and to Parnell's effectiveness as a political leader. Morley, who carried Gladstone's message of excommunication to Parnell, defended the move on grounds of expediency, but acknowledged that the "loss of Parnell" was "irreparable." [83] Two years later, when he returned to Dublin as Chief Secretary in Gladstone's final Government, he saw conclusive evidence of this loss. Without Parnell's

79. Morley to Minto, October 31, 1907, Minto Papers.
80. See P. C. Ray, "Editorial Reflections," *Indian World* (June 1907), p. 533.
81. See Morley's speech to the Eighty Club on June 8, 1886, *The Irish Question*, p. 18.
82. Morley to Gladstone, November 17, 1890, Gladstone Papers, Add. MSS. 44,-256, fols. 72–73.
83. Morley to Spencer, December 1, 1890, Spencer Papers; also Morley to Harcourt, January 7, 1891, Harcourt Papers.

superintendence, Irish nationalism had fallen apart at its ideological and racial seams, and moderate Irishmen, reluctant to impair further their position among their countrymen, could no longer afford to assist an English official, even one who championed Home Rule.

Irish precedents also demonstrated to Morley that an open rupture between the constitutional and revolutionary wings of any nationalist movement invariably worked to the advantage of the latter. For this reason he was unable to share Minto's view that the disruption of the Indian National Congress at Surat in December 1907 "is a great triumph for us." [84] There had been portents of the schism that occurred at the Congress's twenty-third annual Christmastime sitting. A year earlier the moderates had preserved Congress unity as well as their precarious grip upon the Congress leadership by bringing Dadabhai Naoroji, the Grand Old Man of Indian nationalism, home from England to lend his authority to the proceedings. The 1907 session had initially been scheduled for Nagpur, but a confrontation with extremist delegates to an October meeting of the Congress reception committee prompted nervous moderates to shift the event to Surat, allegedly a moderate stronghold. All the while, Minto had observed this dissension with complacent interest: "The split in the Congress . . . is fortunate," he told a member of his council, "in fact, everything looks better." [85]

Morley inferred a totally different, less heartening message from this exhibition of moderate distress. Unlike Minto, he detected neither symptoms of moderate recovery [86] nor evidence that Government officials could afford to "fold our arms and leave the Moderates in the lurch." [87] True, he had not anticipated the shambles that occurred on the opening day of the Surat proceedings, when moderates and extremists openly clashed: "The Congress, so far from being 'flat,' as I had expected, has gone to pieces, which is the exact opposite of flat, no doubt," he confessed to Minto, to whom he predicted that the result would be "the victory of Extremist over Moderate, going no further at this stage than the

84. Minto to Morley, January 13, 1908, Morley Papers.
85. Minto to Sir A. T. Arundel, December 9, 1907 [copy], Minto Papers.
86. Minto to Morley, May 2, 1907, and January 15, 1908, Morley Papers.
87. Morley to Minto, December 26, 1907, Minto Papers.

break-up of the Congress, but pointing to a future stage in which the Congress will have become an Extremist organisation." [88]

The eruption of extremist tempers at Surat effectively dramatized the moderate plight and reinforced Morley's determination to succor India's constitutional fledglings. "Nobody in the world," he had previously told Minto, "has better reason for desiring us to suppress the row than the Moderates among the Congress party, for they will be dished if disorder prevails." [89] The problem was essentially the same one that had confronted British statesmanship in 1886, when Morley had argued that it was preferable to "[strengthen] the hands and [use] the services of the [Irish] party which, though nationalist, is also constitutional," than to "[drive] that party also, in despair of a constitutional solution, to swell the ranks of Extremists and Irreconcilables." [90] On that occasion, he had minimized the threat posed by the "darker forces and more extreme men" who shadowed his Parnellite allies, and asked opponents of Home Rule whether "you [would] rather have these men on your side against those darker forces and more extreme men or not." [91] Nor had Morley been deterred when a dynamite explosion occurred close to the walls of Dublin Castle during his second occupancy; he put down the outrage to "the work of some of the violent and low-class ultras—designing to make success more difficult for the Constitutional Irish, and for us." [92] As Austen Chamberlain remarked after a conversation with the Secretary of State for India at Marlborough House on March 15, 1907: "It was the old problem, the problem of Ireland over again." [93]

Because the Indian events of the prewar years displayed such a déjà vu quality, Morley quickly recognized the direction in which

88. Morley to Minto, December 27, 1907, Minto Papers; also Morley to Bryce, January 6, 1908, Bryce Papers.

89. Morley to Minto, May 9, 1907, Minto Papers.

90. Morley, "Some Arguments Reconsidered," in Bryce, ed., *Handbook of Home Rule,* p. 255.

91. Speech to the Eighty Club, June 8, 1886, *The Irish Question,* p. 19.

92. Morley to Gladstone, December 25, 1892, Gladstone Papers, Add. MSS. 44,-257, fol. 65. Gladstone agreed that "either Nationalists or Parnellites would be delighted to help" apprehend the culprits "if they could," for they realized that this was "a serious blow to them and a blow to Ireland, and to us mainly through them." Gladstone to Morley, December 28, 1892, Gladstone Papers, Add. MSS. 44,-257, fols. 69-70.

93. Chamberlain, *Politics from Inside,* p. 59.

they were leading as well as the disconcerting fact that he was pitted against the forces of historical inevitability. "I have, for my sins," he told Minto, making no pretense to modesty,

> read more than my share of the doings of revolutionary parties in France; I was much in with Gambetta, Clemenceau, etc., after the smash of the Empire, and the battle for the Republic; I saw Irish "rebel" action at close quarters, and for four years I saw them with the eyes of official responsibility. My general notion is that the Moderates are always at a disadvantage. The same forces that begin the move, continue their propulsive power. The only question is whether by doing what we can in the Moderate direction, we can draw the teeth of the Extremists.[94]

The Viceroy, engaged in the thankless task of contradicting a professional historian on his home ground, was brusquely put down for suggesting that "What is going on in India is altogether peculiar in comparison with other revolutions." [95] With a categorical flourish, Morley replied that "Every revolution that I have ever heard of came from above and not from below in the first instance —a few supplying a match, the many bringing torches after." [96] Conceding that the Indian case was different insofar as "Mazzini was only bent on driving out Austrians," while "Tilak's success would mean anarchy and chaos among vast multitudes who could not form a government of their own," Morley refused to qualify his view that "the general course of great revolutionary parties runs in much the same lines as between Moderates and Extremists." [97] Regardless of how many press laws were passed, how many agitators were deported, or how many concessions the British offered, he was convinced that "Indian discontent or alienation or whatever we like to call it" would ultimately "run into the same

94. Morley to Minto, October 11, 1906, Minto Papers. This is a more sincere expression of Morley's intentions than that which he promulgated to the House of Lords when the India Councils Bill received its second reading; then, he elaborated a plan to incapacitate the extremists by "drawing the second class, who hope for colonial autonomy, into the third class, who will be content with being admitted to a fair and workable cooperation." Though he could hardly have afforded to declare so publicly, Morely realized that this was virtually impossible. *Parliamentary Debates*, 5th ser., *I*, cols. 118-19 (February 23, 1909).
95. Minto to Morley, November 4, 1906, Morley Papers.
96. Morley to Minto, November 30, 1906, Minto Papers.
97. Morley to Clarke, October 1, 1908, Morley Papers.

channels of violence as Italian, Russian, Irish discontent." [98]

As Secretary of State for India, Morley appreciated both the need for creative statesmanship and the inescapable fact that any move by an alien authority was doomed to ultimate failure. For India's sake, for Parliament's sake, and undoubtedly for the sake of his own self-regard, [99] he did his best to achieve a lessening of tensions and to rectify the more egregious abuses of imperial rule. But he understood nationalist processes too well to entertain hopes of significant success. Here, too, he displayed keener perception than either critics or colleagues in two hemispheres.

The Morley-Minto reforms, true to their appellation, reflected more the areas of agreement between the two administrators than the dominant influence of either.[100] There can be little doubt that, left to his own devices, Minto, despite a benign nature, would not have embarked on such an arduous venture. On the eve of his departure for India, he had proclaimed his intention to apply to Indian problems the lesson he had learned during his "racing days," that "many a race has been won by giving the horse a rest in his gallops." [101] It is equally improbable that Morley, without the Viceroy's urging and tenacity, would have followed precisely the course that he did. Each made an attempt to placate the other, and the Morley-Minto reforms were, in large measure, the product of these attempts.[102]

98. Morley to Minto, July 8, 1909, Minto Papers.

99. Morley admitted to his private secretary that "he did not want it said . . . that with all his liberal principles he had done nothing." F. A. Hirtzel's Diary, July 13, 1906, *1*, 61.

100. Minto's most recent biographer, who campaigns on behalf of his subject's primacy, concedes that "it was decidedly Morley who on 15 June 1906 asked Minto to set the ball rolling in the direction of reform." Wasti, *Lord Minto*, p. 18. Yet Minto and his wife insisted that the reform policy had originated at Simla, and Lady Minto ascribed Morley's enmity to the fact that her husband had "stated publicly that he was the author of the reforms, for which Morley had hitherto been given the entire credit." Lady Minto's Indian Journals, August 9, 1910, *1910-ii*, 271-72. She later called upon Morley to repudiate *The Times*' unqualified assertion that he had "priority and originality" in framing the measure, and to allow an impartial critic to examine the manuscript of his *Recollections* before publication. Lady Minto to Morley, August 2, 1916 [copy], Minto Papers. Morley refused to comply, and Lady Minto continued her crusade long after both statesmen had died.

101. Cited in "Lord Minto's Viceroyalty," *Edinburgh Review, 212* (1910), 501.

102. Sir Frederic Hirtzel recalled that Morley had been duly impressed by Minto's " 'great pluck' in deciding in favour of a native member of Council, but 'it

Initially, at least, it appears that the granting of reforms mattered more to Morley than their actual content. He was acutely conscious of the geographical and philosophical gulfs that separated him from Indian issues, and was content to accept any advice that did not infringe upon his Gladstonian principles. He explained to Minto that

> I learned some lessons—a good many lessons—in the art of political business from Mr. Gladstone . . . , and I observed that in the case of proposals on which in their aim and substance he had most set his heart, he was always anxious to leave this or that important element in them as long as possible in a state of the Provisional, the Fluid, the Elastic.[103]

His political apprenticeship had also taught Morley the strategic value of recruiting support from both sets of parliamentary benches. He did not require Lord Ripon to point out the valuable "opportunity . . . afforded us of introducing reforms . . . which are recommended to us by a Viceroy appointed by our political opponents." [104] Gladstone had sought a bipartisan solution to the Irish problem in the months before his third administration, and the subsequent defeat of two Home Rule measures testified to his inability to achieve one. For this reason, above all, Morley was prepared to allow the reforms dispatch to bear an Indian dateline. Unfortunately, he proved equally willing to compromise on other seemingly minor points, communal representation among them, convinced that "J. Bull . . . is a fool if he fixes his mind on any one detail—deportation, clause 3, or what you like—instead of criticising detail in relation to the tremendous situation as a whole." [105]

---

would have been simpler for me if he hadn't.' I said I thought poor Lord Minto probably screwed himself up to it thinking he was pleasing *him*." F. A. Hirtzel's Diary, March 18, 1907, 2, 28.

103. Morley to Minto, April 15, 1908, Minto Papers.

104. Ripon was willing "to accept Minto's proposals exactly as they stand rather than lose the advantage of his support," though he never doubted Morley's command of the situation: "I think Minto deserves first credit for the way in which he has dealt with these difficult questions under your very skilful handling which I very greatly admire." Ripon to Morley, April 5, 1907, Ripon Papers, Add. MSS. 43,541, fol. 136.

105. Morley to J. A. Spender, March 19, 1909, Spender Papers, British Museum Add. MSS. 46,392, fol. 7.

To the greatest extent possible, Morley rooted himself in Gladstonian precedent and formulated a policy which his mentor would have been proud to endorse. But this was far less a tribute to his powers of persuasion than an indication of the intrinsic conservatism of the Gladstonian program for India. The Morley-Minto reforms were, almost as much in letter as in spirit, a sequel to the India Councils Act of 1892 which, despite its Tory origins, had profited from Gladstone's eloquent support. According to Gladstonian logic, it was a distinct asset for the 1909 measure, like its predecessor, to remain vague about its ultimate intentions.[106] And Gladstone, without precluding the eventual introduction of parliamentary democracy to India, had emphasized the fact that this was at best a remote prospect.[107] Rather than a departure from his political heritage, the Indian legislation that bears Morley's name is both proof of his continued Gladstonian faith and further testimony to the inadequacies of those precepts.

Few, if any, of the individuals concerned with Indian affairs could doubt the shape that the reform scheme would ultimately take. Virtually all of the provisions of the 1909 program, including the proposal to appoint an Indian to the Viceroy's executive council, had been outlined decades earlier by either Lord Ripon or Lord Dufferin, two Gladstonian appointees to the viceroyalty. Early in Morley's secretaryship, Ripon accurately predicted the contents of the reforms parcel,[108] and Morley reminded Minto that the "points named by me" in his July 20, 1906 address to the Commons "have been under consideration for years." [109] Morley's original suggestions to the Viceroy, casually proffered after a session with Gokhale, proved, on the whole, remarkably similar to the finished product:

> the extension of the native element in your Legislative Council, ditto in local councils; full time for discussing Budget in

106. See Gladstone's reply to C. E. Schwann, M.P. for Manchester North, who criticized the ambiguous wording of the 1892 Bill: "Now, Sir, while the language of the Bill cannot be said to embody the elective principle, yet, if it is not meant to pave the way for the elective principle, it is in its language very peculiar indeed." *Parliamentary Debates*, 4th ser., 3, cols. 78 ff. (March 28, 1892).

107. Ibid., col. 83.

108. Ripon to Wedderburn, June 6, 1906, cited in Lucien Wolf, *Life of Lord Ripon* (2 vols. London, 1921), 2, 289.

109. Morley to Minto, February 22, 1907, Minto Papers.

your Legislative Council, instead of four or five skimpy hours; right of moving amendments. (Of course officials would remain a majority.) [110]

During the dissonant symphony of wrangling and negotiations that followed this harmonious overture, it was decided—much to Morley's credit—to do away with most official majorities, and— much to Minto's credit—to add Indian members to the executive councils at Whitehall and Calcutta.

As Secretary of State for India, John Morley perceived Indian problems through a late-Victorian haze that dimmed his vision. Like his political forebears, he conceived of India's predicament exclusively in social terms. While this approach retained considerable validity, it was no longer either as relevant or as constructive as it had been during the embryonic stages of Indian national growth. Morley clung to the opinion that Indian politicians "craved," as they had decades earlier, "administrative posts . . . a million times beyond political reforms." [111] He wholeheartedly embraced Lord Cromer's dictum that it was preferable to employ a "comparatively inefficient" native rather than a European who might perform the same task "a vast deal better," and he complained that the Indian Civil Service, in its fanatic pursuit of efficiency, had sacrificed a far more valuable premium: popular support.[112] To compensate, Morley was prepared to defy the sacred canons of bureaucratic procedure in order to promote Indians as quickly as possible into the higher echelons of the Indian Civil Service. Impatient to bring Indian spokesmen into his council chamber at Whitehall, he professed to Minto that "to be quite frank, their colour is more important than their brains." [113] Three years later, Sir James Dunlop Smith reported to a scandalized Viceroy that Morley insisted upon the renewed presence of an Indian in the viceregal council "even if he were the second-best man available." [114] But however commendable these efforts, they failed to appease a younger, more militant generation of national-

110. Morley to Minto, June 15, 1906, Minto Papers.
111. Morley to Minto, August 2, 1906, Minto Papers. This view was by no means peculiar to the Secretary of State; it was shared by the Viceroy, who expressed it in his November 4, 1906, letter to Morley, Morley Papers.
112. Morley to Minto, May 3, 1906, Minto Papers; also Morley to Minto, August 29, 1906, Minto Papers.
113. Morley to Minto, June 13, 1907, Minto Papers.
114. Dunlop Smith to Minto, April 20, 1910, Minto Papers.

ist leaders, who clamored for ballots rather than civil service appointments. And Morley soon recognized the futility of any reform policy which stopped short of outright political concessions.[115]

It cannot be denied that Morley was a slow and uneasy convert to the cause of Indian political reform, though he proved a steadfast adherent once the heady scent of constitutional battle had entered his nostrils. His racial views weakened his Radical instincts; his political discomfort, coupled with his intention to retire at an early date, rendered him extremely reluctant "to take part in any grand revolution during my time of responsibility." [116] Much like Minto, he was afraid of proceeding too far too quickly; but unlike the Viceroy, his trepidations subsided at a comparatively early date. Less tempted by the solitude of his library than he alleged, Morley could withhold neither his name nor his labors from the challenge which India afforded her imperial guardians.

But the reform scheme that was painstakingly hammered out was as much the product of successive compromises and responses to daily exigencies as it was the logical outgrowth of ideological preconceptions. It benefited enormously from Morley's frequent consultations with moderate leaders,[117] though he took strong exception to rumors that he was an unwitting tool in Gokhale's hands.[118] The Indian secretary drew a not altogether unjustifiable distinction between the Congress movement and its moderate flank; the former he feared and distrusted, though he recognized its value as a forum for constitutional expression. At the same time, he sympathized with those moderate elder statesmen who clung to the modest goal of "reasonable reforms" instead of chasing after the "mere dream" of autonomous institutions.[119] Gokhale, though he significantly weakened his standing among his fellow nationalists in the process, purchased Morley's confidence

115. As late as the autumn of 1906, Morley endeavored to devise an alternative to political reform which "would interest and attract." Morley to Godley, October 13, 1906, Kilbracken Papers (I.O.L.).

116. Morley to Minto, June 6, 1906, Minto Papers.

117. Gokhale's accounts of his India Office interviews, especially his letters to N. A. Dravid, are quoted extensively in Wolpert, *Tilak and Gokhale,* and in T. V. Parvate, *Gopal Krishna Gokhale* (Ahmedabad, 1959).

118. Morley to Clarke, February 12, 1909, Morley Papers.

119. Morley to Minto, August 2, 1906, Minto Papers.

by fostering the impression that he was "a good deal too sensible to expect any very radical (or revolutionary) changes in his own time." [120]

Though Minto deserves full credit for suggesting the nomination of an Indian to his executive council, it was Morley who subsequently steadied him in their charted course. Morley was not at all surprised by his partner's second—even third—thoughts about the daring step, for he too had serious apprehensions: "In 1881," he told his private secretary, "he would have thought any man (even Mr. G.) a fool who did not make Parnell Chief Secretary; now, looking back he sees it to have been absolutely impossible. So with Native Member. Decision will be unpopular, but he doesn't care." [121] Yet Gokhale's warnings of impending catastrophe, accompanied by a recrudescence of nationalist agitation, convinced both Morley and Minto that nothing less than a bold policy would suffice.

On August 16, 1906, two months after Morley had broached the subject of reform, Minto appointed a committee to consider the matter. A copy of its report reached Morley on November 17, while its chairman, Sir A. T. Arundel, was a guest in his Wimbledon library. Although Minto's committee had discussed proposals for increased Indian representation, a council of princes, and communal and class electorates, its conclusions proved a profound disappointment to Morley. On all but relatively minor points, the Arundel report reflected little more than the divergence of opinion within the committee. And meanwhile, much valuable time had been lost.

Minto insisted that the Arundel report could not be released without a covering dispatch, and this document took longer to prepare than the report itself. His successive pleas for additional time infuriated Morley, who had promised himself that he would cap the promulgation of a reform bill with the announcement of his own retirement. Despite considerable misgivings, Minto forwarded his dispatch on March 21, 1907, a month after Morley penned a blistering condemnation of viceregal heel-dragging: "In this, as in everything else, I have been studiously considerate of your difficulties," he professed;

120. Morley to Lamington, June 29, 1906, Lamington Papers.
121. F. A. Hirtzel's Diary, April 8, 1907, 2, 34; also Morley to Ripon, April 7, 1907, Ripon Papers, Add. MSS. 43,541, fol. 137.

but I declare that I cannot for the life of me see why deliberations originated by you last July should not by this time have
ripened into at least one or two pretty definite proposals,
proper for the consideration of His Majesty's Government.
. . . Well, I am a great believer in the virtues of collective
consultation, and I am all for taking time and giving opportunity to allow men to come round to your own judgment.
But time is one thing, and eternity is another.[122]

Except for the proposal to appoint an Indian member to the
Imperial Council, an item which the Secretary of State found unnecessary and inexpedient to dwell upon in his address to the Commons on June 6, the Government of India's scheme elicited surprisingly little opposition. Quite unexpectedly, the receipt of
Minto's dispatch unleashed an outbreak of reforming zeal at
home, and Morley was caught off guard by the widespread enthusiasm for Indian legislation.[123] The King, to whom Morley
"according to rule" submitted a copy of the proposals, was "full of
laudation," though the Indian secretary had "feared he would say
this is no time for reform, but only for the mailed fist." [124] Lord
Ripon went so far as to label the Arundel report "too conservative." [125] Prepared for another constitutional battle, Morley was
surprised to learn that for once a preponderance of sympathies and
parliamentary votes were in his corner. With intense satisfaction
he counted "A Viceroy, a Cabinet, a H. of C. majority, all looking
in the same direction," and he predicted to Minto that

such a conjuncture of the powerful elements in the firma-
ment must lead to good, unless we bungle. Perhaps I ought to
say unless *I* bungle, for all depends on the way in which the
problem and our solution of it are stated. . . . I am not very

122. Morley to Minto, February 22, 1907, Minto Papers; also Morley to Minto,
February 18, 1907 [telegram], Morley Papers.
123. One month earlier, Morley had wondered whether it might be best to
postpone further reform efforts until the indignation aroused by the Rawalpindi
riots had died down. "That night," Hirtzel recorded, "he dined at H. of C. with
Irish members. 'I am always loyal to those men,' he said." F. A. Hirtzel's Diary,
May 6, 1907, 2, 42.
124. Morley to Campbell-Bannerman, May 18, 1907, Campbell-Bannerman Papers, Add. MSS. 41,223, fol. 245.
125. F. A. Hirtzel's Diary, April 16, 1907, 2, 36; also Morley to Minto, April 17,
1907, Minto Papers.

clever at egg-dances as was my old Chief, Mr. G. But I'll try
my best.[126]

A midsummer steamer carried Morley's reform circular east-
ward to Minto, along with an urgent plea to expedite matters;
"unless your Council make a fidget about it," he asserted, "there is
no reason why it should not be given to the listening earth, with
or without 'the wondrous story of its birth,' before Parliament
rises—which is just now our standard and measure of time and all
its seasons." Morley proclaimed his intention to announce the
appointment of two Indians to his council at Whitehall with the
publication of the circular, "leaving the appointment of an Indian
Member on *your* Council for some other not too distant day." [127]
Later that month, he joined Minto in a long-distance game of
mutual back-patting: "We really, between us, made a move and a
beginning." [128] He paused to acknowledge minor rumblings on
"the extreme Left of my Party" [129] and among certain Indian
malcontents, but consoled himself with the bountiful praise he received from more eminent quarters. "I am not sorry to have
friendly words in newspapers," he told the Prime Minister, "but I
count these as but tinkling cymbals and sounding brass, compared
with friendly words from you." [130]

On August 26, two days after Minto unveiled the provisions of
the reform circular, Morley announced the appointment to his
council of Krishna Gobinda Gupta, a Hindu civil servant, and
Sayid Husain Bilgrami, a Muslim who had formerly served as an
adviser to the Nizam of Hyderabad and as a member of the Viceroy's legislative council. His selections, reached after prolonged
discussions with Minto, were decidedly less popular than his gesture. But this did not discourage Morley, who felt confident that
he had participated in a bold and useful enterprise. Reporting
Gupta's first appearance in his council chamber, he told the
Viceroy:

> 'Tis not vanity that makes me say that I feel I was doing a his-
> toric sort of thing, such as I hope that *you* may do in your

126. Morley to Minto, May 24, 1907, Minto Papers.
127. Morley to Minto, August 2, 1907, Minto Papers.
128. Morley to Minto, August 23, 1907, Minto Papers.
129. Morley to Minto, August 28, 1907, Minto Papers.
130. Morley to Campbell-Bannerman, September 5, 1907, Campbell-Bannerman
Papers, Add. MSS. 41,223, fols. 262-63.

Council one of these days. I fear that neither Gupta nor I would make impressive figures in an oil-painting of the scene.[131]

As successive seasons passed, and Morley received nothing more tangible from Simla than apologies for bureaucratic delays, he grew depressed. "I fear it looks as if our 'reforms' were rather missing fire," he brooded in an early October letter to Minto.[132] It was apparent by the spring of 1908 that the initial display of administrative goodwill had failed to muffle either the cries of agitators or bomb explosions. Equally vociferous was a swelling army of right-wing critics who contended that violence provided a valid excuse to put the reforms project on ice. Yet Morley, increasingly comfortable in the Big Chair at the India Office, drew contrary conclusions from recent Indian events. "I am determined," he instructed Minto,

> that we must persevere with liberal and substantial reforms, perhaps wider than those in your original sketch. Very likely they won't satisfy the educated classes, and it is these classes after all who, in spite of their comparatively scanty numbers, must always set the tune and decide the pitch. Reforms may not save the Raj, but if they don't, nothing else will.[133]

Morley intensified his campaign for the Viceroy to nominate an Indian as an official member of his council.[134] At the same time, he attempted to spur Minto into tackling the reforms project with greater energy. "The delay on the matter of reforms at Simla is like nothing but the old Vatican at its worst," he fumed.[135] The fleeting months aroused disturbing doubts "whether we shall not be laughed out of court for producing a mouse from the labouring mountain. . . . At this pace, Lord Grey's Reform Bill of 1832

131. Morley to Minto, March 12, 1908, Minto Papers; also Morley to Minto, March 26, 1908, Minto Papers.
132. Morley to Minto, October 3, 1907, Minto Papers.
133. Morley to Minto, May 7, 1908, Minto Papers.
134. Morley to Minto, May 21, 1908, Minto Papers.
135. Morley to Clarke, September 3, 1908, Morley Papers. He repeated to Minto Napoleon's explanation to the Pope after he had consecrated his own bishops: "'You and your Cardinals can never decide anything under between three and four years! What's the use? Italy can't wait.' . . . It flashed upon me that the procedure of the Vatican and the Sacred College is not confined to Rome. And India can't wait." Morley to Minto, August 10, 1908, Minto Papers.

would have become law in 1850 or 1860, and Nottingham and Bristol blazing all the time." He deemed it imperative, "quite as much for the sake of India as for parliamentary expectations," to have the measure ready for promulgation before Parliament's Christmas recess.[136] On October 1, the Government of India's reforms dispatch was at last on its way to Whitehall, where it was debated and pruned by a committee composed of members of the Secretary of State's council and Lord MacDonnell, a retired imperial administrator;[137] on November 27, after its perfunctory approval by a Cabinet more concerned with urgent domestic business, it began its journey back to Minto.

By this time, Morley was thoroughly convinced that the reform scheme would have to be a remedy as well as a gesture. He continued to scorn Minto's proposals for either a council of princes or a council of notables, which savored too much of Lyttonian and Curzonian policy.[138] In a letter to the Governor of Bombay, he calculated the need "to go a vast deal beyond the [reform] scheme that started from Simla, though it has been industriously and elaborately worked out there—only without any of the breath of true popular and liberal feeling." He deprecated the view, which he had previously espoused, that officials would have to retain a majority of the places "on every council, from the Viceroy's down to the district or Taluka or Village Council," for this would reduce to "mere sham" the many promises "of giving the Indians a greater share in their own affairs."[139] Nothing less than a "comprehensive settlement," he told Minto, would succeed "in our great object of making an impression on the Indian politicians."[140]

On November 2, a Royal Proclamation, which bore King Ed-

136. Morley to Minto, August 10, 1908, Minto Papers.

137. Morley attempted to add extra weight to his committee by adding Lord Cromer's name to its roster; administrative technicalities, however, made this impossible. Morley to Cromer, September 26, October 1 and 16, 1907, and Cromer to Morley, October 1, 1907, Cromer Papers PRO/FO/633/18.

138. Morley to Minto, June 15, 1906, Minto Papers; also Dispatch from the Secretary of State for India to the Governor-General-in-Council, November 27, 1908, *Parliamentary Papers*, Cd. 4426.

139. Morley to Clarke, September 18, 1908, Morley Papers. "What is the use or sense of offering [a reform scheme]," Morley asked Minto irately, "and then taking it back by means of official majority with a *swamping* vote? And don't you see that in the last paragraph of our dispatch we give a discreet but very intelligible hint to the Lieutenant-Governor to exercise his full authority in case motions or bills should take a wild-cat turn?" Morley to Minto, November 27, 1908, Minto Papers.

140. Morley to Minto, October 23, 1908, Minto Papers.

ward's signature and evidence of Morley's inimitable pen, confirmed the Government's intentions.[141] Morley perceived a mounting restlessness among Indian nationalists, and he reiterated his doubts whether any blend of administrative reforms would win gratitude from either nationalist camp: the extremists would turn a deaf ear "even though we spoke with the tongue of men and of angels"; [142] and the moderates could ill afford to respond too enthusiastically. Still he nursed hopes that the reform scheme, about to emerge from the committee room, "will give them more than they expect from us—which is all to the good." [143]

The reception accorded his December 17 address to the House of Lords in which he outlined the reform proposals augured success. He invited—and received—support from both parties,[144] much as Gladstone, sixteen years earlier, had urged his fellow parliamentarians to exclude the 1892 India Councils Bill from the realm of party politics.[145] Sir Arthur Godley, the Undersecretary of State for India, reported to Minto that Morley's exhortations had been cogent and "audible," despite his chronic throat ailment, aggravated during the closing weeks of 1908 by a severe cold.[146] Sir Frederic Hirtzel, a good deal more prejudiced than Godley in Morley's favor, informed Sir James Dunlop Smith that the Indian secretary had been

> laid up the whole of the previous ten days almost voiceless—
> his colds always attack his vocal cords first. Then he was very
> worried by the ridiculous behaviour of the House of Commons, who insisted upon having a simultaneous statement (if
> they could not have the *only* statement) from Buchanan—
> not out of any particular love of India, but out of mere jealousy of the House of Lords. . . . Things therefore rather
> conspired to make the omens unfavourable. However, the un-

141. The Royal Proclamation "to the Princes and Peoples of India" is included as an appendix in Morley's *Recollections*, 2, 371 ff.

142. Morley to Minto, November 5, 1908, Minto Papers.

143. Morley to Minto, November 12, 1908, Minto Papers.

144. Speech to the House of Lords, December 17, 1908, Morley, *Indian Speeches*, pp. 76 ff.

145. Gladstone insisted, during the 1892 Commons debate: "It is well the people of India should understand the truth—that united views substantially prevail in this House on this matter." *Parliamentary Debates*, 4th ser., 3, col. 84 (March 28, 1892). Morley did not fail to repeat these admonitions when he moved the second reading of the 1909 Bill on February 23. See *Indian Speeches*, pp. 122-24.

146. Godley to Minto, December 18, 1908, Minto Papers.

expected happened. Lord Morley was in better voice than I have ever heard him, and quite master of the situation. He held the House (which was fuller than usual, and keenly interested) from the first, and all his points were well received —none better than his references to Lord Minto.[147]

The opposition Morley encountered in the upper house promised to be fitful and divided. Lord Lansdowne rose to protest against the appointment of an Indian to the Viceroy's executive council,[148] and Lord MacDonnell, who had voiced similar sentiments as a member of the reforms committee, called upon Morley to amend the partition of Bengal.[149] As soon as the initial round of applause stopped ringing in his ears, Morley settled back to await the response from less predictable quarters.

Gokhale, who had considerably more at stake than either statesman, managed to wring a modest declaration of approval from the twenty-third Indian National Congress, which convened at Madras a week after Morley's December 17 announcement. He urged his compatriots, who were fewer and "of a better class" than at recent gatherings, [150] to accord the Morley-Minto program a reasonable opportunity for success "because it must be accepted or rejected as a whole." [151] Largely through his efforts, the moderate politicians held at bay such explosive topics as boycott, deportation,

147. Hirtzel to Dunlop Smith, December 18, 1908, Minto Papers.

148. Lansdowne expressed his apologies and repeated his doubts about the "Native Member" in his December 30 letter to Minto, Minto Papers.

149. Morley, in the account he provided for Minto, described MacDonnell as

a hard-mouthed brute, if ever there was one, [who] did as much mischief as he could, raising the anti-Partition flag, which will encourage my grumblers below the gangway in the House of Commons. Lord MacDonnell does not mean to be malignant, I am sure; but he combines the defects of an Irishman with those of a tip-top Indian civilian, and those two qualifications combined may lead a man very close to malignancy.

Morley to Minto, December 18, 1908, Minto Papers; one month earlier, Morley had brusquely notified MacDonnell that he did not contemplate further consideration of the partition controversy at least until the reform proposals had passed. Morley to MacDonnell, November 5, 1908, MacDonnell Papers (Bodleian Library, Oxford).

150. *The Times* (December 29, 1908), p. 3; the Reuters dispatch added, "Comparatively few Bengalis are present."

151. Gokhale, *Speeches*, pp. 854–56; Sir William Wedderburn, who presided over the following year's Congress, advised Congressmen to *"take all you can get, and make the most of it."* "An Appeal to Congressmen," *Indian Review, 9* (1908), 881-82.

and the partition of Bengal.[152] Morley appreciated Gokhale's assistance and hailed the Congress proceedings as "a remarkable sign that Indians are as capable as other people of sound political judgment and wise political or party tactics." [153] He assured Minto that "the Congress has done all that we had a right to expect," [154] though he probably shared Sir George Clarke's suspicions "that the great majority of the Moderates are cherishing hopes which the Reforms do not justify, and that if their political acumen had been greater, their enthusiasm might have been less." [155] Yet it proved impossible for Morley to sustain his cynicism amid the cries of exultation. When a delegation of Hindus and Muslims presented a joint declaration of gratitude to the Viceroy, he joyfully admitted: "I never have had, and I shall never have, a more splendid Xmas box than when I opened *The Times* on Christmas morning and read about the famous deputation to you about reforms." [156]

The few critics of the Morley-Minto policy were too familiar to be taken seriously. Wilfrid Scawen Blunt alleged that the Government of India had muzzled its enemies while it circulated a doctored version of Morley's historic address to the Lords.[157] Sir Henry Cotton, Dr. V. H. Rutherford, and H. W. Nevinson contributed their criticisms to a symposium in the pages of the *Indian Review*, but these were outweighed by the flattering remarks

152. Minto to Morley, January 7, 1909 [copy], Minto Papers. Minto revealed that Gokhale "is now about to start a tour with the object of preaching co-operation with the Government in the furtherance of our reforms."

153. Morley to Clarke, January 7, 1909, Morley Papers.

154. Morley to Minto, December 31, 1908, Minto Papers. After a "cheerful" dinner with Sir Lawrence Jenkins, Gupta, and Dutt, who convinced him that there now existed in India "a National party more or less committed to our constitutional ways" (Morley to Minto, January 6, 1909, Minto Papers), Morley informed James Bryce that "the Congress wing of the 'Nationalist' Party are committed to loyalty, etc. They broke up with enthusiastic cheering for the King, the S. of S. and the G.G. On the other hand, we have not frightened the Civil Service, or the Anglo-Indian merchant or the British investor. So, for the hour, the sun shines, in spite of bombs and anarchists." Morley to Bryce, January 8, 1909, Bryce Papers.

155. Clarke to Morley, January 28, 1909, Morley Papers.

156. Morley to Minto, December 31, 1908, Minto Papers.

157. Blunt launched his attack in the sheltered precincts of his diary (December 18, 1908, and January 5, 1909), *My Diaries*, 2, pp. 235-37; see his letter of July 27, 1909, to Sir William Wedderburn, cited in the Earl of Lytton, *Wilfrid Scawen Blunt: A Memoir by His Grandson* (London, 1961), pp. 181-82.

offered by prominent Indian spokesmen.[158] In a letter to Minto, Morley scoffed at the accusations leveled by "the pig-headed section of the Ultra-Radicals," and expressed reasonable confidence that "the croaks of these few sour-blooded critics count for nothing." [159] He diagnosed, quite accurately, that

> my difficulties will not arise half so much from those whom I affectionately call my Geese and Noodles in the Radical camp as from the very eminent Fossils of the I.C.S who are now scribbling letters in the papers and pulling wires in all directions.[160]

It was this second group, in its campaign against the appointment of an Indian to the Viceroy's executive council, that threatened to impede the passage through Parliament of the 1909 reform proposals.

Morley realized that diehard peers could inflict less damage upon the contents of the reform bill than upon its timing. But he realized, too, that half the efficacy of the measure lay in the speed with which it was applied.[161] The proposed Indian member for the viceregal council proved the major stumbling block and elicited fierce opposition in the editorial columns of *The Times*.[162] Though the controversial appointment did not in fact require either parliamentary approval or the sanction of either of the reluctant executive councils,[163] there remained the distinct possibility that their Lordships' reservations on this single item might be sufficient to retard the passage of the bill as a whole. "One hears a good deal of criticism of the proposal to put a Native on to your Council," Godley informed Minto in mid-January, adding that "luckily" Morley appeared "so clear and decided" on the matter that further opposition seemed futile.[164] Two weeks later, Morley

---

158. "The Reform Proposals: A Symposium," *Indian Review, 10* (1909).

159. Morley to Minto, December 31, 1908, Minto Papers.

160. Morley to Minto, January 12, 1909, Minto Papers.

161. Morley to Minto, December 18, 1908, Minto Papers; also Sir Harvey Adamson to Minto, January 3, 1909, Minto Papers; Minto to Clarke, January 18, 1909, Sydenham Papers, British Museum Add. MSS. 50,837, fols. 12-13.

162. Sir Valentine Chirol heralded *The Times'* displeasure in a note which Morley paraphrased to Minto, January 13, 1909, Minto Papers; on February 9, *The Times* coupled its criticisms of the projected Indian reforms with a leader on the "Anarchy in Ireland."

163. Morley to Minto, January 21, 1909, Minto Papers.

164. Godley to Minto, January 15, 1909, Minto Papers.

admitted that: "The gale of wind about the Native Member still blows and whistles and even screams in my ear," and he threatened "to end the controversy" by submitting S. P. Sinha's name for royal approval "right away." [165] The Prince of Wales appealed personally to Minto against the Indian Member,[166] and in late February, during a dinner party at Lord Crewe's, the King implored Morley to change his mind.[167] Yet both administrators were determined not to remove "the lynch-pin [from] the car." [168] It became increasingly evident to Morley that Sinha's appointment "will shine out as the most sensible act in the whole story of Reforms," [169] and primarily for this reason, he insisted that another Indian be promptly designated to succeed Sinha, when the latter spoke of resignation the following autumn.[170]

With memories of the fate of two Home Rule bills, Morley apprehensively set the parliamentary gears in motion. "You never can be certain," he instructed Minto, "that the Devil won't insinuate himself into the best men's hearts, until you have got to the Third Reading." [171] In language reminiscent of that which

165. Morley to Minto, February 4, 1909, Minto Papers; Morley was restrained by the knowledge that "neither Parliament, nor our honest public outside has any relish of *coups*."

166. Prince of Wales to Minto, January 26, 1909, Minto Papers.

167. Morley to Minto, February 25, 1909, Minto Papers. On March 3, the King asked Lord Esher to convince Morley "to postpone for two years the appointment of a native member of Council." Journals, March 3, 1909, *Journals and Letters*, ed. Brett, 2, 372; Morley reported his interview with Esher to Minto on March 5, 1909, Minto Papers; an account of the King's correspondence with Morley and Minto on this subject is provided in Magnus, *King Edward the Seventh*, pp. 425-26.

168. Morley to Minto, February 25, 1909, Minto Papers.

169. Morley to Minto, May 14, 1909, Minto Papers.

170. King Edward to Esher, September 10, 1909, cited in Magnus, *King Edward the Seventh*, p. 426; also Morley to Sir Guy Fleetwood Wilson, July 29, 1909, enclosed in Morley to Minto, July 29, 1909, Minto Papers.

171. Morley to Minto, January 13, 1909, Minto Papers. A week later, Morley advised the Viceroy:

It is rash of me, or anybody, to predict the course of any Bill in the two Houses of Parliament, but on the whole I rather look forward to a pretty smooth voyage. . . . My present intention is to introduce it in the House of Lords as soon as . . . the debate on the [Royal] Address is over. . . . I should hope that four or five sittings, or even fewer, would see it through all the stages. Then I should bargain with Asquith that it should be the first Government business (bar perhaps some supplementary estimates) in the H. of C. *There* the Opposition may, in the persons of its less responsible members, commit the heinous, but too familiar crime of obstruction—not from any prejudice

he had employed in 1886 and 1893, he told Godley that "if the H. of L. or the H. of C. choose to wreck the Bill . . . they will do it at their own peril: I mean the peril of Indian confusion." [172]

Because of his keen appreciation of the parliamentary power struggle, Morley concentrated his energies and rhetoric upon potential mischief-makers in the Commons.[173] Aware that "nobody could possibly have produced a scheme . . . that would please everybody," [174] he recognized the supreme importance of carrying the lower house with him, even at the risk of forfeiting support among his fellow peers. "To carry a Bill through the House of Commons was Mr. Gladstone's definition of Ministers' *hard work*," he recalled.

> For 80 days or more I sat on the bench with him sixteen years ago over the Home Rule Bill. I think a twentieth part of that vast span of time will see me through my immediate and personal share of our Indian Bill, and I hope that [Sir George] Buchanan will not be under the harrow [in the Commons] so very much longer. I happen to know that Gokhale has written to Cotton urging him to make as few difficulties as possible; and Dutt is dealing faithfully in the same sense with Rutherford and others of that section.[175]

By early May, Morley's term of trial had ended, and, according to Godley, it remained only "to put flesh and blood on the skeleton (as Lord Morley called it in a somewhat unguarded moment) ." [176]

So far as constitutional practice allowed, Morley did not hesitate to convert his lofty phrases into hard political currency. On March 24, while the Lords continued to quibble about Clause 3 of the re-

---

against our Bill, but from a patriotic desire to keep back other business, and to make difficulties for the most iniquitous of imaginable Governments. However, we will not bid good morrow to the Devil until we meet him, and I am not without hope that we shall *emerge* by Easter.
Morley to Minto, January 21, 1909, Minto Papers.

172. Morley to Godley, February 11, 1909, Kilbracken Papers (I.O.L.) .

173. Lord Midleton, who, as St. John Brodrick, had preceded Morley at the India Office, complained to Minto that the Indian secretary had taken "no pains" to secure adequate support in the Lords. Midleton to Minto, March 26, 1909, Minto Papers.

174. Morley to Minto, March 12, 1909, Minto Papers.

175. Morley to Minto, February 11, 1909, Minto Papers; also Morley to Minto, February 25, 1909, Minto Papers.

176. Godley to Minto, May 21, 1909, Minto Papers.

form measure,[177] he announced the appointment of S. P. Sinha, Advocate-General of Bengal, to the Viceroy's executive council.[178] Less spectacular, though no less successful, were his efforts "to push our India Bill excellently forward." He conceded to Minto that "the pace may seem slack to you," but assured him that "if you were familiar with the parliamentary ground, you would know that not a single available parliamentary hour has been lost." [179] But administrative initiative, like the Morley-Minto reforms, left the environs of Westminster and Whitehall that spring. Thereafter it was again the Viceroy who apologized for delays and the Indian secretary who, with considerably less patience, demanded prompt and decisive action.

An early autumn outburst of violence convinced Minto that it was advisable to place the reforms package in cold storage for a year. The mere suggestion, Morley replied, was sufficient to "make my hair stand on end." [180] A growing uncertainty in British political life, no less than Indian circumstances, dictated an immediate implementation of the scheme: "in a year Lord Minto will be out of office," Morley reasoned, "and possibly myself, too; and the enemies of Reforms may be in power: [Lords] Curzon, Lansdowne, Percy, etc. The miscarriage by delay would be a huge disaster, and nothing less." [181] He had expended too much time and effort to allow the fruits of his labors to perish on the vine.

The Morley-Minto reforms, which received the assent of the King-Emperor on May 25, overhauled the complex network of provincial legislative and executive councils. The former were en-

177. Clause 3, to which the upper house took strong exception, made provision for the Government of India to create executive councils in provinces where hitherto the lieutenant-governor had ruled on his own. It was rejected on March 4 on the motion of Lord MacDonnell, but was soon passed intact by the Commons. In early May, the Lords agreed to a compromise which, in Morley's opinion, "gives away nothing of the slightest substance." Morley to Clarke, May 7, 1909, Morley Papers.

178. "Twenty-four hours after the event," Morley reported that there had been "no shock." Everyone seemed preoccupied, he noted ironically, with Balkan events, which "may well obliterate the case of Mr. Sinha." Morley to Minto, March 25, 1909, Minto Papers; by the time that Lord Roberts offered his "belated protest" in early May, "nobody paid attention, for that is one glorious virtue in our political ways, that when a thing is done, it is treated as done, and people listen no more." Morley to Minto, May 5, 1909, Minto Papers.

179. Morley to Minto, April 7, 1909, Minto Papers.
180. Morley to Minto, October 14, 1909, Minto Papers.
181. Morley to Clarke, October 19, 1909, Morley Papers.

larged to accommodate twice as many Indians, representing new interests—class and communal—and new constituencies. Members of legislative councils—British and Indian alike—were now permitted to debate budgetary matters, move amendments, and call for divisions. In addition, an Indian was appointed to the Viceroy's executive council, and Indian spokesmen were added to the imperial legislative council; only the latter retained an official majority, for Morley had persuaded Minto that this would prove a sufficient check upon the others.[182]

Did the 1909 reforms, by formally conceding the elective principle that was implied in the 1892 India Councils Act, open the way for responsible institutions and a democratic franchise? Both statesmen strenuously denied that this had been their intention, but the question persists whether Morley, despite his oft-quoted disclaimers, realized that he was sowing the seeds of representative government in Indian soil. His admirers have tended to think so, his critics to be divided. Certainly the implications of his policy were pointed out to him by his contemporaries,[183] and shortly after his departure from the India Office he prophesied that the changes he had introduced were "destined in the fullness of time, perhaps no very long time, to prove themselves changes of the first order in their effects upon Indian policy in all its most extensive bearings." [184] Perhaps he was reluctant to clarify his intentions out of fear that he might prejudice Parliament—particularly the upper house—and Lord Minto against his designs.[185] But it is vastly more probable that his Gladstonian myopia prevented him from perceiving exactly where he was leading India, or vice versa. Acutely aware that he was taking a significant step, he appears to have been better able to calculate its effects upon British thought and policy than those upon India.

As Sir Valentine Chirol subsequently pointed out, "the expan-

182. Dispatch from the Secretary of State for India to the Governor-General-in-Council, November 27, 1908, *Parliamentary Papers*, Cd. 4426.

183. See Cromer to Minto, March 10, 1909, Minto Papers; also Morley to Minto, April 2, 1909, Minto Papers; J. Ramsay MacDonald, *The Awakening of India* (London, 1910), pp. 269-70.

184. Morley, "British Democracy and Indian Government," *Nineteenth Century and After, 69* (1911), 197.

185. This is the interpretation offered by Wolpert, *Morley and India*, p. 161 and passim.

sion of Indian representation in the Councils has not been followed by any visible increase of Indian control of public affairs." [186] This was essentially what the authors of the reform scheme had intended. "My own view," Morley explained to Clarke, "has all along been that the Councils would still for many days to come need the guidance of their European chiefs. Only the difference will be that the chiefs will have to pay more attention to the people they are ruling." [187] Yet this policy did not satisfy the constitutional demands of Indian nationalists, nor did it point the way for future Indian political development. For this reason, the Morley-Minto reforms were unable to achieve even the modest durability and results that their authors had envisioned. Though Morley had been confident that his concessions "were quite enough for a generation at least," [188] they were recognized within his lifetime as a palliative which had failed to arrest Indian disaffection and which vindicated his earlier thesis that "A small and temporary improvement may really be the worst enemy of a great and permanent improvement, unless the first is made on the lines and in the direction of the second." [189] A decade later, the Morley-Minto reforms were superseded by the Montagu-Chelmsford scheme, which acknowledged the failure of its predecessor.[190]

The Act of 1909 was at best a stopgap device that afforded both governors and governed valuable breathing time. As such, its value should by no means be underestimated. It failed to furnish a blueprint for the enduring success of the British Raj; but Morley, for one, had never professed that such an achievement was possible. Laden with testimonials, he departed from the India Office in October 1910 confident that he had grappled with India's problems as earnestly and vigorously as any responsible prewar politician could have done: "Don't put my Indian work too low," he cautioned Andrew Carnegie.

186. Sir Valentine Chirol, *India Old and New* (London, 1921) , p. 132.
187. Morley to Clarke, May 7, 1909, Morley Papers.
188. Cited in J. H. Morgan, *John, Viscount Morley* (London, 1925) , p. 21.
189. Morley, *On Compromise,* p. 230.
190. S. R. Mehrotra has explained that as early as 1915, it was apparent that "any further progress on the lines of the Morley-Minto reforms would lead to disaster, for a further increase of the non-official element in the legislative councils would give the latter the power of paralysing government at every turn, but not the power and responsibility of conducting government for themselves." *India and the Commonwealth* (London, 1965) , p. 84.

We have to do our best to put a broken set of communities on
a constructive road: to guide men over a long slow transition.
Maybe they would do it better by themselves. But there we
are, and it is impossible for us to make a clean bolt. My countrymen here, and a good many scores of millions in India,
think and hope that I—whom chance or the stars put there—
may help them through the pressing crisis of the hour. I may
not be so sanguine as they are, but I'm chained to the oar, and
the endeavour is not ignoble, is it? [191]

In a career compounded of public defeats and private humilia-
tions, the Morley-Minto reform policy stands out as John Morley's
saddest failure. Alone among his Gladstonian designs, it bore an
initial promise of durable success. Yet the failure was not that of
an individual so much as of an ideological inheritance which, by
its self-contradictions and uncertainties, proved as irrelevant to the
Indian situation as it did to other urgent problems of early-
twentieth-century British politics and society.

Morley was describing himself, among others, when he asked a
university audience at Manchester in 1912: "Is it not possible that
we are somnambulists, only half awake to strong currents racing in
full blast over our heads and under the ground at our feet, and
sweeping through the world of white men, black men, brown men,
yellow men?" [192] Too sensitive not to perceive the winds of
change, he was prevented by his Gladstonianism from gauging
their velocity.

191. Morley to Carnegie, January 15, 1909, Morley-Carnegie Correspondence.
192. Inaugural Sessional Address as Chancellor, Victoria University, Manchester,
June 28, 1912, *The Times* (June 29, 1912), p. 6.

Bibliography

In accordance with instructions in his will, the bulk of John Morley's private papers was destroyed shortly after his death by Guy Morley, his nephew and heir. Of the items that survived, many were reportedly lost in flames two decades later, when German bombs hit the home of F. W. Hirst, to whom they had subsequently been bequeathed. The remaining papers—reportedly concerned with Morley's early Radical activities—are in the possession of Wadham College, Oxford, where their present trustee has reserved them for his future use. The diverse materials in the Morley Collection at the India Office Library, London, pertain exclusively to his career as Secretary of State for India; it is primarily upon these, the Minto Papers at the National Library of Scotland (a more complete collection), and all known and available Morley correspondence among the papers of colleagues and friends that this study has been based.

Confident that his *Recollections* provided the last word on the subject, Morley made a conscientious attempt to foil prospective biographers who might accord him less sympathetic treatment than his mentor had received. Not only did he request the posthumous destruction of his papers, but he also carefully deleted references to personal acrimonies and prejudices from his speeches and letters published during his lifetime. Although the present study makes use of many items which have previously appeared in print, particularly in the second volume of *Recollections,* these have been restored, whenever possible, to their original form, except where Morley's subsequent revisions elucidated his intentions without concealing his sentiments.

MANUSCRIPTS

Althorp, Northamptonshire
  Earl Spencer Papers
Birmingham University Library
  Sir Austen Chamberlain Papers
  Joseph Chamberlain Papers
Cambridge University Library
  Baron Acton Papers
  Miscellaneous Morley letters

Dublin, National Library of Ireland
  Miscellaneous Morley letters
Dublin, Trinity College Library
  Miscellaneous Morley letters
Edinburgh, National Library of Scotland
  Viscount Haldane Papers
  Earl of Minto Papers
Ithaca, New York, Cornell University Library
  Goldwin Smith Papers
Lincoln, Lincolnshire Archives Office
  Baron Welby Papers
Liverpool University Library
  William Rathbone Papers
London, British Library of Political and Economic Science
  Baron Courtney of Penwith Papers
  Frederic Harrison Papers
  Baron and Lady Passfield [Beatrice and Sidney Webb] Papers
  Miscellaneous Morley letters
London, British Museum
  Earl of Balfour Papers
  John Burns Papers
  Sir Henry Campbell-Bannerman Papers
  Richard Congreve Papers
  Sir Charles Dilke Papers
  Mary Gladstone Drew Papers
  Viscount [Herbert] Gladstone Papers
  W. E. Gladstone Papers
  Sir Edward Hamilton Papers
  Baron Kilbracken [Sir Arthur Godley] Papers
  Marquess of Ripon Papers
  J. A. Spender Papers
  Baron Sydenham of Combe [Sir George Clarke] Papers
London, Imperial College of Science and Technology
  T. H. Huxley Papers
London, India Office Library
  Baron Ampthill Papers
  Marquess Curzon of Kedleston Papers
  Sir Guy Fleetwood Wilson Papers
  Diary of Sir Frederic A. Hirtzel
  Baron Kilbracken [Sir Arthur Godley] Papers
  Baron Lamington Papers
  Sir William Lee-Warner Papers

Earl of Lytton Papers
Viscount Morley Papers
London, Public Record Office
 Earl of Cromer Papers
New Delhi, National Archives
 Gopal Krishna Gokhale Papers (typescript courtesy of Dr. S. R. Mehrotra)
New York, Columbia University Library
 Nicholas Murray Butler Papers
Oxford, Bodleian Library
 George Bentley Papers
 Viscount Bryce Papers
 Sir Sidney Lee Papers
 Baron MacDonnell Papers
 Earl of Oxford and Asquith Papers
 Letters from John Morley to Andrew Carnegie (microfilm)
 Gilbert Murray Papers
 Miscellaneous Morley letters
Oxford, Indian Institute
 Mary, Countess of Minto, Indian Journals
Stanton Harcourt, Oxfordshire
 Viscount [Lewis] Harcourt Papers
 Sir William Harcourt Papers

PRINTED SOURCES

Ali, Mohamed, *Thoughts on the Present Discontent,* Bombay, 1907.
Ali Khan, Syed Sirdar, *The Life of Lord Morley,* London, 1923.
———, *The Unrest in India,* Bombay, 1907.
Amery, Julian, *The Life of Joseph Chamberlain,* vol. 4, London, 1951.
Asquith, H. H., *Fifty Years of Parliament,* 2 vols. London, 1926.
Asquith, Margot, *Autobiography,* 2 vols. London, 1920, 1922.
Aziz, K. K., *Britain and Muslim India,* London, 1963.
Balfour, Lady Betty, ed., *Personal and Literary Letters of Robert, First Earl of Lytton,* 2 vols. London, 1906.
Banerjea, Surendranath, *A Nation in the Making,* Madras, 1925.
———, *Speeches and Writings,* Madras [1920].
Besant, Annie, *Speeches and Writings,* Madras, 1921.
Bilgrami, Syed Husayn, *Addresses, Poems and Other Writings,* Hyderabad, 1925.
Birrell, Augustine, *Things Past Redress,* London, 1937.
Blunt, Wilfrid Scawen, *My Diaries,* 2 vols. London, 1919, 1920.
———, *Secret History of the English Occupation of Egypt,* London, 1907.

Brett, M. V., ed., *Journals and Letters of Viscount Esher,* 4 vols. London, 1934–38.

Bright, John, *Diaries,* New York, 1931.

Bryce, James, ed., *Handbook of Home Rule,* London, 1887.

———, *Studies in Contemporary Biography,* New York, 1903.

Buchan, John, *Lord Minto: A Memoir,* London, 1924.

Buckle, George Earle, ed., *The Letters of Queen Victoria,* 3d ser., vols. 2 and 3, London, 1931, 1932.

Burrow, J. W., *Evolution and Society,* Cambridge, 1966.

Carnegie, Andrew, *Autobiography,* London, 1920.

Chailley, Joseph, *Administrative Problems of British India,* London, 1910.

Chamberlain, Sir Austen, *Down the Years,* London, 1935.

———, *Politics from Inside,* London, 1936.

Chirol, Sir Valentine, *India Old and New,* London, 1921.

———, *Indian Unrest,* London, 1910.

———, *The Occident and the Orient,* Chicago, 1924.

Churchill, Winston, *Great Contemporaries,* New York, 1937.

Congreve, Richard, *India,* London, 1857.

Cotton, H. J. S., *England and India,* London, 1883.

———, *Indian and Home Memories,* London, 1911.

Cross, C. M. P., *The Development of Self-Government in India, 1858–1914,* Chicago, 1922.

Das, M. N., *India Under Morley and Minto,* London, 1964.

Desai, A. R., *Social Background of Indian Nationalism,* Bombay, 1959.

Dilke, Sir Charles W., *Greater Britain,* 2 vols. London, 1868.

Durand, Sir Mortimer, *Life of the Right Hon. Sir Alfred Comyn Lyall,* London, 1913.

Ensor, R. C. K., *England, 1870–1914,* Oxford, 1963.

Everett, Edwin Mallard, *The Party of Humanity,* Chapel Hill, N.C., 1939.

Fitzroy, Sir Almeric, *Memoirs,* 2 vols. London [1925].

Foote, G. W., *John Morley as a Freethinker,* London, 1893.

Fraser, Lovat, *India Under Curzon and After,* London, 1911.

Gandhi, M. K., *Gokhale: My Political Guru,* Ahmedabad, 1955.

Gardiner, A. G., *Life of Sir William Harcourt,* 2 vols. London, 1923.

Garvin, J. L., *Life of Joseph Chamberlain,* 3 vols. London, 1932–34.

Ghosh, P. C., *The Development of the Indian National Congress, 1892–1909,* Calcutta, 1960.

Gilbert, Martin, ed., *Servant of India,* London, 1966.

Gladstone, Viscount, *After Thirty Years,* London, 1928.

Gladstone, W. E., *The Irish Question,* London, 1886.

———, *Our Colonies* (Speech at Chester, November 12, 1855), London, 1855.

————, *Political Speeches in Scotland,* 2 vols. Edinburgh, 1880.

————, *Speech on the Abolition of Negro Apprenticeship* (House of Commons, March 30, 1838) , London, 1838.

Gokhale, G. K., *A Debate on the Awakening of India,* London [1905].

————, *Speeches,* Madras [1916].

Gollin, A. M., *Proconsul in Politics: A Study of Lord Milner in Opposition and in Power,* London, 1964.

Gooch, G. P., *Life of Lord Courtney,* London, 1920.

Gopal, S., *The Viceroyalty of Lord Ripon,* Oxford, 1953.

Haldane, R. B., *An Autobiography,* London, 1929.

Hammond, J. L., *Gladstone and the Irish Nation,* London, 1938.

Hardie, J. Keir, *India, Impressions and Suggestions,* London, 1909.

Hardinge of Penshurst, Lord, *My Indian Years,* London, 1948.

Harper, George McLean, *John Morley and Other Essays,* Princeton, 1920.

Harrison, Austin, *Frederic Harrison: Thoughts and Memories,* London, 1926.

Harrison, Frederic, *Autobiographic Memoirs,* 2 vols. London, 1911.

Himmelfarb, Gertrude, *Victorian Minds,* New York, 1968.

Hirst, F. W., *Early Life and Letters of John Morley,* 2 vols. London, 1927.

————, *In the Golden Days,* London, 1947.

Hobhouse, L. T., *Democracy and Reaction,* New York, 1905.

————, *Liberalism,* London, 1911.

Howsin, H. M., *The Significance of Indian Nationalism,* London, 1909.

Hurst, Michael, *Joseph Chamberlain and Liberal Reunion,* London, 1967.

Ilbert, Sir Courtenay, *The Government of India,* London, 1907 (supplementary chapter, London, 1910) .

Indian National Congress, The, Madras [1909].

International Policy: Essays on the Foreign Relations of England, London, 1866.

James, Robert Rhodes, *Rosebery,* London, 1963.

Jenkins, Roy, *Asquith,* London, 1964.

————, *Mr. Balfour's Poodle,* London, 1954.

————, *Sir Charles Dilke: A Victorian Tragedy,* London, 1958.

Karkaria, R. P., ed., *Lord Curzon's Farewell to India,* Bombay, 1907.

Kilbracken, Lord, *Reminiscences,* London, 1931.

Knaplund, Paul, *Gladstone and Britain's Imperial Policy,* New York, 1927.

————, ed., *Gladstone-Gordon Correspondence,* Philadelphia, 1961.

Knickerbocker, Frances Wentworth, *Free Minds: John Morley and His Friends,* Cambridge, 1964.

Koebner, R., and H. D. Schmidt, *Imperialism,* Cambridge, 1964.

Lajpat Rai, Lala, *Reflections on the Political Situation in India* [Japan], 1916.

———, *The Story of My Deportation,* Lahore, 1908.

———, *Young India,* New York, 1917.

Low, Sidney, *A Vision of India,* London, 1906.

Lyons, F. S. L., *The Fall of Parnell,* London, 1960.

Lytton, Earl of, *Wilfrid Scawen Blunt: A Memoir by His Grandson,* London, 1961.

McCully, Bruce Tiebout, *English Education and the Origins of Indian Nationalism,* New York, 1940.

MacDonald, J. Ramsay, *The Awakening of India,* London, 1910.

———, *The Government of India,* London, 1919.

Magnus, Sir Philip, *Gladstone,* New York, 1954.

———, *King Edward the Seventh,* London, 1964.

———, *Kitchener, Portrait of an Imperialist,* London, 1958.

Maine, Sir Henry Sumner, *Popular Government,* London, 1886.

Major, E., *Viscount Morley and Indian Reform,* London, 1910.

Mallet, Sir Charles, *Herbert Gladstone,* London, 1932.

Masani, R. P., *Dadabhai Naoroji: The Grand Old Man of India,* London, 1939.

Mason, Philip, *An Essay on Racial Tension,* London, 1954.

———, *The Men Who Ruled India,* vol. 2, London, 1954.

Mehrotra, S. R., *India and the Commonwealth,* London, 1965.

Midleton, Earl of, *Records and Reactions, 1856–1939,* London, 1939.

Mill, John Stuart, *Considerations on Representative Government,* London, 1861.

———, *Dissertations and Discussions,* 4 vols. London, 1859–75.

———, *England and Ireland,* Dublin, 1918.

———, *Memorandum of the Improvements in the Administration of India during the Last Thirty Years, and the Petition of the East-India Company to Parliament,* London, 1858.

Minto, Mary, Countess of, *India, Minto and Morley (1905–1910),* London, 1934.

Mody, H. P., *Sir Pherozesha Mehta: A Political Biography, 1,* Bombay, 1921.

———, *The Political Future of India,* London, 1908.

Moore, R. J., *Liberalism and Indian Politics, 1872–1922,* London, 1966.

Morgan, John H., *John, Viscount Morley,* London, 1925.

Morley, John, *An Address to Young Liberals,* London [1906].

———, "Comte," *Encyclopedia Britannica,* vol. 6, 11th ed. Cambridge, 1910.

———, *Critical Miscellanies,* 3 vols. London, 1904–05.

————, *Edmund Burke: A Historical Study,* London, 1867.

————, *The Education Bill* (Speech at Oxford, February 20, 1897), London [1897].

————, *Indian Speeches (1907–1909),* London, 1909.

————, *Ireland's Rights and England's Duties* (Speech at Blackburn, May 28, 1868), Blackburn [1868].

————, *The Irish Crimes Act and Its Abuses* (Speech at London, June 7, 1888), London [1888].

————, *The Irish Question* (Speech to the Eighty Club, London, June 8, 1886), London [1887].

————, *The Issues at Stake* (Speech at Manchester, May 13, 1904), London, 1904.

————, *The Liberal Leaders and Home Rule* (Speech at Newcastle, January 13, 1891) [London, 1891].

————, *Liberal Principles and Imperialism* (Speech at Oxford, June 9, 1900), Manchester [1900].

————, *The Liberal Programme* (Speech at Newcastle, May 21, 1894), London, 1894.

————, *The Liberal Victory* (Speech at London, April 27, 1906), London, 1906.

————, *Liberalism and Social Reforms* (Speech at London, November 19, 1889), London [1889].

————, *The Life of Richard Cobden,* London, 1905.

————, *The Life of William Ewart Gladstone,* 3 vols. London, 1903.

————, *Machiavelli* (The Romanes Lecture, 1897), London, 1897.

————, *Memorandum on Resignation,* London, 1928.

————, *Mr. Gladstone's Irish Policy* (Speech at Newcastle, April 21, 1886), Newcastle [1886].

————, *Notes on Politics and History,* London, 1913.

————, *Oliver Cromwell,* London, 1900.

————, *On Compromise,* London, 1910.

————, *On Popular Culture* (Speech at Birmingham, October 5, 1876), London [1876].

————, *Parliamentary Reform* (Speech at Leeds, October 17, 1883), London [1883].

————, *The Present Crisis and the Future of Liberalism* (Speech at Oxford, February 20, 1887), London [1887].

————, *Recollections,* 2 vols. New York, 1917.

————, *Rousseau,* 2 vols. London, 1873.

————, *Speech on the Occasion of Unveiling the Gladstone Statue, Manchester* (October 23, 1901), Edinburgh, 1901.

————, *Three Policies for Ireland: Coercion, Compromise, Conciliation,* London, 1886.

————, *Two Years of War—and After* (Speeches at Arbroath and Forfar, October 31 and November 4, 1901), London, 1901.

————, *Voltaire,* London, 1872.

————, *Walpole,* London, 1889.

————, *Was the War a Necessity?* (Speech at Forfar, January 24, 1900), New York, 1900.

Mukherji, Panchanandas, ed., *Indian Constitutional Documents,* Calcutta, 1915.

Naoroji, Dadabhai, *Speeches and Writings,* Madras [1915].

Nevinson, H. W., *More Changes, More Chances,* London, 1925.

————, *The New Spirit in India,* London, 1908.

Nicolson, Sir Harold, *King George the Fifth,* London, 1952.

O'Donnell, C. J., *The Causes of Present Discontents in India,* London, 1908.

Pal, Bipin Chandra, *Memories of My Life and Times,* 2 vols. Calcutta, 1932, 1951.

————, *Nationality and Empire,* Calcutta, 1916.

————, *Om Bande Mataram,* London, 1910.

Parvate, T. V., *Gopal Krishna Gokhale,* Ahmedabad, 1959.

Pearson, Charles H., *National Life and Character: A Forecast,* London, 1893.

Quill, Albert W., *Mr. John Morley and Home Rule,* Dublin, 1888.

Radical Programme, The, London, 1885.

Raleigh, Sir Thomas, ed., *Lord Curzon in India,* London, 1906.

Ratcliffe, Samuel Kerkham, *Sir William Wedderburn and the Indian Reform Movement,* London, 1923.

Rawlinson, H. G., ed., *Select Essays from the Writings of Viscount Morley of Blackburn, O.M.,* London, 1923.

Reed, Sir Stanley, *The India I Knew, 1897–1947,* London, 1952.

Robinson, R. E., and John Gallagher, *Africa and the Victorians,* London, 1963.

Shannon, R. T., *Gladstone and the Bulgarian Agitation, 1876,* London, 1963.

Sir Henry Cotton: A Sketch of his Life and Services to India, Madras [1912].

Sitaramayya, B. P., *The History of the Indian National Congress, 1,* Bombay, 1946.

Smith, Goldwin, *My Memory of Gladstone,* London, 1904.

————, *Reminiscences,* New York, 1910.

Spender, J. A., *The Indian Scene,* London, 1912.

————, *The Public Life,* 2 vols. London, 1925.

Staebler, Warren, *The Liberal Mind of John Morley,* Princeton, 1943.

Stansky, Peter, *Ambitions and Strategies,* Oxford, 1964.

Stead, W. T., *Character Sketches*, London, 1892.

——, *The Liberal Ministry of 1906*, London, [1906].

Strachey, Lytton, *Characters and Commentaries*, New York, 1933.

Sydenham, Lord, *My Working Life*, London, 1927.

Taylor, A. J. P., *Politics in Wartime*, London, 1964.

——, *The Trouble Makers*, London, 1964.

Thornton, A. P., *The Imperial Idea and Its Enemies*, London, 1959.

Tilak, B. G., *Writings and Speeches*, Madras, 1919.

Trial of Bal Gangadhar Tilak, The, Madras [1908].

Trollope, Anthony, *An Autobiography*, London, 1950.

Wacha, D. E., *Reminiscences of the Late Hon. Mr. G. K. Gokhale*, Bombay [1915].

Waley, S. D., *Edwin Montagu*, Bombay, 1964.

Wasti, Syed Rasi, *Lord Minto and the Indian Nationalist Movement*, Oxford, 1964.

Webb, Beatrice, *My Apprenticeship*, London, 1926.

——, *Our Partnership*, London, 1948.

West, Sir Algernon, *Private Diaries*, London, 1922.

Whitelaw, W. Menzies, "Lord Morley," in H. Ausubel, J. B. Brebner, and E. M. Hunt, eds., *Some Modern Historians of Britain*, New York, 1951.

Wolf, Lucien, *Life of Lord Ripon*, 2 vols. London, 1921.

Wolpert, Stanley A., *Tilak and Gokhale*, Berkeley, 1962.

——, *Morley and India, 1906–1910*, Berkeley, 1967.

Yajnik, I., *Shyamaji Krishnavarma*, Bombay, 1950.

JOURNALS AND PERIODICALS

(Place of publication is London except where otherwise noted.)

Bengalee, Calcutta, 1905–10.

Contemporary Review, 1906–12, 1923.

Economist, 1906–10.

Edinburgh Review, Edinburgh.

Empire Review, 1907–09, 1923.

Englishman, Calcutta, 1905–10.

Fortnightly Review.

India, 1905–10.

Indian Review, Madras, 1905–10.

Indian World, Calcutta, 1905–10.

Nineteenth Century (And After).

Pall Mall Gazette, 1880–83.

Pioneer Mail, Allahabad, 1905–10.

Quarterly Review, 1907–11, 1918, 1924.

Spectator.
The Times.
Times Literary Supplement.
Times of India, Bombay, 1905–10.

Ali Khan, Syed Sirdar, "The Present Discontent in India," *English Review, 1* (1909), 576–83.
Cecil, Algernon, "Mr. Morley," *Monthly Review, 23* (1906), 5–17.
Cotton, H. J. S., "The Unrest in India," *North American Review, 190* (New York, 1909), 392–401.
Eustis, F. A., and Z. H. Zaidi, "King, Viceroy and Cabinet," *History, 49* (1964), 171–84.
Galbraith, John S., "Myths of the 'Little England' Era," *American Historical Review, 67* (Washington, 1961), 34–48.
Gandhi, M. K., "A Confession of Faith," *Young India,* Ahmedabad, July 13, 1921.
Harper, George McLean, "John Morley," *Atlantic Monthly, 108* (Boston, 1911), 805–17.
Jenkins, Roy, "From Gladstone to Asquith: the Late Victorian Pattern of Liberal Leadership," *History Today, 14* (1964), 445–52.
"John Morley," *New Statesman,* September 29, 1923.
"John Morley's Speech on Human Progress," *New York Times,* November 27, 1904.
Johnston, W. J., "Mr. Morley and Ireland," *Westminster Review, 165* (1906), 475–92.
Moore, R. J., "John Morley's Acid Test: India, 1906–1910," *Pacific Affairs, 40* (Vancouver, 1968), 333–40.
Morgan, J. H., "More Light on Lord Morley," *North American Review, 221* (New York, 1925), 486–94.
Morison, J. L., "John Morley: A Study in Victorianism," *Bulletin of the Departments of History and Political and Economic Science, Queens University, Kingston, Ont., 34* (1920).
Morley, John, "The Expansion of England," *Macmillan's Magazine, 49* (1884), 241–58.
———, "Some Thoughts on Progress," *Educational Review, 29* (New York, 1905), 1–17.
Robinson, Ronald, and John Gallagher, "The Imperialism of Free Trade," *Economic History Review,* n.s., *6* (1953), 1–15.

OFFICIAL PUBLICATIONS AND REPORTS

H.C. 203 *Report of the Joint Select Committee of the Government of India Bill, 1919.*

Cd. 4426 *Proposals of the Government of India and Dispatch of the Secretary of State*, 1908.

Cd. 4435–36 *Replies of the Local Governments, etc., to Letter from the Government of India, No. 21, dated 1 Oct., 1908.*

Cd. 9178 *Addresses presented in India to His Excellency the Viceroy and the Right Honourable the Secretary of State*, 1918.

Native Newspaper Reports, 1905–10. (India Office Library).

Parliamentary Debates.

Reports of the Indian National Congress, 21st through 25th sessions, 1905–10.

Index